Praise for *A Modern Woman's Guide to a Natural Empowering Birth*

"I am thrilled to see a book that encourages women to take birth back. That is our only hope. We can't wait for the culture of fear to subside. We women have to address fear with truth: Birth is a natural function of biology. Birth is inherently safe and interference is inherently risky.

The culture of fear that separates women from their biology also robs them of their power. *Thank you for making women's power and truth the theme of your book. I know that many women will have better births because of this empowering book!"*
~ Carla Hartley, Founder of Trust Birth Initiative and Director of the Ancient Art Midwifery Institute

"One of the best things you can do to prepare for birth is to saturate yourself in positive birth stories"
~ Dr Sarah Buckley MD, Author of *Gentle Birth, Gentle Mothering.*

"Reading it is very much like being *surrounded by wise women teaching the lessons of birth we wish we all had received as young women*. ... a great blessing to those women who go seeking for birth wisdom."
~ Jenne Erigo Alderks, Board member and Grassroots Advocates Co-Chair of the Coalition for Improving Maternity Services

"I loved reading A Modern Woman's Guide to a Natural Empowering Birth.... We really need get back to a place where women trust birth, trust the process and above all else, trust themselves and their ability to birth their babies and your book will encourage readers to do just that.*I think you are onto something powerful here.... Love it!"*
~ Simone Snyder CMT, CD, ICCE, International Childbirth Education Association (ICEA)

"I have always believed that mothers are the true experts of birth, and it is to them we must turn for insights and inspiration. Katrina Zaslavsky proves this adage is true. Her book is interesting, informative and will not only inspire today's modern woman, but women for generations to come." ~ Laura Shanley, author of *Unassisted Childbirth*

"... opened my heart and eyes to how childbirth can and should be. *I now know exactly how I want my labour to be and am looking forward to experiencing every second of it. No fear, no worries*. Thanks Katrina for giving me and other mums-to-be this incredible gift." ~ Shannon Dunn, first time mother-to-be, Conscious Life Media

"...*mandatory reading material!* The modern and ancient wisdom contained within these pages are vital to restoring a culture that views birth as the *healthy, happy, natural function it should be*, and has always been." ~ Rebecca Dettman, intuitive, journalist, homebirther

"... a must for mothers looking for real and positive information. *You'll be inspired, enlightened and empowered to overcome your fears* and liberated by the insightful stories. So put down the birthing textbooks, throw away the how-to's and run to the shops for this inspiring book! *Highly recommended*." ~ Heather James, Inspiring Mums Founder & mother of two.

"Such a *refreshingly 'real' book to inspire, encourage and empower women* for their most sacred rite of passage. Thank you Katrina." ~ Sonya Wildgrace, VBAC counsellor, doula and natural birth educator

"... *brimming with positivity* and should be *essential reading* for expectant parents." ~ Kristen Morrison, Naturally Better Kids and author of *Naturally Better*

"... *amazing resource for any woman thinking of getting pregnant or is pregnant*, whether the first time around or not. It is certainly something I will consider gifting to my clients, as part of my new mother's program." ~ Vicky Gardner, former president of Infant Massage Australia and wellness creator at Sanctuary for Souls

"*I love the sisterhood*: women empowering women, women supporting women ... sharing our stories. Thank you." ~ Vickie Mg, mother

"*I love your message to women to own their magnificence* by living consciously, naturally and empowered. Keep spreading your light and love into the world, beautiful lady." ~ Suzy Manning, Sizzzl transitional coach for women, speaker and author of *Wise Women, Circle of Wisdom*

"... *everything you need & want to know* ... double thumbs up!" ~ Rachel Eslick, mother

"... beautifully compiled stories ... *wealth of expert opinions* to create a resource that empowers women to *take control of their birth experience* by arming them with knowledge and instilling faith in their ability to choose what's right for themselves." ~ Micky Marie Morrison, P.T., ICPFE, author of *Baby Weight: The Complete Guide to Prenatal and Postpartum Fitness*

"*This is how birth is meant to be*. This is how nature intended it. Positive, inspiring and wonderful. These stories show you that *labour can be amazing* if you believe in yourself and what your body can do." ~ Amanda Santoro, mother

"Well written and presented, it will become a *valuable resource for expectant mothers everywhere*. Well done." ~ Robyn Stitt, complementary therapist from Overcoming Overwhelm

"The true beauty of this book is that it is not telling women how they 'should' birth – *it presents them with options* other than to hand some of the most important decisions of their life to a stranger in white coat." ~ Katia Leonaite, mother

"*I love the powerful message* that Katrina is spreading and the support and understanding it offers women. Thank you." ~ Natalie Hennesey, Spirited Women's Network

"This book can help you realise what you are capable of and that *you are indeed a beautiful birthing goddess*." ~ Leonie, mother

"... encourages us to *take back the reins on our body and trust that they have been created to serve this very purpose*" ~ Katie Blewitt, An Empowered Life

"As a proud new mum to a baby boy, I can't begin to explain how much I learned. Some first-time mums like me who knew nothing have really gotten empowerment from you—you taught me that it's about me and that I have a say and not everything a doctor says is final. It's all about me! *I'm very grateful and lucky I came across you* two months before I gave birth. I learned so much in that space!"
~ Nalo, mother

"Sure to be a wonderful resource for birthing women, with *stories straight from the heart*, from women, doulas and midwives."
~ Cas McCullough, mother and doula, Mumatopia

"Katrina, I love the way you are helping so many people to improve their life and health with a *natural, holistic approach*; you are truly inspirational." ~ Tegan Benfell, Additive Free Kids

"What a *wonderful resource for women looking for birth support*. Every woman has the right to a 'natural, empowering birth'." ~ Rina Joye Bly, mother

"Beautifully written Katrina. You have done a great job in providing women with *knowledge in order to make empowering choices* for birth." ~ Jo Thomson, midwife

"... *fundamental resource for women looking to own their birth experience* and achieve a fantastic natural birth."
~ Kathryn Williams, homebirth midwife

"Childbirth can be one of the most ecstatic experiences for a woman if she learns to trust her body and her baby. I hope this book helps more women *find the confidence and belief in their bodies to discover the joy of natural birth*!" ~ Kate, mother

"*I absolutely love A Modern Woman's Guide to a Natural Empowering Birth*. It's such an important resource for women. I just loved reading your story…" ~ Rebecca Mugridge, author of The Pram Diet

"*It's always good to read about other women* who have also had a positive experience giving birth." ~ Eva Miles, mother

A Modern Woman's Guide to

A Natural Empowering Birth

*A Collection of Inspiring Birth Stories,
Expert Tips & Practical Insights to
Reclaim Your Natural Birth Power &
Overcome Your Fears in a Modern World*

Katrina Zaslavsky

Copyright

A Modern Woman's Guide to a Natural Empowering Birth

ISBN: 9780987234209

Copyright (c) Katrina Zaslavsky 2011

Copies are available at special rates for bulk orders.

Contact us at *info@inspiringbirthstories.com.au* or (+613) 9578 2798 for more information.

www.inspiringbirthstories.com.au

A Modern Woman's Guide to

A Natural Empowering Birth

*A Collection of Inspiring Birth Stories,
Expert Tips & Practical Insights to
Reclaim Your Natural Birth Power &
Overcome Your Fears in a Modern World*

Katrina Zaslavsky

Copyright

A Modern Woman's Guide to a Natural Empowering Birth

ISBN: 9780987234209

Copies are available at special rates for bulk orders.

Contact us at *info@inspiringbirthstories.com.au* or (+613) 9578 2798 for more information.

www.inspiringbirthstories.com.au

Acknowledgements

I would like to express my heartfelt gratitude to all the beautiful women who shared their inspiring birth stories from the heart, as well as the wisdom gained on their journey into motherhood. Also our wonderful professional contributors who generously shared their expertise in order to empower other women around the world (in no particular order):

Tammy Haikal, Rebecca Oliver, Heidi Vine, Rebel Belinda, Rebecca Dettman, Rachel Averbukh, Cory Andrews, Kiera Pedley, Rachel Eslick, Kristen Morrison, Heidi Claire Adams, Davini Malcolm, Kate Filmer, Heidi Merika, Natalie Gay Hennessey, Wendy Grenfell, Miren Kruse, Hayley Rynderman, Amanda Santoro, Vickie Michelle Gibbons, Eva Miles, Ellie Burscough, Kate Clark, Tess Dwyer, Kayla, Bronwyn Davis, Rebecca Colefax, Wendy Grenfell, Rina Joye Bly, Leonie Wimberger, Anneliese Fitzgerald, Brooke Gough, Nicole Kopel, Meagan Genovese, Rebecca Pizzi, Debbie Barber, Stacey Hart, Brooke Veldwyk , Karlene Whittaker, Robyn Stitt, Diane Gardner, Sonya Wildgrace, Cas McCullough, Shivam Rachana, Nicole MacFadyen, Jo Thomson, Unmani, Kate McBride, Kathryn Williams, Deanne Schmid.

A special thank you to *Dr Sarah Buckley, MD*, for sharing her valuable insights in her interview featured in the afterword of this book.

Thanks to my fabulous editor, *Shannon Dunn* at Conscious Life Media, who went beyond the call of duty and gave her heart and soul to the project.

To my amazing husband who believed in me, even before I believed in myself, and supported me every step of the way to bring my dream to this world.

To my precious daughters who had to share their mummy for many months during the birth of my new "baby". You light up my world and you are the reason I have done all of this.

To my dearest mother who has given me the gift of life, unconditional love and foundation of good health and then continues to keep on giving. To my dear father who has a heart of gold, has shown me the lighter side of life and has instilled the values that helped me to write this book. To my dear sister who shared my joys and challenges and to my brother who taught me to go for my dreams and that everything is possible. May others be so blessed.

A Note from the Author

Please note I am not a doctor or midwife and the information contained within this book should not be taken as medical advice. It applies to the majority of normal healthy women and there will always be exceptions to the rule.

The information contained in this book is based on the author's experience and that of numerous other mothers and birth professionals who have kindly shared their story and expertise. While care has been taken to ensure accurate and safe information has been given, the author and publisher do not accept responsibility for any problems arising out of the contents of this book.

Every woman has the right to be properly educated and informed when it comes to her birth and make the right choices for her and her family from that educated place. Whatever she chooses is her responsibility.

Be aware, the information contained within this book is not intended as a substitute for consulting with your healthcare provider. Therefore, always check with your preferred healthcare provider before embarking on any major changes to your lifestyle.

Please also understand that in no way do I seek to diminish the importance or validity of modern medicine. I believe the medical establishment plays a critical role when it comes to dealing with real medical emergencies and to save lives, and I am so grateful we live in modern times when this is the case. It is the over-reliance on medical interventions, general lack of education and therefore lack of perceived choice when it comes to birth options, and possible risks of interventions, as well as negative beliefs about birth in the first place, that is of real concern.

Table of Contents

Preface
Secret Women's Business

The one thing that never ceases to amaze me is the lack of sisterhood when it comes to bringing babies into this world. It's either secret women's business that nobody likes to talk about, or we delight in comparing notes about who had the longest, most complicated and painful experience, all the while scaring the wits out of each other.

If somebody has something negative to say, we tend to be all ears, yet—in the majority of cases—when someone has something positive to offer, they're quickly shut down (I know, I was one of them). Nobody, it seems, wants to hear about it.

No wonder positive birth stories are so rare—and not because they don't happen (you are about to hear a whole lot of them!)—it's likely mums with happy birth tales don't want to sound like they are bragging, and tall poppy syndrome prevails.

And so, empowered mothers tend to keep it to themselves. Yet, by keeping their heartening stories under lock and key, women are doing each other a great disservice and only perpetuating a one-sided view of the journey into the first moments of motherhood.

It's time to change that. It's time to stand up tall and proud while sharing our positive birth experiences to pave the way for other women, so they too may have their own empowering journey.

Bringing Back the Magic: the Miracle and Beauty of Birth

I remember being pregnant, searching library shelves; hungry to devour everything I could on the subject to prepare me for a natural birth.

Only I found most books were downright clinical, boring and uninspiring. I was left dissatisfied and disappointed.

It felt like every negative account and symptom just added to the fear and mind pollution. I craved stories that would blow me away. I wanted to revel in the magic, the miracle and beauty of birth. Surely that wasn't too much to ask?

Finding real accounts from everyday mothers who had inspiring birth experiences was indeed a challenge. Rather than be defeated, I took to the streets and compiled the book I had been looking to find on those library shelves. You're now holding it in your hands.

Some may sound like fairy stories compared to the negativity you may have become accustomed to hearing, but I assure you, these accounts are very real. Magic happens when you unlearn and strip away everything you thought you knew about giving birth. It's time to start with a fresh canvas.

Birth can be beautiful. Women were designed for it. The knowing of this is at our very core. Every stage of birth is a gift and a miracle.

Understanding this, embracing your pregnancy and giving birth the natural way is the best preparation for motherhood and the road of life that's ahead. It makes you stronger, more confident and courageous, and able to handle anything that comes your way. A truly empowered woman!

This book was written for every woman in bloom, especially first-time mothers. Regardless of your stage of motherhood, it's never too early or too late to hear positive, real stories from empowered women.

Behind the Scenes, an Empowered Book in the Making

Why inspiring birth stories, you may ask? Like most modern women, I was filled with fear and anxiety, as well as positive anticipation as a first-time mother-to-be.

The natural birth course I attended was filled with inspiring stories and this really helped to "normalise" the whole experience in my mind, to restore confidence in my body and nature's perfect design, and to overcome my fears.

Also, chance encounters (I prefer to call them synchronicities) with the right people at the right time who shared their amazing birth stories with me that I needed to take the road less travelled, despite the enormous fear of the unknown.

Ina May Gaskin sums it up beautifully...

> *"The best way I know to counter the effects of frightening stories is to hear or read empowering ones. I mean stories that change you because you have read or heard them; because the teller of the story taught you something you didn't know before or helped you look at things from a different angle."*

> *"Birth stories told by women who were active participants in giving birth often express a good deal of practical wisdom, inspiration and information for other women. Positive stories shared by women who have wonderful childbirth experiences are an irreplaceable way to transmit knowledge of a woman's true capacities in pregnancy and birth[31]."*

In life, there are some things you plan and others that life plans for you. This book is a result of the latter. A very inspired idea to say the least, and a message that needed to be told, even with two beautiful kids at foot!

After interviewing dozens of women from different cultural and family backgrounds—each with different values, belief systems and from many walks of life—common patterns began to emerge. It has been a fascinating and exciting process of discovery to say the least!

This was something I had anticipated and was looking for—much like a detective seeks out clues to solve a mystery or puzzle. So too, we seek to solve the mystery of birth by learning from other people's experiences, rather than having to live many lives and take notes.

As my mother always says, it's better to learn from other people's experiences than from your own mistakes. These common threads, together with my own experiences and lessons, helped form the key insights of this book.

A Modern Woman's Guide to a Natural Empowering Birth was inspired and a labour of love (don't mind the pun!) and I truly believe each woman's story can be a source of strength and inspiration for those who have chosen to take the natural path.

Although each story is unique and some will speak to you more than others, there are vital lessons to be learned or gems you will find in each one.

My sincere hope is this book serves as a valuable source of guidance, strength and inspiration for modern women who would dearly love to go natural, yet are not sure if they can, and are overcome by fear.

I hope this guide will help you to learn to trust in yourself and in nature's perfect design and reclaim your birth power. This is particularly important for first-time mums who don't know what to expect or what their bodies are capable of.

Others may need healing and the reassurance that they can still go natural after a disempowering, traumatic or negative experience the first time around—often a medical or caesarean birth they had not planned for or wanted.

> *"If we are to heal the planet, we must begin by healing birthing."*
> ~ Agnes Sallet Von Tannenberg

As you will see, it can be done naturally in most cases. You can do it too! But don't take my word for it, or anyone else's for that matter. I hope this prompts you to do further research, question advice you have been given, get a second opinion if you need to and discover that natural births, breech births, twin births and vaginal births after caesarean (VBACs) are happening safely all the time.

How to Use This Book

This self-help, inspirational guide, is a collection of inspiring birth stories, expert tips and practical insights to help women reclaim their birth power and overcome their fears in a modern world.

A Modern Woman's Guide to a Natural Empowering Birth features real, personal, stories: gems from the heart of other mothers, who have walked the path and come out stronger, positive and more empowered on the other side. There are also inspirational and thought-provoking quotes, tools and resources you can use to take charge of your birth experience to create a magical story of your own.

The real beauty of this book is that it focuses on the positive and spiritual aspects of birth that we don't often hear about, so you can immerse yourself in a world where everything is possible.

Yet it also gives you valuable food for thought with vital birth lessons within each story.

If you read nothing else on the subject of birth, this can stand alone as a complete mind-body preparation guide, with everything you need to know to empower yourself for a positive birth experience. Or it may send you on a whole new path of self-discovery and hopefully change your life forever, for the better!

Pregnant women are encouraged to slow down from the hectic pace of modern life, take time out from our busy schedules and nurture ourselves. What better excuse than a precious baby growing inside of us to do so!

Yet I am well aware this is not always possible. Busy modern women don't always have the opportunity to read for long periods. With this in mind, this guide has been designed so you are able to open the book to any insight and still get what you need to hear in that moment, rather than having to read the entire book from cover-to-cover in order to receive the full value from it.

An Empowering Gift

This book can be the perfect empowering gift to yourself to enjoy anytime while you sit back with a cup of tea and put your feet up. Just dip into one or two of the insights at your leisure. This is particularly helpful when you feel any negatives, doubt or fear creeping in and you need a good uplifting dose of inspiration.

There are 21 insights, each with a birth-related theme. Within each insight, you will find empowering birth quotes, commentary from my life-changing journey into motherhood, including practical suggestions and tips from myself and other empowered mothers in **Mothers' Wisdom**.

Our professional contributors include leading experts and pioneers in the birth field, who share must-knows to help you enjoy a beautiful, natural and rewarding experience. These women offer important birth lessons and tips in **Experts Say** to inspire, educate and celebrate women as they journey through this powerful, life-giving experience.

This is followed by an inspiring birth story from an empowered mother and a thought-provoking quote to leave you with powerful food for thought.

In the afterword, I share a special interview with internationally recognised natural birth author and speaker, Dr Sarah Buckley, MD, well known for her bestselling book, *Gentle Birth, Gentle Mothering*.

In this interview, she answers some of the big questions and shares valuable insights from a doctor's perspective, including the real risks of medical interventions (that your doctor won't tell you!) and the vital role of ecstatic birth hormones in natural birth.

In the last chapter titled **Continue The Journey**, you will find useful links to empowering birth tools, including a sample birth plan with a full explanation guide to help you take charge of your birth experience: a must-read resources list, as recommended by the empowered mothers and birth professionals we interviewed.

There are also empowering birth affirmations for you to use daily to prepare and re-program your mind for a positive birth experience!

Mum on a Mission

My mother never spoke about her birth experiences. It was considered "secret women's business" in her era in Eastern Europe and nobody really talked about it. All I know about my own birth was my mother had to be strong.

She was proud that I was born naturally and drug-free, as were both of my siblings. She had no support from my father and had to do it alone (with the support of the hospital midwives) which was perfectly "normal" in those days, since men were not allowed to set foot beyond the hospital entrance.

So I am told, my father only came for my mother one cold, snowy evening, followed by collection of the "parcel" the next day. He knew nothing of what happened inside those walls. My mother is amazed by how involved husbands or partners are these days—in the labour and in bonding with their babies. She thinks it's so special to have your loved one there to hold your hand.

My health journey started a long time ago, as far back as childhood. Growing up in a close-knit family of five, it was my mother who first gave me an appreciation of "natural is best".

I am blessed with an unconventional mother who doesn't believe in relying on doctors or taking medication when sick. She made a firm decision very early in life to never give medicine to her children.

So I grew up with my mother as my family "doctor" and her "strange" natural remedies on the rare occasion when our health was not quite right. On all my school forms where it asked for family doctor, I wrote "Mum"—much to the confusion of my teachers!

I never had antibiotics or so much as a pain reliever in my body under my mother's care. Instead, she had natural remedies for everything, from an earache to a sore throat—knowledge she had gained from stories, her own maternal wisdom and from speaking to doctor friends about what they gave their own children (often not their own medicine they prescribed) and she had an uncanny knack of storing these gold mines of information in her mind.

While some were certainly strange at the time, they were usually effective. With lots of love, home cooking and a few organic fruit trees in the garden that I picked in the summertime with my two siblings, we all grew up strong and healthy.

I'm so grateful for this gift of a natural start in life. I have appreciation for the power of the plant kingdom and our own incredible healing nature, given the right conditions.

I now have two beautiful little girls who have come into this world naturally and completely drug-free; each has been breastfed for as long as they needed and are being raised on real food rather than junk.

My little miss four, enjoys green "crocodile" smoothies (they don't bite but are packed with dark green leafy veggies!), happily munches on apples and raw veggie sticks as "normal" snacks and eats healthy home cooked meals with us.

There are no "kids meals" or junk food snacks on the menu and she has not developed the taste for sugar (beyond dried fruit as the ultimate treat) unlike many of her peers.

We have managed to avoid the artificial "glow in the dark" cakes and lolly bags at kids' parties and our children have been exceptionally healthy. They have never had any medication in their bodies or seen a doctor for anything and I intend to keep it that way.

It makes me feel really proud as a mother to know I am giving our precious children the very best start in life. As parents, we have to be the best example and set a strong foundation. So I am committed to continuing the legacy as a "natural mother".

My journey into motherhood, and the knowledge I have gained along the way, have had such a profound impact on me, that it has led me on a whole new pathway: to become an advocate of natural and conscious parenting, committed to supporting women in bloom to give birth naturally without drugs or interventions (if that is what they choose) and to overcome their fears about birthing in a world that has become so medicalised and fearful of something so perfectly natural.

As a natural mother, formerly a public health professional, founder of Inspired Wellness (*www.inspiredwellness.com.au*) and more recently Inspiring Birth Stories (*www.inspiringbirthstories.com.au*), together with a lifelong passion for healthy living, my calling is to awaken people around the world to live a more natural, conscious lifestyle. I am so inspired to walk this path personally and professionally.

Born in Eastern Europe, raised in Adelaide and now happily nested in Melbourne, Australia, with my amazing husband and two beautiful girls, I continue to follow my passion and spread the message of natural, conscious living worldwide.

While my own birth experiences and knowledge had such a profound, positive impact on me, I was surprised to discover expectant friends generally didn't want to hear about it. Apparently, I was the "lucky" one, the "superwoman" with the high pain tolerance, or so they thought.

The truth was, I was none of these things and yet I noticed significant differences in my approach or mindset and level of conscious preparation than those around me who went down the opposite path and then wondered why they were so "unlucky".

My biggest question became, "Why is it some women have such positive experiences while others are left traumatised?"

This became an endless source of fascination for me, which turned into an obsession, as I was hungry to learn what was really going on. This is something we will uncover and explore together in this book.

I sincerely hope *A Modern Woman's Guide to a Natural Empowering Birth* opens your eyes to beautiful new possibilities and brings fresh inspiration and positivity into your world—as well as real tips and insights you can really use to prepare your mind and body, to empower yourself for a positive pregnancy and birth experience.

Thank you for joining us on this empowering journey and may you have a beautiful and rewarding birth!

Blessings,

Katrina Zaslavsky

1st Insight:
We Need a Reality Check

"Pregnancy and birth are the most crucial and powerful passages in a woman's life. Most births around the world lead to some degree of preventable trauma for the mother and baby ... preventable because much of it is iatrogenic, that is, caused by the doctor or midwife. In many cases, if the mother, baby and birthing process had been treated with respect, the trauma would possibly have never taken place... Instead, the mother likely would have had the most miraculous experience of her life."

~ MIDWIFERY TODAY

We live in times when people are more technologically connected yet more socially isolated than ever before. Add to the mix, the modern day "disease" of passing on horror stories, overwhelming fear, negativity and misconceptions about birth. This is why birth support—in the way of sharing inspiring stories, insights and positive community—is essential!

As women, we have been given an incredible gift of creating and nurturing new life. This is no small matter! It is something to be honoured, respected and celebrated in the highest sense, and carries with it many long-term ramifications for mother and baby.

Yet, many of us are walking in the darkness on our journey into motherhood, as we generally don't see other women giving birth in the normal course of our lifetimes (it is still very much a mystery and most of us have no concept of what is normal or what to expect).

Meanwhile, there is often too much focus on procedures and drugs in antenatal classes and we generally look to our obstetrician for all our answers—and the only ones he or she knows are medical ones.

Unless we actively seek out information ourselves, all we have to go by is what our mother's friend's aunty and authority figures tell us—which is often far from positive or inspiring—and what we see in Hollywood movies, which is dramatised for entertainment value and bares little resemblance to reality.

Why a perfectly healthy pregnant woman would be driven in a wheelchair at high speed, kicking and screaming wildly into the hospital delivery room and then lie down obediently on a bed like a patient, is beyond me!

What is the result of all this? We have allowed something perfectly natural, miraculous and beautiful to be reduced to the equivalent of a medical condition to be carefully controlled and managed—a "nasty" process to be endured or an emergency just waiting to happen.

We have lost touch with nature and our value as women as powerful creators and nurturers of new life. Modern women are expected to achieve and perform in the corporate or business world in order to receive any sort of recognition as valuable members of society.

Being a mother doesn't count. Yet from the moment of conception, and even beforehand, we carry the incredible gift and responsibility of the most important job in the world.

Not enough women are consciously birthing their babies or doing their health, and that of their baby, any favours by the choices they make (or make by default by not making them, thus allowing health decisions to be made for them).

To me, this is all part of the need to move towards a conscious and natural lifestyle, which I feel so strongly about. Having babies is a bit like chocolate. If you have never tasted it, you would never know the sweetness and what you are missing out on.

Likewise, if you have never experienced a peaceful, gentle or beautiful birth on your own terms you would not know any better and would accept whatever happens as normal and acceptable, even if it compromises the safety and wellbeing of you or your baby.

Common Doesn't Mean Normal and Normal Has Become Uncommon

When you think about it, birth is something that should come naturally. We have been having babies since the beginning of time. This is what we are designed to do as women, so why do we even need a book like this one?

Have our bodies suddenly become "faulty" in their design or is there something else going on that is responsible for the unreasonably high caesarean rates and common use of medical interventions to birth our babies into this world? This is exactly what we will explore in this book.

If natural birth is what we have been designed for and is the way it has always been done until recently, why is it other women start raising their eyebrows when you mention you have had a natural, drug-free labour? It's simply because "normal", natural births have become uncommon in our modern Western world.

To give birth naturally and drug-free these days is the exception and not the norm. So it's official, I am not "normal" and very proud of it!

I still find it surprising though, that the large majority of my female friends with children have had medical or caesarean births. I could count the number of natural births on one hand. However, in my mother's era, only 35 to 45 years ago in Eastern Europe, a natural birth was how it was done in most cases.

There weren't all those drugs on the menu, so very few women used them. Caesareans were only performed in absolute emergencies, not as a common practise, so you didn't hear of it happening much. When you did, people would gasp in horror.

Hospital midwives also encouraged women to be strong and not use drugs in order to not harm the baby in any way. It's an interesting contrast to today's drug-pushing world, where they will generally offer drugs unless you specifically ask them *not* to in a written birth plan!

Having said that, there are some wonderful doctors who are less interventionist in their approach and are happy to deliver breech, twins and multiple-birth babies naturally, and I was fortunate to find one of them.

"It is not female biology that has betrayed the female... it is the stories and myths we have come to believe about ourselves." ~ *Glenys Livingstone*

Keep in mind, medical births have only been around for the last 200 years or so[42]. Throughout history and since the beginning of time, women have been doing a fine job having babies all by themselves (aside from the support of other women) and not a doctor in sight.

That's not to say we don't need doctors (it's a very personal choice) but it's important to remind ourselves that doctors don't deliver babies—we do!

According to the Australian Institute of Health and Welfare Report latest statistics, in 2008 the number of caesarean births was 31.1 percent[34]. Meanwhile, in the United States, around one-third of all American women have a surgical birth. In some Australian private hospitals it is now 50 percent of all births.

Therefore it might be a wise idea to find out the caesarean rates of your hospital of choice before booking into a fancy birthing suite that has the right decor and offers five star luxuries as part of your stay.

How could something so natural have gone so wrong? Surely Mother Nature couldn't have made such a grand mistake when the survival of the human species depends on it?

"What is normal today is not the same as what is healthy." ~ *Barbara Patterson and Pamela Bradley, authors of Beyond the Rainbow Bridge, Nurturing Our Children from Birth to Seven*

There Has Got to Be a Better Way. Tough Lessons on Empowerment - Anneliese's Story

Anneliese settled on a private hospital with an obstetrician for her first labour. She didn't know anybody who had had a natural birth. All of her friends carried past term, were induced and ended up having an emergency caesarean.

Knowing only these outcomes, Anneliese expected the same. She did her best to take care of herself during pregnancy, including chiropractic care to be aligned and ready to go. Meanwhile, she walked the dog every day and did water aerobics to keep active.

Anneliese, who went into labour early one Saturday morning, had to learn important birth lessons the hard way. In the midst of labour, she sensed her obstetrician was impatient to go home and have her weekend free.

" Without any real explanation or consultation, her obstetrician announced, "One and a half hours is long enough, let's get him out. "

Being her first labour, she was unaware she could say "no", as nobody had told her that in the hospital antenatal classes. All she knew from the classes were "all the bad things that could go wrong" and the only options for pain relief they taught were medical ones.

During her pregnancy when she had asked her obstetrician about having a birth plan, Anneliese was told there was "no need", so she didn't bother making one and convinced herself that "you can't plan these things".

Following the birth, Anneliese found out another woman was waiting for her labour room, as the hospital had an influx of 10 to 12 babies that day—a lot for a small private hospital to handle. This meant she was unable to birth in her own time.

Extra interventions such as an episiotomy[6] were used to hurry things along. Because of the episiotomy, she struggled to feed her baby for the first week-and-a-half after he was born, as it was difficult to sit down for any length of time.

The pethidine used during labour for pain relief, meant her baby came out groggy and had difficulty feeding. She also believes it made her feel detached from her own baby, which affected the natural bonding process straight after birth.

She remembers thinking: "Is he really mine?"

Needless to say, this was not an empowering or positive experience! This fuelled Anneliese to do things very differently the second time. She knew there had to be a better way.

Later she discovered pethidine stays in the baby's body for up to four weeks, yet nobody had told her that. For the first six weeks, he wasn't feeding or sleeping properly and she was not coping at all.

In fact, she would feed him and then quickly hand him over to her husband, as she didn't want anything to do with him. Sadly, as a result of all of this, she suffered from postnatal depression.

Anneliese's story illustrates the cascade effect of intervention and the importance of understanding what is going on with your body.

It also shows how crucial it is to know your options—including the pros and cons of the different interventions—your right to question your care providers and say "no" if something doesn't feel right.

Also the importance of being involved in the decision-making process, rather than having things done to you without your knowledge or consent. As you will discover, knowledge is the first step to empowerment.

A Healing Experience: "I Did It-Just as Nature Intended!"

The good news? Anneliese's second birth was far more empowering than the first and was exactly the healing she needed. Being a very strong person, she decided to give it another go.

This time she was going to do things differently. She was determined to have a natural birth without drugs, even though she couldn't imagine how that was possible.

She decided on a public hospital with her own midwife (she had considered a birth centre, however, the one-night stay wasn't long enough for her).

For Anneliese, this was much better than the previous experience she had in a private hospital with an obstetrician. "I cannot fault it, it was much better," she says. "I was much more mentally prepared the second time around thanks to the birth course."

After lots of reading on the subject, Anneliese was armed with a birth plan and knew what she wanted.

With her husband, she had prepared her mind with a special hypnobirthing course that taught her how the body works, as well as relaxation and breathing techniques.

As a result, she found it was much easier to get into "the zone", which is where she stayed most of the time. She took charge of her birth experience with, "This is my experience and I want to do this right. I don't care what's going on around me."

** ** *She found the more deeply she breathed, the easier the contractions were. Therefore it was much more manageable.* **"**

Only once did she say, "I don't think I can do this", to which her newly empowered husband responded with, "Just breathe, you are doing really well!" This was exactly the kind of support she needed.

Thanks to the course, her husband knew how to support her, also saying reassuring words such as, "She's nearly here!"

Anneliese was so relaxed and in a different zone this time, that her husband didn't think she was listening—so he started casually talking about the unfortunate events of the last experience to the midwife.

Anneliese was still aware and all she needed to say was "Mat, don't!" and he stopped. She didn't want those thoughts in her head. As far as she was concerned, they didn't exist.

Anneliese had pre-warned her husband that if she asked for any pain relief this time, to get her through another couple of contractions before making any decisions and not give in straight away. Yet she didn't ask for a thing.

This time she was a little bit vocal but not nearly as much as the first time (she had much more internal focus) and she wasn't squeezing her husband's hand like the first time. She just focused on relaxing and getting rid of any tension. She also knew it couldn't last forever.

Besides getting in "the zone", she used other drug-free tools such as music, a hot shower in which she held onto the chair while breathing through contractions, and a face washer.

Her state of focused relaxation meant she could feel the baby moving down but wasn't as aware the head was being born. The birth happened only two-and-a-half hours after arriving at the hospital. Her labour lasted for only four-and-a-half hours from start to finish.

When her baby girl was born, she was immediately placed on her chest and fed beautifully straight away on both sides—Anneliese says she is still "on a high" from this experience. "Wow, and all of it with no pain relief!" she adds.

There were no effects on her or the baby from the drugs this time, which made a remarkable difference to both of them. She was able to bond with her baby girl instantly: "She is amazing, I just love her to bits!"

Her baby became a great feeder and sleeper, settled well and even put herself to sleep—the exact opposite of her first experience.

" She believes going natural and drug-free meant her second baby was "a lot calmer and more at peace internally". "

For her second labour, she had learnt her lesson and ensured there were minimal visitors in the hospital and her newborn baby wasn't passed around.

It was all about the three of them bonding and getting to know each other, and that's all that mattered.

She was head-over-heels after the birth: "I couldn't believe it, I did it—just as nature intended!" Anneliese says.

While she felt she had missed out on something during her first birthing experience, this time made up for it. She now firmly believes nature intended women to birth naturally. Anneliese now encourages other women to "give your body a go".

Anneliese's Keys to a Natural and Empowering Birth

- Gain knowledge. Do lots of reading and find a good quality independent birth course.

- Create a birth plan.

- Trust your instincts. Hers were always there but she didn't have a chance to trust them in a hospital environment.

- Be prepared physically, mentally and emotionally as to what is going to happen.

- Enjoy the experience. She actually looked forward to the labour as it was a chance to put everything she had learnt into practise and she wanted to see if she could do it.

- Respect the importance of relaxing between contractions, so the uterus can function as it should.

> *"…Birth is a rite of passage of women. Their journey should be honoured, their rights should be fiercely protected, and their stories should be shared."*
>
> ~ MARCIE MACARI

2nd Insight:
Make a Commitment

> *"Stay committed to your decisions, but stay flexible in your approach."*
>
> ~ TOM ROBBINS

*I*f there is one thing I have learned about birth, it's that you can't just sit on the fence and see what happens. Deciding what you would like upfront—a natural and drug-free birth or a medical labour—and committing to it, means you can begin making conscious preparations towards achieving your desired outcome.

For instance, if you have not made a firm commitment to go drug-free and haven't written it in your birth plan with something such as, *"Please do not offer any medical pain relief,"* then you may get to a point in the labour where you don't know if you can do it anymore. At your most vulnerable point, you will likely be offered the drugs and in that weak moment, it's easy to give in unless you have made a very strong resolve not to beforehand.

When I've asked my pregnant friends, *"Are you planning to go natural?"* They would often say, *"I'm not sure yet"* or *"hopefully"* or *"I will see how I feel when I get there"*. Their experience would likely be unpredictable unless they made some definite decisions between then and the birth.

I have seen this pattern again and again. If there's anything predictable about childbirth, this would be it! Those who sit on the fence and leave it to chance are likely in for a bumpy ride. I knew from experience that my friends' indecision would almost certainly lead to medical intervention.

I'm so grateful I was prepared with a thorough birth plan, thanks to the research I had done during the previous nine months.

...utcome was always a natural, drug-free and gentle birth, free ...edical interventions.

Being a "natural woman" in every other part of my life, it simply made sense and was non-negotiable. I didn't want to hear about any other option. I wanted to be undisturbed, left to my own devices, the way nature had intended.

Above all, I have always believed natural is best. That trust in nature really helped me stay strong and have faith in everything working out for the best.

Having had two natural, drug-free births, this was my single most empowering decision. It is also the healthiest and most selfless choice you can make for your baby, which is the first step to thinking about another person before yourself—lesson number one of being a conscious mother!

We can then carry this strength and courage throughout our lives and bring those same qualities to everything we touch, starting from parenthood itself.

Giving birth naturally, prepares us so much better for the incredible journey of motherhood, where we are often called upon to push through challenges and access more of ourselves than we ever realised we had inside or thought was possible.

Like myself, the large majority of women who shared their stories, had made the conscious decision to give birth naturally and made firm decisions regarding the use of interventions well before the event started.

> *"You are constructing your own reality with the choices you make... or don't make. If you really want a healthy pregnancy and joyful birth, and you truly understand that you are the one in control, then you must examine what you have or haven't done so far to create the outcome you want."* ~ Kim Wildner, Mother's Intention: How Belief Shapes Birth

Natural Birth By Choice or Chance? - Mothers' Wisdom

"I always knew I wanted to have a natural birth and very little, if any, medical intervention and my wish came true. The birth was just the way I had visualised it. I definitely thought about it and made decisions on, 'this is how it is going to be'—deciding not hoping." ~ Amanda

"I knew the gas might upset the baby and wanted as low toxicity as possible. No one was going near my spine with a needle! Therefore I had no drugs during labour and was very set on it beforehand." ~ Robyn

"I decided to have a natural birth as I wanted to allow my body to do what it was made to do. I also wanted to be aware and available for my baby." ~ Rachel

"I had decided to go natural before I went into hospital and took steps to ensure that it would happen. My midwife is a powerful woman who knows the hospital system really well. My birth team were also all advocates of natural birth. If you want a natural birth in a system that favours intervention, you have to make sure you have a team with you that is strong enough to ensure a natural birth outcome." ~ Heidi

"I opted for natural all the way but kept in mind if medical intervention was needed and it was safer for the baby, then that was okay too. I recall friends who wanted a natural birth and didn't end up having one and they were very disappointed—I believe they held onto the idea too tightly. You need to be happy anyway. I knew what I wanted in my heart, but I was going to be happy anyway." ~ Kate

"Having a natural birth was worth the few hours of pain and I knew the benefits for me and my baby. The recovery time is much less and I feared being cut open far more than the birth pain." ~ Leonie

"I chose to go natural because birth is a natural process!" ~ Natalie

Making a Decision: Why Go Natural?
- Experts Say

Sonya Wildgrace, professional birth counsellor (VBAC), independent natural birth educator and doula[4], says it's "very important" to make a commitment to going natural.

"If you do not commit, you secretly believe that there is something not right with your ability to birth naturally and that you are not willing to explore for some reason, usually an unexpressed seed of fear or anxiety," she explains.

"Sitting on the fence means you have doubts in your own ability. Whether that is to know your body well enough, or whether you believe that your birth support may not be adequate."

She believes it could also indicate the mother and partner aren't aligned enough to be able to hold (their) own ground with strong personalities in the medical team.

"Whatever the reason, your inability to commit means a lack of trust in someone or something that makes your desire to sit on the fence a safer bet," **Sonya** says. "Sitting on the fence creates more anxiety and mistrust. Inevitably, prolonged sitting on the fence makes someone else have to choose for us."

Shirley-Anne Lawler, midwife, coach and birth facilitator, agrees the commitment to go natural is a choice. "That commitment and choice will hold you in great stead during the process—a constant reminder that your body and baby deserve a joyful easy relaxed birth experience. This ease and joy naturally flows on in the hours after birth and over the months and years ahead."

"Birth ceases to be a debate at all when you ask an expectant parent whether they would like their child to have the best possible start in life, or would you like to shorten their life span and rip them off of their health and longevity?" says **Sonya Wildgrace**.

"Humans tend to have a quick-fix approach to life. If I can't see the damage with my own eyes, it does not exist. Put quite bluntly, if we cut corners in birth, we just may be shortening the life expectancy and compromising the health of our future generations. I hear parents say, 'Prove it!' I reply with, 'Do you really want to take that risk with your infant?'"

Kathryn Williams, homebirth midwife and natural birth educator, also says it is important to be committed to natural birth so you can prepare and surround yourself with fantastic support. "Why Natural? Why not?" she asks. "It's as nature intended; our bodies and babies are designed for the birth journey and doing it naturally has lasting benefits for mother and baby."

According to **Jo Thomson**, private hospital midwife, many women have different ideas as to what constitutes "natural". "For some, delivering vaginally is enough to warrant saying they had a natural or normal birth, regardless of whether they have used pain relief or had other interventions," she says. "Yet, some pain relief options and interventions can have long-term effects.

Recovering from a c-section or other intervention will take much longer and affect the mother's ability to care for her baby and may impact on breastfeeding as well."

All I Was Interested in Was a Natural Birth - Debbie's Story

I was 20 when I had my first baby boy. I had little-to-no trust in doctors. Hence, I didn't visit a doctor while I was pregnant and didn't go to any antenatal classes. I did, however, search the secondhand shops for a book to give me some understanding and guidance. I found a little guide called Birth Without Violence by Laboyer. It was very inspiring.

Nearly nine months had passed when I woke early one morning with a feeling of strong period pains. This continued for about two hours. I woke my partner and told him, "It's happening, this baby is coming today." It was about 7am and it seemed like forever waiting for him to get ready to drive me to hospital.

❝ When we arrived at reception, I told the lady I was having a baby. She must have thought I meant in a month or so because it wasn't until I had my third contraction in about five minutes in front of her that she realised I meant right now! ❞

The contractions turned my legs to jelly and I dropped down into a squat until they passed. I was asked to wait around the corner as someone would come and see me soon. With my back against the wall, I slid down into a squat as another contraction took over my body.

I heard footsteps coming towards me; it was a lady and she was pulling on a rubber glove. I knew it was me she was coming to see. What a moment, no time to be shy. She told me she wanted to see how dilated I was so I lifted up my skirt. I was still squatting against the wall, probably only 10 metres from the entrance of the hospital but just around a corner, out of sight.

She said, "Wow, you're 10 centimetres dilated, you really are ready, come with me." We walked down the corridor and were joined by a few other hosptial staff. I was panicking, worried they would just take over.

So I decided to speak up and tell them I wanted a "Laboyer style" birth and, lucky for me, they knew what I meant and agreed. I was taken to a room and a bean bag was brought in for me.

Someone went to get a full length mirror and they asked us if we had brought any music, which we hadn't. This all seemed quite funny to me.

" All I was interested in was a natural birth. "

I sat back into the bean bag and began to feel quite an intense lower back pain like you can get with your period, but stronger. I thought it was just a progression of the birthing process. I began to curse and curse. This went on for about 15 minutes.

I was a bit of a rebel and was only concerned about myself at this point. I wish I had gotten up and moved around but I didn't. I had no idea at the time that my position was contributing to my discomfort. My whole body was pushing down and it was intense.

My baby's head was crowning and as my partner was invited to look, just at that moment my waters broke, splashing him in the face. He quickly retreated to the safety of behind my head. He was stroking my hair, telling me I was okay, which annoyed me.

As the head came down further I began to tear—now I really had something to complain about. I silently laughed at myself, when a strange man walked into the room and took front stage.

I asked him who he was and he said quite proudly, "I'm your doctor, I'm here to deliver your baby." I thought that was a joke, I was the one delivering my baby, not him. Anyway, no time to argue.

My baby was born shortly after and an amazing sense of calm came over me... "It's a miracle," I thought. "A baby has grown inside me!"

The doctor held my bubs on a slight angle to allow his lungs to drain; they clamped and cut his cord and passed him to me wrapped in a little cloth. The placenta came out with the next contraction and it was in perfect condition. My baby was born just five or six hours after I woke that morning.

I was asked when I wanted to go home and I said "right now". I was told that was fine. I had a shower while daddy bathed our brand new little son. I came out of the shower to find a nurse inspecting my son, so I asked her what she was doing.

She told me she was just checking his Apgar score, a visual observation that tells the condition of a baby. My baby's score was seven out of 10. She told me he had the highest score she had seen in her career. He weighed 2.7 kilograms.

I was very proud, considering I had experienced nearly all-day sickness for much of the entire pregnancy.

" I held the point of view that my body knew exactly what it was doing. I had a strong sense of trust in nature's intrinsic design. "

We left the hospital shortly afterwards, just one hour after we walked in. I was very appreciative for their help even though I didn't show it or say it to anyone. The respect they showed me was enormous. I am forever grateful.

Two years later I was in labour again. This time I was having my baby in the squat position, supported by the doc and nurse. I was squatting on the bed with my arms wrapped around their necks, with my face just millimetres from the nurse when she said, "I know you, I was the one there when (pointing to my now toddler) was born. You are a legend. To this day people still talk about you: the lady who had her baby and was in and out of the hospital in an hour."

I felt so proud; totally chuffed with myself. I had had no idea. Wow, how cool, this lady was not a stranger at all. This was a pretty special moment... I smiled from ear-to-ear.

A few minutes passed and another contraction or two.

66 Little did I know the next one was it and it didn't hurt at all. I just felt a sensation which pushed my baby down through my birth canal and out into the room. 99

I leaned my head forward to see only a little head popping out. I began to panic... had I given birth to an alien? The doctor read my face and reassured me the rest will be out with the next contraction and sure enough he was right. As the doctor moved forward to catch my baby, he had to ask me to let go of his neck. That was funny.

The doc passed me my baby and I held him up to have a good look. It was another boy. I thought, "Oh it's you," like I knew him very well. The doctor had to prompt me to tilt him sideways, to lower his head so his lungs could drain.

I could feel a tug below and became confused. The doctor reminded me the placenta would be out in a minute with the next contraction.

They didn't clamp or cut the cord straight away. They waited until my little boy was breathing with his own lungs first. The atmosphere in the room was very gentle and I got my wish, my number one son was there to witness the birth of his little brother.

About 18 months later, I fell pregnant for the third time. I had planned the first two, but this third one was my birthday surprise. Yes, I had conceived on my birthday. I wasn't ready to have another baby.

It took me about four months before I decided to stop blaming and cursing myself. I knew I had to make peace and apologise to my unborn baby or it might decide it doesn't want me either and things could go horribly wrong.

My waters broke around 4.30am on the morning of the night I'd stayed in hospital with my three-year-old son who had broken his arm. We were relocated to a labour ward. While we sat waiting for something to happen, I decided to experiment with various positions.

I had no sensations, pain or anything at that time, it was just that my waters had broken. My stress from my son breaking his arm had brought on my labour. It was only one week earlier than the other two who had come of their own accord so I was not too worried, but I was a bit concerned that my unborn bubs was stressed.

The staff seemed a bit frantic, so I asked them what was going on. I was told it was a high risk delivery because I was only 36 weeks pregnant. "Really?", I thought, I wonder how they worked that out, no one had asked me one single question.

So I thought I'd better tell them the truth but they seemed to just dismiss me. With that said I went on with my experiments.

I tried out the hands and knees postion, which was very comfortable. I had a go at squatting, hanging onto the bed head for support, as my team wasn't there to help me. Then I sat back down and arranged the pillows like a bean bag and leaned backwards.

" Wow, what a surprise, that lower back menstrual-type-pain was right there just like when I had my first baby. I was amazed and excited. I played with it a few times sitting up at 90 degrees then leaning back. "

Each time I moved backwards past vertical, my lower back became uncomfortable. I felt like I had been the first one to discover this! I was content with my experimenting and returned to my hands and knees.

About 20 minutes had passed when someone came to check on me. They wanted to check my dilation, so I got into squat so they could have a good look. "Wow," they said. "The head is there, you're crowning." So the word got out.

Within a minute, I had about six people forming half a circle around my bed. Now I had an audience, who would have guessed? I couldn't be bothered arguing so I chose to ignore them instead. Then someone said, "Get the kid (my son) off the bed, he is in the way."

Someone put him on the ground and he ended up on the outside of the circle. All I could hear was his tiny voice saying, "Mummy I can't see, mummy I can't see." I was thinking, "Great one, everyone else can see but my own son." Yes, I was angry and just at that moment someone else heard him and picked him up so he could see. I wanted to give that person a star sticker for being so thoughtful.

" I was so happy he was now part of the excitemen
at him, my whole body relaxed and my baby was born
whoosh. I didn't even feel a contraction, let alone any pa
awesome and wow was it quick. "

Someone stepped forward and caught my baby boy. He was ju..fine.
They gave him a little wipe down, wrapped him in a cloth and passed
him to me. By that time, the placenta was out and gone.

They asked me when I wanted to leave and I said "now" but then it all
came back to me: we had to wait until the doctor gave my other son
the all clear. It was only 6.30am and the doctor wasn't even on duty
until around 9am. At least I had my son there with me to witness the
arrival of his new little brother.

Giving birth was the most fun thing ever. I enjoyed it so much I had
to share. If there is one message I would like to share, it's do your
perineal massage[(2)]. *It is so worth it, you'll be amazed.*

Much love and best wishes to all the mums-to-be.

"Giving birth to a new life is about so much more
than just the moment itself. The power of finding
your strength as a woman through birth resonates
for the rest of your life. It shapes you as a person,
and as a parent."

~ GINA SEWELL

3rd Insight:
Knowledge is Birth Power

"If I don't know my options, I don't have any."

~ DIANA KORTE

*W*hen it comes to birth, ignorance is certainly not bliss. Knowledge is the key to unlocking the door to a wonderful birth.

Taking charge of your birth experience begins with knowing all your options, determining what is right for you and making informed decisions as to who, where and what you will accept for you and your baby's welcoming into the world. These are important decisions to be made for the special occasion of your baby's birth-day and need to be worked out beforehand. This of course is unique to each woman and a process each one of us must explore for ourselves.

This can mean the difference between having an amazingly positive and joyous experience or wondering why you were so "unlucky" or what did "I" do wrong?

As you will discover, achieving a natural, empowering birth is far more than just a matter of "good luck". There is a lot you can do to influence the outcome and give yourself the best possible chance for a positive and rewarding experience for you and your baby.

I Am Woman, Hear Me Roar!

Women have choices and rights. Most of us just don't know about them, as we have been kept in the dark for too long. There's a saying: *If you don't stand for something, you will fall for anything.* I feel there are close parallels with the subject of birth, as we are really being led astray and not being told the full story.

Our society leads us to believe giving birth is only one day or so out of our whole lives and just a means to an end (or a new beginning in this case). Having spoken with countless women who are traumatised or deeply affected years later by how they were treated during labour, or by not having the birth they wanted, I am convinced now, more than ever, that *birth matters*!

The process and the woman's mental and emotional wellbeing are just as important as the result and will actually influence the outcome. The same process can either lead to trauma and ill feelings—or personal satisfaction, empowerment, pride and the greatest joy.

This feeling and memory stays with you for the rest of your life. Also, your baby only gets one chance to come into the world, so isn't it worth taking the time and care to give them the very best start in life?

It seems to me we let our professionals off the hook too easily with the one line—"*as long as there is healthy mummy and baby*"—that covers or justifies all wrongdoings and supposedly makes everything "okay". Even when the woman is traumatised by her experience, she is often made to feel it doesn't matter. It's time for a positive birth revolution!

Understanding the Cascade Effect

What is one of the biggest pieces of the birth puzzle? Becoming aware of the Cascade Effect. As we heard in insight one, one little step of intervention can lead to another (and another and another) and have massive implications and complications down the track for mother and baby.

For instance, being hooked up to a foetal monitor for a long time causes the labouring woman to become inactive. This can slow labour down (due to distraction of the monitor), cause tension, and result in an inability to move around, so her membranes may need to be artificially ruptured to speed things along.

This only decreases her ability to focus and makes the woman more likely to request medical pain relief, leading to further intervention and making a caesarean birth a more likely outcome[19].

In birth, things are designed to work in a specific, intricate and uniquely individual way. If we mess with one thing, no matter how "harmless" it may seem, it will always have consequences.

When your body is ready—and not a minute sooner—everything will happen perfectly all on its own, as it is meant to. So, if knowledge is birth power, were our empowered mothers properly informed before they gave birth? Yes they were!

Ripe And Ready - Mothers' Wisdom

"I was well-educated and informed for my three home births with very detailed birth plans, support people and very tuned into what I needed and when. I belonged to an education group supporting women's rights to be informed on their birthing options." ~ Vickie

"I did an awesome birth preparation course that prepared my mind and gave me all the knowledge I needed to take charge of my birth experience." ~ Tammy

"I believe I was fairly well informed but nothing could prepare me fully for my first experience of birth!" ~ Rachel

"(We) asked lots of questions, read lots of books, watched videos and decided on a natural birth in a private hospital." ~ Eva

"I read a lot about the process and also birth stories on both sides (positives and things that went wrong)—so I went into the process with a wide view of what happens. I was open to the needs of the baby during birth.

Although I wanted a natural birth, if the baby needed medical intervention, I would be okay with that because ultimately the health of the baby is the most important thing, not my desire for a natural birth." ~ Kate

"Do your research. Don't take everything you are told at face value. Empower yourself by busting all the myths. My best suggestion is to stay away from hospital births altogether. Birth in a place of your choice that's beautiful, peaceful and known to you—not ugly, rushed, timed and unfamiliar." ~ Leonie

The Beauty of Hindsight

"I wouldn't go to hospital birthing classes! However, I would do it exactly the same—it was perfect." ~ Amanda

"I would do it exactly the same. I would love to do it over and over again as it is so exciting and such an empowering experience for the whole family."
~ *Kristen*

"In hindsight, I wish I had never had my waters broken. My body was working fine until it was intervened with and I believe that I would not have required pethidine if I had been encouraged to continue in my own way." ~ *Rachel*

Do Your Due Diligence - Experts Say

Cas McCullough, a birth and postnatal doula, suggests new mothers figure out what is important and find the option that best supports what they want.

"If you want a natural birth then it is unwise to go to a private hospital with high caesarean rates," she says. "You'd be better off finding a midwifery program or having a home birth. In any case, hiring a doula and having someone there for you continuously throughout labour is of real benefit."

Meanwhile, **Jo Thomson** says the caesarean rate of most Australian hospitals is 30 to 40 percent, regardless of whether it's private or public. "(It's a good idea) to look at individual obstetrician c-section rates, rather than the hospital as a whole, as some have much higher rates than others—and also to avoid having epidurals[1]."

Jo adds: "Most midwives, at least at the hospital I work at, support natural birth. Many have done a course on acupressure in childbirth, and it is hoped our unit will be able to provide women with the option of water births within the next couple of years."

Cas strongly advises doing an independent childbirth education class or hiring a doula who will provide childbirth education as well as labour support: "Book into a few different options in the first few weeks so you don't feel rushed to make a decision.

Make a decision that fits with your needs and not with the needs of your grandma, aunty or sister. Make sure you have continuity of care by a supportive midwife and or doula wherever you are birthing."

Cas firmly believes the best gift you can give your child is to make informed choices about birth. "A positive birth experience gives you a great start to parenting and breastfeeding," she says.

Shivam Rachana, principal of International College of Spiritual Midwifery, teacher and author, believes there is great value in a woman's endeavour to create a human being and the long-term ramifications of doing so.

"Women need to embark on a process of learning and having the full experience. Give her information. It is a new state and she may be frightened. Helping a woman to have the experiences and feel confident about them is important," she says.

Rachana's words of wisdom: "It is a challenge. You do not decide to run a marathon and then get up the next day and run it. You need to prepare for it mentally and your body needs to prepare.

You need to treat your body in a particular way so you don't arrive tired to the labour. Pregnancy is a great point of personal growth—a great spiritual awakening.

With the emotional body and hormones, it is energy that is moving— allow the emotions to move through you during pregnancy. It is a time of heightened health … return to our mammalian nature … follow Mother Nature's blueprint and we will get a good response."

> *"The truth for women living in a modern world is that they must take increasing responsibility for the skills they bring into birth if they want their birth to be natural. Making choices of where and with whom to birth is not the same as bringing knowledge and skills into your birth regardless of where and with whom you birth."* ~ *Common Knowledge Trust*

More Than Just Good Luck

A lot of women would say birth is nothing more than a matter of "luck" or "outside of our control". How much influence do we really have over our birth outcomes and why do mothers have such vastly different experiences?

"I hear this from many women who have become detached from their own birth story," says **Sonya Wildgrace**. "It's easier to blame their loss of control on outside influences than to take any responsibility for the outcome.

Some genuinely don't even know they have ecstatic hormones. They are among the large majority that are influenced by the media and the medical model of birth.

They don't want to explore the reasons why, because 'why' means pain and suffering. These women believe there is only birth with great pain relieving drugs, or natural birth with all the pain.

Then we have women who know about natural undisturbed birth. They have the secret and they know they are the strength that they invoke."

"The mothers who really 'mean' it, have already researched birth well before they meet me. They know what they want and they are committed, they do their homework and they are willing to talk about the dark stuff.

They explore birth to its end, including all of their fears and they voice them too. They leave no sneaky fear or belief stone unturned. I work a lot with fear and what fear can do if not given a voice."

Diane Gardner believes there is much we can do to achieve a positive outcome. She encourages women to believe their body can do it and teaches them to listen to their body.

She also suggests they become familiar with the documented Fear-Tension-Pain Syndrome[5], and teaches women to use their mind to keep their body relaxed so the most blood can flow where it is needed.

Naturopath and natural fertility specialist **Nicole MacFadyen** agrees, "There is a phenomenal amount we can do to influence our birth outcomes. Everyone is different, however, if we have confidence in ourselves, then this makes a big difference."

A Positive Mind Reaps Positive Rewards

Diane has observed that the mothers who have taken on the hypnobirthing tools and used them, have had "easier, calmer births and calm babies". She suggests using the tools, however, "be flexible with birth and just listen and work with your body".

Unmani, a teacher of conscious birthing and a rebirthing practitioner, says, "There are so many stories of women changing their mindsets and having a positive experience. Also choosing the right person to support them.

For example, a midwife who may delay the decision to go to caesarean if things are taking too long by putting the mother on the toilet and then allowing the urge to push to come about naturally.

A midwife who will override an obstetrician's decision if they think it's the right course of action at the time. There is heaps of power women have and it's time for women to reclaim their power."

Jo Thomson believes those who go into it with a positive outlook and haven't thought about everything that can go wrong, and who are willing to work through it by breathing and staying calm, find birth easier to cope with.

As a hospital midwife, she had not considered birth alternatives, as even the midwife training does not focus on the emotional impact of birth.

She began to realise the effect when looking into post-traumatic stress disorder, identifying that those women who had traumatic birth experiences felt disempowered, as they believed they had no control over what was happening.

Nicole MacFadyen believes calmness and excitement going into it, set the scene for parenting. If the birth is peaceful and what was expected, the mother is not exhausted, traumatised or devastated and it gives her the confidence in her ability to mother. "Positive birth sets up the scene for positive parenting," she says.

Nicole says the key patterns she has observed in women who have a positive experience is knowledge, calm birthing, confidence, trust and knowing.

Know Your Options

Too many pregnant women today are unaware of the different birthing options available to them—and there is a big price to pay for it. It seems too many women do not have enough knowledge in order to make informed decisions of their own.

"Ignorance about childbirth is certainly not empowering and leads otherwise intelligent women to just submissively follow whatever their provider tells them to do[43]."

Dr Michael Klein states, *"Even late in pregnancy, many women reported uncertainty about the benefits and risks of common birth procedures."*

For instance, a shockingly high number could not answer basic questions regarding the pros, cons or safety issues associated with epidurals[1], episiotomies, caesareans and other childbirth options.

This is worrisome because a lack of knowledge affects their ability to engage in informed discussions with their caregivers[43]."

What hope does any pregnant woman have of experiencing an empowering birth if she doesn't know what is happening to her own body and is uninformed of the pros and cons of her decisions?

Blissful Birth in the Comfort and Privacy of Her Own Home - Natalie's Story

I chose to have home births for both of my babies. I have never been one for doctors or medical intervention unless absolutely necessary and had opted for alternative therapies instead. To be honest, I was fearful of giving birth in a hospital.

I did a lot of research. I always had my head in books, especially the first time around— anything that I felt would empower me to actively contribute to the birthing and nurturing of my child.

I took in what felt right for me and took nothing as gospel. I understood every woman's birthing and parenting journey is unique and one size does not fit all.

Also, I went to natural pregnancy and yoga classes and ensured I was completely comfortable with the decision I had made. I could not think of anything more beautiful than birthing my baby into an environment that was purposefully created to provide the most blissful energy I could.

I loved the fact it was my home and that after the birth I could have the comfort and privacy of my own room. I spoke to people who had had home births; I watched videos, met with midwives and visited the hospitals. I also "went within" and tuned into my own higher guidance and awareness.

Ultimately the decision was easy for me. I also wanted water births because it made sense that the pain relieving benefits and the transition from watery womb to warm water help create a much gentler birthing process.

My two extraordinary midwives visited frequently prior, during and after the birth and became like family. I had complete trust in their abilities and advice. I knew I was going to have their full support and focus throughout the entire process.

Having the follow up after the birth also made such a difference. They were embracing of all my ideas and needs and were also excellent support for the other people who attended.

Mum was coming all the way from Queensland, Australia (I was in Western Australia at the time) for the birth of my first child. I kept saying to the baby, if you want grandma to be here, you have to wait until at least the 22nd (when grandma would arrive).

Sure enough, on the morning of the 22nd, I went into labour and was well into it when they arrived. I had my partner, his mum, my mum, the midwife and a close friend (who was videotaping in our tiny apartment)—with the birthing pool in the kitchen.

Both grandfathers were waiting in the lounge room. It was beautiful to have all those women to share it with and to be able to bring the men in immediately after the birth to be involved.

It was a little crowded but so supporting and encompassing.

My first labour was four hours and textbook perfect. Tahlia was born in the water and we spent time just floating before getting out. I found the water to be really soothing and supportive. I had my music playing, low lights, incense.

❝ I was fully present and aware throughout the whole experience. I felt centred, attuned, powerful. I was amazed at what my body knew to do. ❞

I felt I had done all I could to birth this baby with awareness and now I had to just trust the natural process to unfold. It was the most amazingly beautiful experience.

It was a different story altogether with my son's birth. I had very few contractions, and had the urge to push way before my mind had caught up with what was happening. I didn't feel as centred but very instinctual.

I had no time to think or plan, to mentally prepare myself or meditate. It was purely a physical knowing and flowing. We (me, mum, stepdad and baby) were all a little shocked at the abruptness of his arrival.

My husband was away at sea and I had sent my daughter to my aunt while we filled the tub in readiness. But my little man was in a hurry and was born 45 minutes later.

Even though I wanted my daughter to be a part of the birth, we didn't have time to get her back (she had been such a part of the lead up whenever the midwife came, including listening to the baby's heartbeat).

As it was, the midwife didn't make it in time either and my mum had to deliver him! She was so grateful she had experienced my daughter's birth and knew what to expect. Was she scared? Absolutely, but she got in the tub and helped me birth.

My stepfather was roped into filming because everyone was missing it. The dog was a constant companion too. The midwife arrived in time for the delivery of the placenta and the check over. Dad (my husband) arrived eight days later.

I didn't have enough water in the tub to submerge and mum wasn't comfortable with him being born in the water where she couldn't see, either. When he was born, the cord was around his neck and mum simply undid it.

Once he was born and with the midwife administering to us all, we relaxed and marvelled at what we had accomplished. He came in a rush and has been into the fast and the furious ever since!

I think even with all the best intentions, the experience is never what you think it will be. Better to surrender and accept that who is there is meant to be, and those who aren't, aren't.

I also believe every woman should take the time to research—this is your body, your baby, your choice. Always get a second opinion and trust your instincts.

Remember birthing is a natural process, not a disease or illness.

"Research your birth options and decide on your wants/needs in pregnancy prior to labour as much as you do before you buy a cell phone plan, new computer or car. Those things can all be returned or exchanged, your pregnancy, labour and birth cannot."

~ DESIREE ANDREWS

4th Insight:
Get In The Zone

"When you have come to the edge of all the light you know and are about to step off into the darkness of the unknown, faith is knowing that one of two things will happen: there will be something solid to stand on or you will be taught how to fly."

~ PATRICK OVERTER

Learning to relax or meditate is a wonderful tool for life and especially important to cultivate in preparation for labour. This mind-body preparation pays off later, as regular practise makes it much easier to go to this relaxed space during labour, and is especially helpful for the transition from home to hospital (if you choose a hospital birth).

It also ensures your body stays in a relaxed state for the entire process so everything flows smoothly and you are able to go into a different state altogether—also referred to as "getting in the zone". This is a vital piece of the puzzle.

Empowered to Rearrange the Furniture!

While creating a relaxed internal environment is the first step to getting in the zone, it is important to recognise that choosing the right birth conditions where you feel most comfortable—and then creating a safe space, no matter where you are in your external environment—is just as important for feeling at ease for birth.

It is interesting to note, mammals will not give birth until they feel completely safe and private, away from any predators. We are no different[42].

Our internal state is impacted by our external environment. For instance, the mere sight of the hospital medical equipment made me feel uneasy. To create a safe space, my husband asked the nurses to hide any medical equipment on arrival to hospital so I would "feel more at home" (I didn't want to feel like a patient). They thought this was a strange request, but they had no choice but to go along with it.

He then asked them to remove the clock from the wall in the labour ward. This meant I could lose all sense of time and space, instead of clock watching and minimise the distraction of a constant ticking in my ear, while making "getting in the zone" easier.

Thank goodness he did, as I was completely unaware of being in hospital for the next 12 hours! It would have felt like an eternity, had I known, and would have impacted on my confidence.

Thank goodness for the knowledge I had gained from my wonderful birth course, as I would never have thought to do any of these things, or have the nerve to rearrange the furniture! In essence, I was doing everything in my power to make myself feel comfortable, safe and create a homely environment in a private hospital.

The Power of Hypnosis and Going to a Happy Place

How did I get in the zone? As soon as I set the scene with my husband and the initial monitoring was completed, the first thing I did was lay on the floor on my side with my favourite big soft pillow and cosy "safety" blanket from home. I then turned my attention inward, rather than focusing on what was going on around me and listened to my trusty hypnobirthing CD.

It was like an old friend. It calmed me instantly. It was the same one I had used throughout my pregnancy, so my body responded immediately by going into a deep state of relaxation. It felt like I was going deep within myself... into a dream-like state, or going to another place.

This was all part of the "plan" to ensure everything would proceed normally and not slow down events as I had read about so many times. It worked wonders!

Tips for Zoning Out - Mothers' Wisdom

"I think I tried to block out everything that was going on around me and not worry about what I looked liked or sounded like, and just focused on myself." ~ Nicole

"I used breathing and put myself into a meditative state, into my zone, which is what got me through. I wanted to deal with it my way, rather than numbing it with drugs. I wanted to feel any changes—if you are numb during the experience, you can't voice anything or control it." ~ Kate

"Getting in the zone is what gets us through and we do it instinctively. Human mammals are the most vulnerable during birth and stress disrupts this state and can shut labour down so you need to relax for everything to work properly. The best medicine is to be in the zone." ~ Tammy

"The whole time I was in my head, in the zone. I didn't even notice a girlfriend who came into the room." ~ Rebecca

"What helped me to get in the zone? My doula! She was priceless! I had a really fast intense labour and really started freaking out during transition and she talked me through it." ~ Christen

"I did six months of pre-natal yoga to prepare for my birth, so when the time came, I was able to go to my 'yoga-place'." ~ Robyn

"It is sort of like an out-of-body experience. I clearly remember the sensation of… 'This is my body… working very hard, stretching and opening, breathing… and then this is me… the emotional part that is watching a miracle happen'… so difficult to explain, but so unforgettable. I never tried to 'try' and everything really worked out beautifully. I think relaxing is the key and you just need to let go and ride the wave." ~ Jill

The Relaxation Response

Dr Herbert Benson, author of *The Relaxation Response and Timeless Healing,* describes the relaxation response as a bodily calm that all of us can evoke, that has the opposite effect of the well-known 'fight or flight' response.

Many long-term benefits in both health and wellbeing and can be brought on with very simple mental focusing or meditation techniques.

People eliciting the relaxation response open a kind of door, clearing and rejuvenating their minds and bodies, readying themselves for new ideas and suggestions."[46]

According to Marie Mongan, founder of the Hypnobirthing Institute in New Hampshire, United Kingdom, a deep state of relaxation during labour through self-hypnosis can help alleviate the fear and discomfort many women feel.

"Tension and fear can get in the way of labour and prevent it from running smoothly," she says. "Hypnosis can relax a labouring mother and ease anxiety which allows the uterus to be relaxed and work more efficiently and therefore cause less discomfort and pain during labour."[32]

Riding the Waves - Experts Say

"Getting into your own zone or rhythm is important to ride the intensity of birth: there are many ways to do this and it doesn't necessarily need to be taught," says **Kathryn Williams**. "However, learning techniques, thinking it through and visualising or practising how it might happen is great preparation. Key words, thoughts, counting, hypnosis, vocalising your own pattern are examples my clients have used."

Shirley-Anne Lawler recommends a relaxation technique that involves the birthing woman placing her hands loosely face down in the palms of her partner. "The support person gently wriggles the hands up and down, encouraging the woman to stay relaxed, focused on the breath, and loose, keeping eye contact at all times."

She continues: "If the hands of the birthing woman grip at all, there is tension in her body, which inhibits the birthing process. If she loses eye contact, there is lack of presence.

If she restricts her breathing, she is in her head and not in the moment—having a support person who is used to being totally present will encourage the birthing mother to stay present and focused in the moment."

Her second top tip? "Between waves, laugh, tell jokes, watch funny videos," she says. "Laughter really does work!"

Complementary therapist **Robyn Stitt** says don't try to "wish the pain away". "Look at it as a strong stretch—there is a difference—you can't breathe and hold stress at the same time, so by breathing you're actually relieving the tension," she says.

"Muscles send messages to each other. Clenched fists, a tight mouth, a furrowed brow, all send signals to the birth-passage muscles, the very ones that need to be loosened. Opening up to relax these upper-body parts relaxes the lower ones." ~ William and Martha Sears (Birth Without Fear)

A Positive Hospital Birth in the Zone - Amber's Story

When I became pregnant, my doctor told me if I wanted to give birth at a private hospital, I had to book in as soon as possible, as hospitals and obstetricians book out quickly.

I hadn't really thought about what I wanted to do, and hadn't done any research at all about birth, so I immediately booked into a private hospital with an obstetrician my general practitioner had recommended.

I assumed that is how you get the best care, in the most comfortable environment. I was also paying hundreds of dollars for private health insurance. Wouldn't you want the best medical care in case something goes wrong?

I knew I wanted a natural birth and to avoid medical intervention, but soon heard the chances of medical intervention at private hospitals were much greater.

Shortly after starting a natural birth class, the instructor, who was very passionate about what she did, made it seem like I almost had no hope of a natural birth in a hospital. I was pretty scared I had made the wrong decision.

I always wanted a natural birth, but I guess in the back of my mind I wouldn't have been disappointed if, when the time came, I found I needed something for the pain.

❝ What scared me was being in a situation where it was other people, such as the midwives or obstetrician, who were pushing for intervention during birth, when I wasn't able to communicate what I wanted or not in a state to fully understand the risks of not agreeing. ❞

The natural birth classes were helpful. There was not a lot of practical assistance, but just the knowledge it can be done increased my confidence. However, the classes put fear in me about medical intervention and even about going to a private hospital. The classes also focused on the spirituality of birth, and that wasn't something I was very interested in at the time.

After my second meeting with my obstetrician, I left in tears. I wanted to discuss my fears with her, and thought this is what you were meant to do with your doctor. I also read in all the books that you should discuss with your doctor about the birth, what to expect, what their procedures and policies are.

However, I felt she didn't have the time to hear my concerns, and couldn't get me out of the room quickly enough (I later realised she had to rush to the hospital for a birth. Of course if she told me, I would have understood).

After that appointment, I should have changed obstetricians, but couldn't bring myself to do it. This doctor never said anything about her procedures during labour, and I was too chicken to ask, as I could foresee the answer: "Why would I do anything (intervention) if it's not needed?"

Even when I did build up the confidence to ask her a question, the answers were very brief and I felt silly for asking.

I soon discovered, after talking to other health professionals, that this obstetrician wasn't the most empathetic doctor. I will always go by other people's recommendations from now on, as I need someone with a better bedside manner.

❝ I do feel much more confident now in making sure these specialists take the time to care for me in the way I am paying them to! ❞

When I was pregnant, I was quite anxious about whether I was doing the right thing about going to a private hospital and also about my obstetrician, as I didn't know what she would be like at the birth and how much she would dictate what would happen.

I was also anxious about induction—I didn't want to be induced and was scared the doctor would want to induce me too early for my liking. However, throughout the nine months, I gained confidence.

We had gone to the hospital classes, and it actually helped to lessen my fears. The midwives I met seemed lovely, and I left feeling they would always assist a woman to have a birth without medical intervention if possible. I also took up the offer to allow a student midwife to follow my case before and after the birth.

She attended visits with my obstetrician, and I felt like I could speak to her easily about everything, which I didn't want to talk to the obstetrician about. Once she started attending, my obstetrician also changed demeanour—I felt relieved I chose to have her involved. I had also been seeing a physiotherapist who was amazing.

She took the time to talk with me about everything, even the birth. She was the hospital physiotherapist too, and also the instructor of the prenatal water exercise class I was attending, so was a wonderful support before the birth.

Going into the birth, I felt quite positive. I felt like I knew so much about birth and birthing aids, and I had organised my bag with everything I thought I may need during birth... music, a TENS machine[9], heat pack and essential oils. I was also drinking raspberry leaf tea two to three times a day.

" Most importantly, I had the confidence that it can be done—through the natural birthing classes, but also through knowing my mum had three births in a hospital without intervention, and her sister had two. Hopefully it was genetic! "

As my due date approached, I was ready for it to be over! My mind had already started to turn to natural induction methods. I was doing lots of walking, and was ready to go out and buy castor oil. On my due date, my obstetrician said she would give me an internal exam at the next appointment.

We had heard that sometimes if your body is ready, the internal exam could trigger labour. However, at the appointment, the doctor said she wouldn't give me an internal as it was too early and we could still wait a week.

As we settled into sleep that night, I already started feeling light cramping. I watched the clock and realised the cramping was regular and was getting heavier. I lay there for about an hour-and-a-half before I woke up hubby.

We had planned to have my mum and husband at the birth, so hubby called my mum straight away. The contractions became heavier quite quickly and by the time mum got there about 20 minutes later, I was slumped over the fit ball getting into "the zone" for each contraction.

I had the TENS machine out, but I found focusing on the contractions helped more, and the distraction of the TENS machine only made it worse. For a while, a heat pack on my front helped. I thought one on my back might help too. Mum called my sister and asked her to bring one over, and she never left (I ended up needing cool towels, not heat packs).

My husband called the hospital, and the nurse said to wait and call back in an hour. We were keen on staying at home for as long as possible, so weren't in a rush to go to the hospital. I don't really remember what happened after that, but I think mum must have suggested we should think about going.

We weren't timing contractions—they seemed to be coming pretty quickly, but not lasting long. We called the hospital, and after the nurse heard me going through a contraction, she said we should come in. She didn't seem concerned that we weren't timing them.

I had heard the move from home to hospital was usually quite hard. At the time I think I was uncomfortable, but not too bad. I couldn't sit on my bottom. I had to have it off the chair and I was leaning to the right. I could also feel the sensation to push already, but it didn't occur to me to mention it.

I didn't push because I knew if you did it too early you were at risk of tearing, so I fought the sensation. I was thinking quite rationally about what was going on including what part of labour I was up to.

We arrived at the hospital. I had gotten into a pattern of being quite still and moaning through my contractions, rather than moving. The midwife met us. I felt she was quite pushy. I had gotten through everything myself so far, and suddenly without knowing me, she was telling me to walk to the lift and that movement helps with the contractions.

I was thinking I didn't need her to tell me what to do. I was hanging onto my mum while we were walking quite slowly from the lift to the birthing suite, stopping along the way when a contraction came. Again, I felt like I had a rhythm going yet was being forced to move at a certain pace to get to the room.

❝ Eventually we arrived at the birthing suite. The midwife must have given me an internal exam (I don't remember). I didn't really mind having an exam or foetal heart monitoring, unless it disrupted me in my "zone". ❞

My membranes hadn't broken but by the time the midwife examined me, I was already almost fully dilated. She said it was too late for any pain relief if I wanted any. My midwife felt there was no point in breaking my membranes as I was already so far along—I wouldn't have wanted them broken artificially anyway.

As I walked into the room, I sat up on the bed. I felt like a zombie, and although my mind was very aware of what was going on, my body was just doing what it was told. I never envisaged I would be on the bed.

I thought I would be on my hands and knees in my zone, but I went along with it and they checked whatever they needed to. After all of that, my zone had been re-established whilst lying on the bed, so I actually never got up from the bed again. I gave birth on my back in the classic childbirth position you see in the movies!

❝ The midwife kept asking me if I wanted to get up and move around, or go onto all fours, and I just knew if I moved, I would get distracted and come out of my zone, so by my own choice, I stayed there! ❞

The midwife called the student midwife who was assisting me and eventually called my obstetrician once I had begun pushing. At one point the midwife said to me: "That sounded like you wanted to push." I said I had wanted to since the car. She hadn't realised how far along I was, or it must have progressed quite quickly.

Even though I had confidence in what my body was telling me, I was scared of tearing and stitches. After a while of my pushing by myself, they started talking me through it. The student midwife was the one who was most involved, and when my obstetrician arrived, she stood back and didn't say much.

She let the student have the experience, which I am grateful for, as she knew me—and what I was hoping for during the birth. She was assisting me with my breathing during the pushing, and telling me to push down into the baby.

During that phase, nurses kept coming in to have a look, as seeing a baby being born in its membrane was rare.

What helped most during this phase was the midwives, obstetrician and my mum, who told me after each push they could see his head—and knowing every push was one step closer to him coming out. I think hubby was in a bit of shock during the whole thing, but was also offering encouraging words.

With my sister taking the photos, hubby and mum were able to stay up near me—I was holding one of their hands the whole time. They kept asking me whether I wanted to have a look in the mirror, or feel his head, and surprisingly, I didn't want to because again, as soon as I contemplated doing something different, my zone would get disrupted.

Feeling him, seeing what was going on and feeling him as he came out was something I had really wanted to do, but I just couldn't move my body or do anything else other than focus on what I had to do.

Throughout the labour I was thinking, "This isn't that bad… I'm getting through this." Knowing what part of labour I was up to, and how I was progressing helped with getting through it. I kept thinking, "These contractions aren't that long."

It must have been a while on the bed, trying not to push through the contractions, when my mind started to get a bit tired.

❝ I think I muttered, "I can't," but this was counteracted with the midwife and my mum saying, "You can, and you are doing it. ❞

With every contraction, I was giving a low, long moan. Vocalising helped me to get through them. There was no screaming, until the push in which his head came out. I didn't realise I had screamed until it happened, and I think I may have laughed afterwards.

My mum described it as a "primal animal wail", and it was just an instinctual thing to do. Hubby said he had never heard a scream like that in his life—it was just a sudden, one-off loud yell, which my dad and brother said they could hear from the waiting area.

As the end was getting nearer, I started to leave my zone and become more aware of my mum, hubby, midwives and sister. We even have a photo of the midwives and I was laughing at my sister while she was taking photos at the end of the bed, in between pushes.

Bub eventually popped out and was given straight to me. I was told to blow on his face, because he was in shock and wasn't taking a breath properly. I wasn't scared, because the obstetricians and nurses were calm about it.

They asked who was going to cut the cord but I said I wanted to keep the cord connected for a while. They calmly said they needed to cut it now because they needed to move him to give him oxygen. I remember them asking if it was okay.

I'm sure if I said it was important to me for the cord to stay connected, they would have moved the oxygen machine, or my bed. Just knowing they were not doing anything without my approval made me feel relieved, and I said "that's fine"—and my mum cut the cord.

As they had our baby in the corner on the bed with the oxygen, my husband asked if everything was okay, but I knew everything was fine. They gave the baby back to me and we watched as he was making his way to my nipple.

My mum, who is a breastfeeding counsellor, was there eagerly awaiting the photo of bub latching on by himself! Eventually, the midwife attached him.

Overall, I'd describe my birthing experience at the hospital as positive. I was lucky enough to have midwives who allowed me to give birth in the way I felt comfortable. I was also lucky enough to have a quick seven-hour labour, and wasn't faced with a situation where the birth I had hoped for was challenged by any complications.

I think the most important things, which made it possible, were my preparation and mindset in the lead up, reading and watching positive birthing stories, doing yoga and keeping active during pregnancy.

I had read about lots of positions and how to cope during the labour, but in the end I just did what my body was telling me.

I also believe the raspberry leaf tea I was drinking a few times a day helped with my contractions and strength of my uterus. Also, the support and confidence my midwives and support people showed me during the birth was important.

I did have a positive birthing experience in the private hospital, but perhaps next time I'll choose to have my birth in a homier environment of a birth centre.

"Birth is an opportunity to transcend. To rise above what we are accustomed to, reach deeper inside ourselves than we are familiar with, and to see not only what we are truly made of, but the strength we can access in and through Birth."

~ MARCIE MACARI

5th Insight:
Give Up Control

> *"Birth is not something you DO, it is something you allow."*
>
> ~ **AUTHOR UNKNOWN**

*I*n our Western world, especially in the business or corporate sector, modern women are praised and respected for "making it happen" and controlling everything. In birth it is just the opposite. It's more a matter of letting go, going with the flow and allowing it to happen, rather than making it happen. As such, a very different energy and approach is required.

Therefore, giving up control is a big part of the birth preparation process. A lot of us live in our head most of the time. We need to get out of our heads and back into our bodies. Birth is a very primal and instinctual thing, so we need to go to "that place" to allow it to happen.

A girlfriend of mine was pregnant for the first time and was proud to announce she had snared the very best high-risk obstetrician in town. When I politely asked why she needed a high-risk obstetrician when she was low risk and had a perfectly healthy pregnancy, she replied with, "I am a lawyer and like to have all my bases covered… I like to control all risks just in case."

She was a self-confessed control freak. What she didn't realise is she had more probability of intervention, being treated as if she was high risk and of having a surgical birth, just by making this choice.

> *"Treating normal labours as though they were complicated can become a self-fulfilling prophecy."* ~ *Rooks*

Empowering Tips

So what to do for the control freaks out there?

Unlearn what you think you know about giving birth *by attending a recommended independent natural birth course. Consider skipping hospital classes (as I did) which may, in many cases, only feed the fear, and instead, shift your mind to a different reality. Plus it will give you new practical tools along the way.*

Use the power of affirmations. *Make a list of quotes that resonate with you—or turn your fears into powerful positive statements by putting them in reverse, that is, what you would like to experience. Read them daily, dare to say them aloud and really imagine it, feel it… "I go with the flow and allow my labour to unfold naturally." (See www. inspiringbirthstories.com.au for inspirational birth cards with empowering quotes and affirmations for daily use).*

Find positive role models *who have already been there and done it to help instil the belief and confidence that you can do it too. When I was pregnant for the first time, I met a lovely lady who was very naturally-minded like myself. She had given birth naturally and drug-free at home. At the time this sounded revolutionary.*

What really amazed me is she spoke about her births as such fond memories. It was exactly what I needed after being shaken by some stories I really didn't need to hear! Guard your mind against mental pollution, particularly horror stories!

Meditate or quiet your overactive mind daily *with total present-moment awareness, or practise living in the now[44]. With the right mind space, even washing the dishes can be meditative! This will help you get out of your head and back into your body, which is exactly where you need to be during labour.*

Channel the need for control *into writing a comprehensive birth plan detailing how you would like it to be, then put it away and let it go. You may also want to plan for every possible eventuality in this document so you are prepared for everything without actually dwelling on it. This will clear the mind, help to put you at ease and allow you to focus on the positive.*

Feel organised *by packing your hospital bag with all sorts of tricks to feel organised and prepared.*

Harness that nesting instinct *to create order in the house— housework will be the last thing you will want to do with a new baby! This is the time to cook up a storm, especially healthy soups and casseroles with loads of vegetables to freeze for later. Get stocked up with cloth or disposable nappies, so you don't have to leave home more than necessary. This will come in very handy for the first few weeks of cocooning with your newborn baby.*

Look Beyond Birth. *We often place so much emphasis on the pregnancy and birth that we forget to look beyond it at how to raise a healthy, happy well-adjusted child or simply think about what to do next. Then we wonder where to find the instruction manual for this beautiful little person who has taken our world by storm. It's a bit like creating the perfect wedding day and then forgetting to think about nurturing and growing an amazing relationship with your partner after the big day.*

Get Set for a Positive Birth - Mothers' Wisdom

"Do lots of reading and watch videos, stay positive, don't listen to horror stories, believe in yourself, do not panic, breathe and don't scream and swear. Stay calm. Meditate, use positive affirmations—and don't overeat— you don't need to put on 30kg." ~ Eva

I practised breathing and visualisation techniques religiously. The most valuable thing I did to prepare was to stand up for my rights and outline how I wanted to be left alone during my second birth." ~ Rachel

"Be actively responsible for creating what you want in the birthing experience. Spend the pregnancy doing whatever you need to build confidence in yourself, your birthing custodian (doctor or midwife) and your partner. Be proactive. Know yourself well enough to discover what you will require to support and honour yourself in this process. Ultimately it is about you!" ~ Natalie

"Your best chance for a natural and drug-free and relatively painless birth is to believe in yourself and trust your body and look into independent birth courses to help you do so." ~ Maria

"I was very relaxed about things for my first birth. When my waters broke, I drove into work, and between contractions, managed to pay everyone their wages and get that sorted out!" ~ Kate

"I was happy to experience everything and just relaxed between contractions. Don't stress about what's to come—just take it all in, listen to all the sounds around you, do what you need to do and just take it as it comes." ~ Rachel

"With my third, I really let go of my need to know everything and just listened to my body and my baby; tried to tune in to my needs and follow my instincts. Without a doubt, the most valuable thing I did to prepare was going to Birthtalk meetings, pregnancy yoga and having my own midwife." ~ Cas

"I thought, 'what if I can't do this, what if I'm not a good mum?' I dealt with this by telling myself I am not the only one; everyone has gone through it before and had the same silly fears. If they can do it, so can I. The fear factor didn't wreck the whole thing though—it wasn't scary. I was enlightened by everything happening around me." ~ Rachel

The Art of Letting Go - Experts Say

Robyn Stitt says embrace "what is" and go with the flow to enable a positive birth experience. "It's going to happen anyway, so relax and wonder at the power of the human body," she says.

Deanne Schmid, a natural birth advocate and former Homebirth Network South Australia committee member, agrees: "Trust and surrender—keys for a natural birth!" she says. "Once labour kicks in you have a choice— to be frightened and want to run away or be in awe, gratitude and respect of the way your body takes over and just does exactly what it is meant to do.

You cannot stop the contractions coming, so you might as well enjoy the ride! You can go with the flow and trust that each contraction is bringing you closer to having your beautiful baby in your arms.

The more we resist pain with fear, the more it hurts and slows down the birthing process. The more we surrender, 'let go' and trust, the easier it goes. The best thing to be in control of is your attitude!"

"Control usually is where we have to 'have control over everything'," adds **Shirley-Anne Lawler**. "That, you have to let go of!"

In the birth experience control becomes something quite different. Being in 'control' in the birth experience is most important, as the birthing woman must remain very present—in the moment with total focus.

In control of her breath, in control of what she requires and desires, aware that her body is comfortable and relaxed, in control so that she can make choices.

She must be in control and present so she doesn't get out of control, lose focus, which increases the need for possible intervention. Once you lose control it takes a bit to regain that."

A Personal Victory After Learning to Let Go - Heidi's Story

The mere thought of having another baby was not only thrilling and exciting but also worrying and overwhelming. Of course we had enough love, time, cuddles and energy to give. However, there was a huge mountain that loomed over my heart, mind and tummy.

I was extremely fearful about how to deliver the baby into the world in a far more pleasant way than how my first baby had been born. I am a bit of a perfectionist and feel better about life knowing detail, outcomes, planning, and timetables.

I guess I am not one to "go with the flow". So when it came to having my first baby, I was way out on a limb, in the dark, alone and frightened.

After a gruelling 32 hours of labour, high forceps and "lower region" repair, not to mention the dreaded postnatal depression cloud that followed, I decided there had to be a better way to deliver. A caesarean was not one of my options.

In the months that followed until Jeremy's birth, I engaged in a determined focus to learn about hypnobirthing and try to deal with any fears I had in the past.

❝ It was an intense time of discovering what I feared, what I could imagine, how I trusted myself and others and collecting new skills to deal with labour that would ultimately lead to an easier, happier, more comfortable birth. ❞

There was an element of knowing when to hand over my body and baby in the case of things going pear-shaped. Medical professionals have studied long and hard and have far more medical knowledge than me.

I therefore returned to the private hospital where I had given birth to my baby girl, Imogen, 19 months before. However, I knew what I wanted this time: a natural, uninterrupted drug-free labour and birth, and as painless as possible.

" To me, hypnobirthing was the development of knowledge, skills and confidence required to have a positive labour and birth experience. I managed to attend a couple of workshops with a group of other expectant couples. "

We learnt about hospital protocol, deep breathing, lung capacity, "hot chip huffing", hip and perineum positioning, crowning and the role of the "gorilla": the partner, husband, boyfriend, family member or doula who accompanies and supports you in the birthing suite.

They should be skilled and confident in knowing your physical and emotional needs and also in relaxation techniques and basic hospital procedures. I spent as much time as possible at home in labour before leaving for hospital.

My bags were packed and my friend Mish, who had experienced a hypnobirth, came over to accompany me. I bathed quietly in warm water and did not make a fuss or react as the surges began slowly creeping in. I was still uncertain whether I would instinctively 'know' when to leave home but Mish kept whispering, "You will know Heidi, you will know."

The course taught me deep relaxation techniques and visualisations. I often listened to an affirmation CD in the car, especially on longer car trips. My biggest challenge was letting go. I found it difficult at first to give in to the idea that my body would know what to do.

I did understand the physiology behind the woman's body and birthing experience, having studied anatomy. It was more an emotional cling onto the ledge of fear: the dreaded "what ifs".

I often thought back to the animal kingdom and the women, who centuries before me in cultures long ago, did not have monitors, stirrups, sterilised equipment, mediballs and surgeons. To help my body relax, I kept thinking of a rag doll, lifeless and limp, with no strength in their cotton limbs, torso or neck.

When surges became stronger I simply flopped wherever I was and closed my eyes, delving into hearing my heartbeat, breath and observing the tightness across my tummy.

My uterus and cervix were simply expanding, moving, warming up for the main event. It was exciting to think my baby was not far away from its first cuddle and kiss.

> **" Thanks to my state of relaxation, I don't know how many hours labour lasted. "**

It crept up like the soft wave on the shore. I scrambled into the car at 1.30am, cat-like across the back seat and on top of my blanket. I felt every bump on the freeway, as my body was incredibly sensitive. We arrived at the hospital the same time I was born 32 years before.

Despite a routine internal examination being hospital protocol, I opted against this. **First victory!**

I also requested for the foetal heart rate monitor to be switched to minimum so I did not hear the "beep beeps", and only the midwife could see the heart rate on the monitor. **Second victory!**

I wished not to be spoken to unless there was intervention required, based on medical fact and observation. My midwife only spoke to my husband outside the door. **Third victory!**

I used whatever was in the room and listened to what my body wanted to do. I pulled the cushions off the couch and knelt over them on the floor. I was not going to be put into stirrups or lay on my back on the bed. **Fourth victory!**

The lights were low and dim in the hospital and I had clasped my own pillow from the minute I left—my little comfort aid.

I instinctively got up on the bed on all fours, head biting into my pillow and legs apart. My voice was a growl; a deep moan, a release, a relief, a throated howl to the depths of my perineum, and at the in-breath of a further gruelling "surge" I released—with gusto and relief—the embryonic sac that had enveloped my little baby for the past 38 weeks.

The intact bag of fluid came out. The midwife whispered, "Bubs is coming sweetheart, concentrate and let go." Confused but focused (as I thought that could not have been the baby) I filled my lungs with air and breathed down, concentrating, allowing, freeing and propelling my baby down and outwards as my body expanded to its limit.

Two surges later, my little boy arrived with a short umbilical cord, so as I rolled over, I cuddled him on my tummy, as he didn't reach my chest. When his perfectly positioned head moved through me, it was not "pain" as such; it was more of an intense heat, a burn without the fire.

It was a valve of pressure released... a soothing floodgate of relaxation and muscle fatigue; a delicious sense that the "worst" was over, and my miracle took his first breath. The midwife did not cut his cord straight away. **Fifth victory!**

My baby Jeremy was gurgling, cooing, curled up the way he was inside, and had very blonde hair, eyelashes and brows.

" Deep, dark pools of blue gazed up at me, and a flood of pride flushed over me as I had just encountered my wildest dream without a mil of analgesic. Good on me! "

It was a moment in time of bliss, fatigue, the odd shock shiver (as it had been rather quick) and a thirsty mouth. His nails were perfect; lips, pale pink. The lights remained low, as were their voices and a tear of joy ran down my husband's face.

The midwife was astounded. Smiling, she wrapped us up before cutting the cord and leaving us to make me a hot tea. It's an encounter that still fills me with pride and disbelief when I recall my marvellous achievement.

I have no doubt in my mind that any willing, able and confident mother can and has the ability to create her own magical experience through determination, study, focus, health and drive.

Women have been blessed with amazing bodies. You can do it. At least open your mind to what could be. I am a living testimony that anything is possible!

Jeremy became an avid breastfeeder; a smiling and happy boy who makes me laugh, sleeps well, loves riding with Uncle Ben on the motorbike and continues to astound me at three-and a-half-years with his depth of concern for others and his light and cheerful disposition.

There's an important difference between giving up and letting go. Surrendering to the labour is sometimes hard for those who like to be in control."

~ JESSICA HATCHIGAN

6th Insight:
Consciously Prepare Your Mind and Body

"What I love about stories the most is the power they have to teach us of possibilities that might not occur to us without them."

~ INA MAY GASKIN, AUTHOR & BIRTH ACTIVIST

It's interesting that we spend so much time preparing the nursery with all of the must-have items including pretty baby clothes, yet we often don't spend the time to properly prepare ourselves for birth itself. But what does it really mean to prepare for birth?

It's important to protect your mind from mental pollution and those who believe they have a duty to tell you about their own horror story or recount the gory details of "so and so" who had a caesarean or complications.

As curious as you may be, do not let them unload on you. They can gossip or get therapy elsewhere. Your internal environment and emotional health is paramount—they form a sacred space you share with your baby. It's your job to protect its sanctity.

Instead, immerse yourself in positive stories, affirmations, mantras or thoughts, and surround yourself with a community that supports your direction.

Now you're showing off your precious baby bump, there's no better time to take extra care of your body, mind and spirit. I remember having an internal struggle, believing self-care was "selfish". Now I realise it's essential as the air we breathe and the wholesome food we eat.

Looking after myself (and the growing life inside me) meant daily meditation and visualisation, pre-natal yoga, walks in nature and eating the most nourishing foods I could get my hands on.

I also removed myself from negative or stressful situations and did my best to stay calm and centred, all the while avoiding extreme emotions. I found I needed to slow down my work pace, have relaxing massages and listen to my body.

Generally staying active like a normal healthy person (I even managed to climb the Great Wall of China when I was five months pregnant with my first baby!) but tuning in and taking naps if I needed it.

My Empowerment Toolkit

These invaluable tools took me from healthy pregnancy to happy labour:

- Staying active;

- Listening to my body;

- Pre-natal yoga classes or DVD;

- Regular professional massages;

- Meditation and visualisation CDs;

- Walks in nature, such as parks and beaches;

- Eating the most nourishing foods for my baby and I;

- Listening to soft, soothing sounds or classical music;

- Removing myself from negative or stressful situations;

- Avoiding extreme emotions and choosing peace instead;

- Slowing down the work pace, less demands, honouring myself.

Conscious Mind Body Preparations

> *"If you were about to climb Mount Everest you would prepare for it emotionally, physically, psychologically. Research, look at your fitness levels. This is our Everest! Honestly own and befriend your deepest fears and seek help to express and resolve them. Dare to look at everything that feels like a holding out of fear or trauma… then surrender and trust the journey no matter where life and birth takes you…"* ~ Davini

Mothers' Wisdom

"I copped a lot of flak for staying vegetarian—I felt judged (as if) I was doing my child an 'injustice'. I did have apprehensions but I knew this felt right. My iron levels were fine and my child was born perfect in size and in every way.

The midwife commented that my placenta was perfect and healthy! I also drank raspberry leaf tea towards the end of my pregnancy—I believe this helped me to have two smooth births." ~ Kate

"I did yoga, swimming and spent a lot of time squatting in preparation for my birth. Both my babies were born in the squatting position—it allows everything to be open and gravity can assist." ~ Natalie

"(I did) yoga, acupuncture, naturopathy, massage, reading, speaking with positive people who are like-minded. The prenatal classes the hospital ran were interesting. While many others who attended seemed happy to go with the flow, we challenged things that seemed illogical or converse to what we had learnt from books. There were some very interesting discussions." ~ Cory

"I took a liquid iron tonic and did water aerobics, meditation, yoga and lots of walking. The most valuable thing was to keep a journal. Get educated; get to know your body, take yoga classes … get informed. Get to know your body, clear any emotional 'stuff' (about) your mother and really be clear about personal relationships, especially with the father or main partner, as their emotional support is crucial." ~ Vickie

"I rested before the birth, ate well, took supplements to prepare my body. Following a fitness program was helpful in maintaining tone and assisted in recovery." ~ Kristen

"I supported my body with yoga, great food, water and regular exercise. I went to birthing classes that were aligned with my values and spiritual ideals. I spent a lot of time in nature. I wrote and drew and dreamed!"
~ Natalie

Been There, Done That: Words of Wisdom from Empowered Mums

"Let go of the fear. It's a 'positive pain'. Remember that what is happening is natural; research techniques. Don't give your power away, take control of it. Go with what feels right, don't listen to other people. Relax into it, it's a natural process." ~ Wendy

"Empower yourself with research and knowledge. Don't trust everything that you are told by the medical profession. Know that to them, time and money comes before you and your baby. Do not be pressured into doing something that doesn't feel right. Home birth is an option. Not only an option, but a very safe option." ~ Leonie

Empowering Tip:
Honour yourself with increased rest and self care during pregnancy or you may suffer from fatigue, premature labour or toxaemia[10]. Women need to be supported during this time or avoid high stress situations or responses in order to reduce risk of complications. [22]

The True Cost of Not Being Prepared - Experts Say

"You need to consciously prepare for birth or you are more likely to suffer from postnatal depression which affects vitality, mental health and physical health", says **Unmani**.

Nicole MacFadyen agrees. She believes postnatal depression and other emotional and physical health implications can result from not becoming empowered for one's own birth—including possible paralysis from epidurals and the cascade of intervention from drugs.

"If you prepare for it, then the chances of labour being straightforward and having a fast recovery are very high," she says.

"Breastfeeding is also affected if you are not prepared properly because of stress and other factors. Other health implications include possible haemorrhaging. These risks are all unnecessary."

Preparing for a Healthy Pregnancy

In *Alternative Medicine, the Definitive Guide*, naturopathic doctor and midwife, Dr Molly Linton says to prepare for a healthy pregnancy, a woman needs to "realise the physiological impact carrying a child has on her health" and that she listens to the body's needs.

She continues: "Adequate rest, including naps, 'mental' breaks and sufficient sleep are essential. Maintaining a positive outlook and keeping stress to a minimum are beneficial to both mother and baby.

Comfortably paced, regular non-jarring exercise, such as low impact aerobics, walking, yoga and swimming, can increase stamina for labour, strengthen muscles used during delivery and may enhance the ability to cope better with labour."[22]

Eat Right, Birth Right

"Adequate nutrition during pregnancy is the single most important physical factor in determining the outcome of pregnancy." ~ Anne *Frye, author, Holistic Midwifery*

Our body is a temple and we should treat it with the utmost care, eating only the highest quality nourishing foods. Would you put junk in a temple? Of course not.

Yet we often think nothing of filling up the "tank" mindlessly with poor-quality fuel just to get it done quickly in our busy lives; easily, as we often can't be bothered to make the extra effort and cheaply, as we are counting dollars instead of return on investment: that is, eating for all the wrong reasons[37].

Don't just do it for yourself—do it for your baby! After all, the baby doesn't come from nowhere. It is made out of what you are eating (pregnancy nutrition) and have already eaten (pre-conception nutrition).

So if you are really committed to a natural birth, it cannot be emphasised enough to eat right, since this is one of the key factors that will ensure a smooth ride through pregnancy and an easy uncomplicated birth with everything working as it should[19].

Good nutritional status prior to conception and during pregnancy and breastfeeding has been shown to increase the likelihood of a healthy, full-term pregnancy, a shorter and more straightforward labour with less medical interventions and a more successful breastfeeding experience[19]. Your baby's physical, mental and emotional health is worth the extra effort and it's only nine months of preparation until you see the fruits of your labour!

For more information and nutritional tips for pre-conception, pregnancy, breastfeeding, postnatal recovery and beyond, visit *www.inspiringbirthstories.com.au*

Keep in Condition for Body and Bump

Ellie Burscough, a professional fitness trainer for mums says, "Most women think when they become pregnant that they can eat what they want and stop exercising. However the opposite is true. You are growing a little being inside your body.

It is important to eat as healthily as possible to help your growing baby. It is important to continue exercise throughout pregnancy. This differs from person to person. If you are used to running, then running right up until birth may be normal for you. However do not start an exercise program that you are not accustomed to.

Avoid abdominal exercises, exercises where you are laying on your back and contact sports. Be aware of the relaxin (hormone) in your body, which makes you extra stretchy and make sure you don't overstretch. If you are unsure whether any particular foods or exercises are unsuitable in pregnancy, consult a naturopath/dietician or personal trainer."

She adds: "Benefits of exercise in pregnancy can be an easier pregnancy and labour with less complications and less need for intervention. Your body is more prepared, it can help to ease pain and you may have a shorter labour.

Exercise in pregnancy can help to boost your energy, (help you to) sleep better, reduce discomfort, reduce stress and boost endorphins, gain a healthy amount of weight and maintain some strength and muscle tone. It also means it is much easier to bounce back after pregnancy and get back to your pre-pregnancy weight."

A Conscious Approach to a Natural, Joyous Birth - Rebecca's Story

I've always had a robust, down-to-earth philosophy about health. I haven't taken so much as a cough drop since I was about 15, and I don't have a doctor.

I believe if you eat green veggies, exercise, sleep properly, get some sunshine, play in the dirt and think happy thoughts, you'll rarely encounter illness... and when you occasionally do, not only is it excellent for your immune system, but it's usually masking an emotional upset that needs to be addressed.

I first fell pregnant in May 2008 and I remember walking through the house on a sunny day and saying to my husband, "I don't think I want to go to hospital. I just want to have the baby at home."

❝ No fears or worries ever entered my head. The idea just felt right, relaxed and natural. ❞

We searched Google and immediately found a phenomenal midwife who has birthed thousands of babies in hospitals and homes (everything from breech births to twins and cords wrapped around necks) and has an awesome holistic philosophy.

Throughout my easy pregnancy, Lisa, my husband and I met monthly for cups of tea. I had no ultrasounds, because I didn't want to blast my foetus with radiation, and I never saw a doctor or obstetrician; Lisa performed all my check-ups and gave me positive, empowering books to read, such as Ina May Gaskin's "Spiritual Midwifery".

I ate properly, consumed no caffeinated, carbonated or alcoholic drinks, and used nothing on my skin and hair but organic herbal oils. We had a plastic pool all ready to fill for a water birth, but when my waters finally broke—nine days early, at 1am—I realised I didn't desire it.

I filled the house with candles, played soft music and let my body guide me. I did lots of wriggling and stretching on hands and knees, and as my cervix slowly opened, so did my throat. I made louder and louder noises, which greatly assisted the pains.

The contractions went throughout the night, while the midwife sat and knitted, and my husband sipped cups of tea in the corner. It was very quiet and beautiful, and rain pattered on the roof. I kept my eyes closed and focused within.

**   My body was releasing so many natural chemicals; I was sailing high as a kite! It was an awesome natural high. I honestly don't remember the "ouchy" bits!**

Around 5am, Lisa suggested I sit so that gravity could assist with pushing. I delivered my baby half-standing up, hanging off my husband's neck at 8.28am. My baby boy went to the breast and fed within about one minute (his appetite hasn't ceased since!).

After a while, the placenta was delivered and I felt wide-awake, exhilarated and glowing. I held him against my chest, skin-to-skin, for most of the first 24 hours for bonding and natural temperature regulation.

I had a three-dimensional tear but declined stitches. The midwife told me to "keep my knees together" sitting and standing for a week, and it healed back together naturally. I also bathed it in saltwater and swam in the ocean.

After my homebirth I found myself intuitively doing lots of "natural parenting" things such as co-sleeping, and later, feeding him only pureed organic fruit and vegetables. I found my body was incredibly in tune with my baby's—we could awaken from a sound sleep simultaneously!

It was like we had a very strong energetic cord still linking us, and this lasted for months. Afterwards, my husband, a chiropractor, was telling one of his patients how fantastic our birth was.

She asked, "Did you have a homebirth?" "Yes," he said. "How did you know?" "Because you only hear people who've had homebirths talking like that," she answered. "Never hospital births."

I got pregnant again in May 2010 and this time I really took it in my stride. I was almost brutally efficient. I woke up with labour pains around 5am the day after my due date, and the contractions deepened over the course of the day, textbook-style, while I walked around the garden, watched TV and ate chocolate!

The pain was actually stronger the second time or in any case, I can remember it more vividly as it was during daylight. However, I simply told myself, "It's just muscle fatigue from the cramping," and also, "It's totally natural and in about two hours it will be all over for the rest of your life!"

When I felt "pushy", I knew exactly what I had to do this time, and how it would feel. Halfway through, I stopped and gasped, "Is the head out yet?" "Not yet," said Lisa, who was of course helping me once again.

So I kept pushing and out slithered my baby girl—in one long push—and no tear this time. The placenta emerged 10 minutes later, again much quicker and easier than the first time, because I knew what it felt like and what I needed to do.

Breast-feeding was also no problem. My daughter had a slightly twisted foot and some conjunctivitis, but we squeezed a bit of breast milk in her eyes, and regularly straightened out her ankle with stretches and some chiropractic adjustments over the following days, and it sorted itself out naturally within a few weeks.

" Having had two such fun, happy, easy, fear-free birth experiences, I now wholeheartedly cringe whenever I hear hospital horror stories. "

In my opinion, most girls do not have the confidence or health philosophy to feel strong enough to say "NO" to doctors, obstetricians, gynaecologists and bossy hospital midwives who seem to make every personal decision for them, and teach them from the word go, that birth should be "unbearable", "frightening" and "dangerous".

The body really is perfectly architecturally designed to give birth, and the less it's interfered with, the happier and calmer the baby (and mummy) feel.

Doctors are so jumpy and quick to introduce drugs, needles, vacuums, surgery and other forms of butchery when often, the body and/or baby still needs a little time to turn, descend and birth naturally.

We do not run out into the field every time a goat or a sheep gives birth with white coats, stethoscopes and machinery, and nor do we expect blossoms, trees or vegetables to perform "on time" in our gardens, forcing them to follow our own tightly controlled, impatient human timelines.

According to the World Health Organisation, only 12 percent of births are "high risk" enough to actually require the sorts of procedures that hospitals offer. And yet your average pregnant woman receives all of them.

Lots of mums begin labouring nicely at home, but lapse into "shut down" mode when they arrive at the hospital and are told they have to give birth within a time limit.

Mum freezes up with adrenalin, the labour halts, the doctors rush in with forceful procedures, and... well, it's easy to see the downhill series of events that happen after that.

We need to stop drugging our babies and dragging them forcibly out of the womb into glaring, noisy, negative environments, injecting them immediately with toxic chemicals and slathering their skin with petroleum-based skincare products.

Don't even get me started on elective caesareans! I don't know what's worse—the mum who deprives her baby of the natural yeasts, bonding chemicals and vital cranial moulding from the vaginal tunnel, and herself of an incredible life rite-of-passage, or the doctor who selfishly schedules his caesarean so it doesn't interfere with his Christmas holidays!

Another thing that worries me is that often women feel, deep down, they'd quite like a home birth, but their husbands get scared and talk them out of it. We need to honour and support pregnant mums' intuition.

I would love to live in a society that is less medical and more trusting of life's natural flow; a society where women who choose homebirth are not publicly vilified or threatened with fines and jail. At the very least, I'd love to hear more joyous words used to describe pregnancy and birth, and for women to share more heart-warming birth stories.

"If you were told you could have one of the most physically, emotionally, and spiritually transcendent moments of your life and here's the map to get there, would you really say no?"

~ ELIZABETH DAVIS, BA, CPM, AUTHOR OF ORGASMIC BIRTH

7th Insight:
Expect Only a Positive Outcome

"I discovered I always have choices and sometimes it's only a choice of attitude."

~ JUDITH M. KNOWLTON

When my father would visit while I was in bloom, he would hear me saying my affirmations, such as, *"My birth happens easily because I am so relaxed."* He would be quietly sniggering in the corner at my positive self-talk. To him, it was all nonsense.

Yet, I knew it worked, as I had proven it to myself the first time around. So I decided to program my mind daily with only positive thoughts, leaving no room for the negatives to take residence.

During my second pregnancy, it wasn't so much the fear of the birth process that I needed to overcome, or even the unknown, as I knew what to expect—but could I be so "lucky" to have it so "good" twice in a row?

Things didn't work out this time with my midwife so I needed to know I could still do it without her support. It's almost as if I thought I had created the perfect formula for a natural birth. If one element of that formula was missing, would it alter the outcome?

The lesson here was to be flexible, stay positive no matter what, and realise I was the source of power. I did it once and I could do it again!

By the time my baby was ready to greet the world, I had dealt with my fears. Baby was ready for launch and I was feeling incredibly calm and filled with positive anticipation.

This time it began with a nice gradual build-up of light "waves" over a couple of days. We had interstate visitors due to arrive; with their visit falling on the same day I went into labour.

For some odd reason, I decided we would still go along with the original plan and catch up. So, they came over and we shared a meal—and my labour—as a family around the table.

It must have been a very unusual meal for them, as I had to stop to breathe through waves in between sentences, mid conversation! They kept commenting on how well I was handling it all and couldn't believe how calm I was, considering I was in active labour!

As it picked up in intensity and the waves became more regular, I continued to breathe through it while watching the clock for time intervals and taking notes to indicate a pattern of how far along I was, all the while our guests were there with us. I would never have planned it this way but they were great company and certainly served as a pleasant distraction!

Envision an Easy, Peaceful Birth - Mothers' Wisdom

"I envisioned daily, an easy peaceful birth, and that is exactly what I received." ~ Leonie

"I focused on a quick, easy birth, stayed calm and thought positive thoughts at all times and believed in myself. I used my mind to visualise a quick easy birth for many months beforehand." ~ Eva

"Expect only positive, then let go—do not dwell on what could go wrong. Let your birth carer worry about that. Put it on the birth plan and then put it away, that's why you employ them." ~ Tammy

"I told myself that I would be fine and wouldn't need or use drugs during the birth. By talking to myself and creating a positive mindset, this created a positive birth experience. If you are scared, then the fear can create a negative experience." ~ Kayla

"It doesn't have to be a medical thing and you don't have to have doctors and pain killers. It can be lovely and quick and easy." ~ Amanda

"It's not only possible (to experience birth without drugs), it's achievable and most definitely one of the most rewarding experiences of my life!" ~ Rachel

"People say 'I am having all the drugs' before they have experienced any contractions. People need to know they can get through it. Some people find power in saying 'I am having all the drugs that they can give me,' however they are straight away giving away their power and control. Some women just don't know they can do it." ~ Kate

"I would dispel the myth that it has to be difficult—it doesn't have to be! Knowledge is power. Gather all the information that you can. You can prepare for birth to make it easier. Squat instead of lying down! Birth can be easy if you are more conscious and aware." ~ Shirley

Do Anxious Mothers Produce Anxious Babies?

If babies are aware and listening, does that mean they are affected by the mother's anxiety or negativity? Pregnant women have secretly wondered—and ironically worried—whether their negative emotions during pregnancy impact their baby, and researchers have been on the case.

Dr Marcy Axness, PhD, explores in her book *Parenting for Peace*[25] how the lifelong emotional health and wellbeing of a child is directly affected by the experiences of the mother during pregnancy. Scientists have acknowledged a pregnant mothers' moods significantly impact the brain development of her baby.

While occasional stress is not a real concern, a pregnant woman who is in a state of constant anxiety will have elevated stress hormones that "communicate" to her baby that he or she is in an unsafe environment, despite the fact this may not be true!

The constant stimulation by the stress hormones causes the baby's cells to mutate and prepare for a delivery into the unsafe environment that it perceives is the world outside the womb.

Dr Axness writes, *"Chronic stress in pregnancy tends to sculpt a brain suited to survive in dangerous environments: short of attention, quick to react, with reduced impulse control, with a dampened capacity to feel calm and content.*

This makes for a temperamental baby, difficult to soothe and calm, a baby who is challenging to parent".

Therefore, if the mother experiences chronic stress during pregnancy, it can create a temperamental baby who is a challenge to the parent and difficult to soothe and calm. This sadly sets the initial relationship up between parent and child as one of struggle, while being unable to connect in a loving and satisfying way.

The scientific evidence from the field of neuroscience is backing up what spiritual wisdom has been alluding to throughout time; that our experience in the womb is preparing us for our lifelong lessons about who we are and how we are going to fit into the world around us.

We can use this amazing knowledge to ensure we feel supported, loved and safe in order to influence the fundamental brain development of the foetus in a positive way. Thus setting the child up to be born with the idea of love and safety and not ready to tackle a dangerous world![25]

Fear-Free Birth - Experts Say

Diane Gardner empowers women by helping them to understand the documented Fear-Tension-Pain Syndrome[5], which forms the basis of her natural birth preparation course.

This fascinating theory is based on the research of Dr Grantly Dick-Read. The young doctor was profoundly impacted by a single birth experience in his obstetric career that changed his life. He had attended a home birth, where for the first time, a young mother refused his offer of pain relief[40].

He was amazed to observe the young woman birth her baby without any medical help whatsoever. He recorded afterwards that, *"There was no fuss or noise; everything seemed to be carried out according to an ordered plan and to make matters even more incredible, she appeared to be have little or no pain whatsoever!"*

This was a striking contrast to his common hospital experience. Before he left, he asked the woman why she had refused the pain relief. She was quiet for a moment, then looked up at him and said, *"It didn't hurt. It wasn't meant to, was it doctor?"*[40]. These words shocked him and turned all of his beliefs and training about birth upside down.

Dr Dick-Read had always been fascinated by nature and how animals birthed without any fuss or complaint, and wondered why humans perceived their births as frightening and dangerous.

As he later explained in his book, *Childbirth Without Fear*, the experience with this young woman was, "The seed that would eventually alter the course of my life."

From this seed, he eventually developed the Fear-Tension-Pain Syndrome, which still holds true and is more relevant today than ever before. It all starts with our belief. What are your beliefs about birth?

In essence, fear creates the pain by setting off the "fight or flight" response, which takes blood away from the uterus muscles and causes unnecessary pain. Knowing this about the body, **Diane Gardner** teaches her pregnant clients to use the mind to keep the body loose and relaxed so oxygen-rich blood can go to the uterus where it is needed to prevent or minimise unnecessary pain during labour.

> *"Deep relaxation, surrender, letting go: when midwives are asked to disclose the secret of giving birth with relative ease, these are the words we choose."* ~ Elizabeth Davis, author of Orgasmic Birth

Preparing for a Calm Birth - Kate's Story

In the weeks leading up to my baby's birth, one affirmation I struggled most with was allowing my labour to unfold whenever it did.

❝ Being a young professional, married to another young professional, each living by their Blackberry calendar and having a schedule mapped for each day, allowing my body to take over was a challenge. ❞

But take over it did. The week before the birth, I felt myself gradually pass into a different state, the body getting ready for something and the brain getting out of the way. By Tuesday I didn't feel like driving anywhere, by Wednesday I didn't really feel like leaving the house.

I had Braxton Hicks contractions all through that week—comforting physical "warm-ups" for the coming event. My husband was working long hours, and I started to get annoyed with his phone calls asking, "Are you in labour yet, do I need to come home?" To which I could only reply, "I'm not sure, it would be nice to have you home, but it's not urgent."

On Friday night I had a bloody show[11]. I was grateful my course instructor had mentioned this because it had been skimmed over at our hospital classes. My mother was impatient for the arrival of the first grandchild, and had instructed us to take the dog for a long walk.

So we walked, and periodically I would pause a moment for something I assumed was a surge, give my husband a cuddle, and then go on. I went to bed that night, sure tomorrow would be the day.

Saturday was a spectacular early spring day. My mother came over in the morning for a cup of tea while my husband went out for a ride (I didn't fancy being alone). We sat outside in the sun knitting and chatting, and I realised the surges had changed; they were lower down, a bit like period pain, but not painful. By the afternoon they were getting more regular.

I played piano for a while, fascinated that some other part of my brain must have taken over because the things I had previously found difficult were easy. At around 5pm, we took the dog for a walk to the park, and again, I would stop and cuddle my husband each time a surge came.

He was anxious to start timing them so the cuddles were a nice way of letting him start and stop the clock. When we got home, we called the hospital. Surges were regular and about six minutes apart.

The hospital midwife asked if we had a birth plan, and I said we were hoping for a calm birth. She said labour wasn't really established yet, and it could be another day or so, so best to stay home and try to have dinner and go to bed as usual.

She gave some "helpful tips" about the system: try to be admitted to hospital after midnight, as if I'm admitted at 11.55pm, those five minutes would count as a "day" of my stay; it was policy that on the third phone call, the hospital requires you to come in. I'd just used my first, so be careful about what I called for!

" After the call, I did some yoga breathing exercises, and some gentle floor exercises, all the while feeling surges periodically but remaining relaxed and happy to be at home on my yoga mat. "

My husband and I had dinner, after which I said I'd quite like to go to bed and listen to my hypnobirthing CD. He was eager to time surges, so he sat next to me while I lay there with my headphones. My breathing changed—almost instinctively—between surges and rest, so he could time things easily just by watching.

At the end of the CD, he knew how far apart they were, and that they were regular. I knew I wasn't going to last until midnight! We called my mother to come and collect the dog, and my husband finished packing the hospital bag while I had a bath. By then the surges were very strong, and I found it helpful to exhale loudly— rather like a gentle roar—through each surge.

I had been worried about how to make the call when to go to hospital. I had hated our hospital tour, and been worried about midwives and systems and the medicalisation. But I didn't really want to have a home birth either.

Our obstetrician was great and happy to be paid handsomely for doing nothing other than showing up for the last few pushes, provided all went smoothly.

Sometime before 10pm, I said to my husband it was now or never. Surges were strong by then, and closer together, and I couldn't imagine that car trip with surges any stronger or more frequent.

He called the hospital. The midwife asked if I wanted to come in for pain relief, assuming I still had many hours to go! My husband said no, it wasn't for pain relief—we were coming in because I said it was time.

The car trip was a bit of an ordeal, despite my husband's careful driving. I put on my headphones with my hypnobirthing CD again, laid out my old yoga blanket in case my waters broke, and closed my eyes. I laughed as I felt my husband drive over a speed bump slower than I thought was possible. Every three minutes or so I roared gently, and then settled back to resting.

As we pulled up to the hospital, I didn't want to be left at the door while he parked. I needed my husband with me, even if that meant having to walk further from the car. I had two surges in the car park, where my trusty yoga blanket came in handy to kneel on.

I had one while crossing the laneway, and my husband almost had to carry me to the other side as I was more inclined to be on all fours in the middle of the road.

I had another surge at the front door as we buzzed reception, and one more at the front desk of the delivery suite, which was the first time I felt the urge to push. We hadn't managed to wait until midnight.

The midwife attending us was a younger woman, and through my half-closed eyes I saw her baby bump. She was 34 weeks pregnant herself, and had just finished Calmbirth classes, so I knew we would be in good hands.

❝ The room was dimly lit; she kept her voice low and asked just a few questions about how to make me more comfortable. ❞

She never asked about pain or offered pain relief. I asked to be on all fours, leaning on the back of the bed. It was more comfortable during the surges that way, and I had worked out using the Epi-No[8] that it was an easier position for me to push.

Hubby was summoned to the desk to do paperwork. While he was gone, a second midwife came in—older and bossier —wanting to check the baby. She fiddled and fiddled, trying to find the heartbeat. I started to get worried and the next few surges were harder to manage, seemed less regular, and the urge to push went away.

Eventually she told me I would have to move onto my back, which I did reluctantly. She found the baby's heartbeat straight away, and of course he was fine.

I was pleasantly surprised to find there was a benefit to being on my back. The surges were stronger, but the rest in between was better, and I relished these in-between moments. My husband came back during one of these rests, and was momentarily distressed— he thought I had fainted or been drugged, such was my complete lack of responsiveness.

Things went smoothly from there. The bossy midwife left, the younger one asked if I might undress, which seemed like a good idea, as my waters still hadn't broken.

There was no need for a vaginal examination as she could see the membrane "just there". Soon after she called the obstetrician, and between surges I heard how our obstetrician had been at the hospital ball that evening, no doubt dancing the night away.

I was now pushing on each surge, still happily roaring each time to steady the exhale. The bossy midwife made another appearance to recommend I try some other breathing technique, as I "would have a sore throat if I kept that up".

I couldn't be bothered paying her attention and was grateful when she stopped talking—needless to say, I stuck with what worked for me!

❝ The surges were never "painful" but they were certainly a very strong, all-absorbing sensation, and exhaling loudly was the right thing for me. ❞

A sore throat in the morning (it's true, I did have one) was a small price to pay! I felt the baby's head moving down.

Having used the Epi-No, I recognised the sensation straight away and was happy that our boy was on his way. Our obstetrician arrived, and was clearly in a good mood from his evening of dancing.

He asked if I wanted to have my waters broken, which I declined, so he just observed. The baby's head was now partly out, still with the membrane around it, and for a moment I lost my confidence. I wished the waters would break. It felt dry, and as though the surges weren't coming often enough. But I knew giving up at this point was not an option.

My husband said a few days later that this was the only moment he thought I was in pain. For the rest of the labour he said I looked "in control"—an onlooker's way of saying fearless and content to go with my body.

On the next surge, little bub's head appeared. The obstetrician unwound the cord from around his neck and unwrapped him from the membranes. On the next surge he was all out.

> **❝ Almost immediately I heard my baby's lusty wails, and a warm, slippery, wriggling bundle was put on my tummy. The joy of meeting him and satisfaction of giving birth was indescribable. ❞**

He is now nearly five weeks old, and is a beautifully alert and settled baby. He arrived three days before his due date, and was 3.55 kilograms at birth with Apgar scores of 9 and 9. I had very minor tearing, which didn't require any sutures and has healed well.

The hospital documented the labour as three hours and 45 minutes But the numbers don't convey the subtleties of how the body prepares for labour, nor the joy and pride of giving birth the way women are designed to!

"For far too many women, pregnancy and birth is something that happens to them, rather than something they set out consciously and joyfully to do themselves."

~ SHEILA KITZINGER, AUTHOR & CHILDBIRTH ACTIVIST

8th Insight:
Words Have Power

"Since beliefs affect physiological functions, how women and men discuss the process of pregnancy and birth can have a negative or positive effect on the women that are involved in the discussion. Our words are powerful and either reinforce or undermine the power of women and their bodies."

~ DEBRA BINGHAM

Words are powerful. We get what we focus on in life, and birth is no different. In fact, there is a saying, *thoughts become things*. While this concept may sound rather esoteric or far-fetched, if you stop and really think about it, it is incredibly profound.

Whatever you choose to believe, one thing is certain, humans are made with such incredible built-in intelligence—better than any computer—and we are only starting to scratch the surface. Having that underlying respect for nature's brilliance in the human design certainly helps create trust in the birth process.

Protect your Mental Space

The language we use is so important. Our beliefs, thoughts and words about birth have a significant impact on our experience. Used negatively, they can work against us, or used positively, they can be our greatest ally. My suggestion is to focus on positive inputs only.

Pregnant and birthing women are particularly vulnerable to suggestion, so this is the time to protect your mental space, in much the same way a mother bird will protect her nest.

As a prime example, my friend Karlene thought she was progressing well with her labour in hospital until she asked the midwife, "Do you think it will take much longer?" to which the midwife responded with, "It could still take many hours," and "It's not really happening for you."

In that instant, everything changed for her—her confidence dropped, fear crept in and an otherwise smooth labour turned into a complicated one.

Begin a Positivity Diet

I would often refer to negative inputs throughout my pregnancy as *"mind pollution"*. It really felt that way and is the reason why I did my best to guard against negative comments or stories from well-meaning friends and strangers, and consciously decided not to attend hospital birth classes.

I felt so empowered after doing the hypnobirthing course and it really helped me overcome my fears. I didn't want to spoil the good work I had done and pollute my mind by attending the hospital one afterwards. My feeling is it would only instil more fear. That was the right choice for me personally, however it's different for each person.

Word Games or Recipe for a Pain-Free Birth?

Knowing the immense power of words, how did I apply this to my experience? I used it to have two virtually pain-free and 100 percent drug free-births! They were certainly challenging, intense and uncomfortable at times but I never experienced anything I couldn't handle.

Maybe I didn't allow myself to feel actual "pain" as I never gave it that horrible name—in fact, no one was permitted to use the "p" word during the event, not even myself. It's a word that is more suited to when you hurt yourself or when there is something wrong, which was clearly not the case.

These sensations—although unlike anything I had previously experienced—had a definite and positive purpose.

I didn't even name these sensations as "contractions". Instead, I referred to them as "waves". "Riding the waves" was a very peaceful and beautiful analogy and I have always loved the ocean.

There are also striking similarities between the ebb and flow of ocean waves and labour waves, the way they build up in tension and then release, giving the body a chance to rest in between. All part of nature's brilliant plan.

Empowering Tips

Give in and ride the waves. *If you spend the "in-between" time fearing or resisting the next wave, you have wasted that chance to conserve your energy and rest, while also creating unnecessary tension in your body, which will only create the very pain you wish to avoid. So I can't stress enough the importance of being relaxed!*

Take charge of your space, *no matter where you choose to give birth. That means setting the scene (and all the people in it so they know the rules of the "game") in accordance with your birth wishes, yet staying open and flexible at the same time.*

For example, when we checked in at the hospital and were shown into the labour ward, I made myself comfortable while my husband (my "gorilla") primed the staff about my birth wishes to make sure everyone was on the same page. His role was to protect me and my wishes so I could focus solely on what was going on within and feel completely supported.

We set the mood with dim lighting, soft music and hushed tones. Negativity was not allowed—all staff had to respect that—and any problems or concerns regarding how I was progressing were to be discussed with my support team in private, not in front of me (this was all outlined in my birth plan). I figured that way, it wouldn't impact on me and I could stay totally positive and calm, as my emotional state was everything.

Our Thoughts Create Our Reality

For thousands of years, spiritual teachers have taught that our thoughts and language have the power to alter our physical state from one of disease to health, or to create our reality. More recently, respected authors such as Louise L. Hay and Deepak Chopra, have delivered the same message.

Now we have scientific proof to back this up. Groundbreaking research by Russian scientists has shown DNA within living tissue will react to language-modulated laser rays and radio waves when the proper frequencies are used.

With this knowledge, the scientists are working on devices that are programmed to the correct radio and light frequencies to influence the way our cells process and create the very substances that sustain life.

Although the devices being created can work all the time because they are attuned to the correct frequency, we can still obtain the same result if we also tune into this frequency. We can achieve this by going within and developing a higher consciousness in order to connect and communicate with our DNA.

In other words, one can simply use words and sentences of the human language!

This, too, was experimentally proven. "Living DNA substance (in living tissue, not in-vitro) will always react to language-modulated laser rays and even to radio waves, if the proper frequencies are being used"[18].

What has this got to do with birthing? With this information, it is clear, practises such as meditation, affirmations and hypnosis have a real basis and are of great value, as they allow you to attune to the frequency that can alter your physical being, and create a happy, healthy, positive body and mind.

Also, within this research, it has been discovered what we call "intuition" also has an explanation through a process called hypercommunication. This process has been used in nature for millions of years. Take an ant colony for example, when ants are building a colony, they will continue to do so as long as the queen ant is alive.

She does not have to be physically present at the colony to ensure the building is being undertaken correctly. However, if the queen ant dies, the building of the colony stops. It appears the queen ant sends the building plans to the ant colony via group consciousness. Without this information being sent, the ants do not know what to do.

In a similar way, we can receive information that is outside our current knowledge in the form of inspiration or intuition. In order for individuals to receive this intuition or hypercommunication, it is important to be in a state of relaxation, as any stress or worries prevent this information from being transmitted effectively.

The message is clear, we can alter our reality if we attune to the correct frequency through relaxation, meditation or hypnosis. So sit back, relax and allow inspired information to come to you and allow your body and baby to attune to perfect health![18]

Positive Self Talk - Mothers' Wisdom

"I attended the standard birth class in hospital but it didn't help. I believe that everything comes down to your mindset. People in the birth class didn't have any self-belief at all. There were lots of women who ended up having caesareans and drugs—only one other lady had a natural birth like me." ~ Kate

"Create a positive affirmation about the thing you think will scare you the most and then use it all the time and tell other people about it. Our affirmation, 'sliding right out', really helped to refocus anytime something seemed difficult." ~ Cory

"Be aware—be conscious of the thoughts you are having—choose to not listen to the negative experiences and only focus on the positive. Decide what you want to listen to." ~ Shirley

"I prepared by reading, watching videos and talking to other mums, but I was only interested in listening to positive stories. I also did lots of positive affirmations daily. Meditate, use positive affirmations, believe in yourself, stay calm and don't forget to breathe. Read lots of books. You can do it!" ~ Eva

"I prepared mentally with positive self-talk and took naturopathic remedies and made diet changes. I took antenatal classes, however I found they just scared me and I had to do a lot of positive self talk to recover from them." ~ Kayla

"I felt in control and calm throughout my labour by virtue of my own positive self talk—when I was in pain I told myself it was 'all good and natural' and that I was doing a good job. I was happy and pleased with myself that I was doing it." ~ Wendy

"When I read about the process of labour, all the blood drained from my face. My husband took one look at me and said, 'What's wrong?' When I told him, he promptly removed the book from me and we started some positive affirmations together and after that it was all good.

I knew how the whole process worked but the gory descriptions were just a bit much, so we changed focus and all was good in the world again." ~ Cory

"Keep your own counsel and don't take on others' negativity. Write your own birth plan—it is empowering to visualise how it will happen. It is intensely personal, private and intimate. You can plan it to a degree if you are educated but it is also something that you ultimately have to do on your own." ~ Kristen

Seeds of Power - Experts Say

"Beliefs are like seeds, if you plant the right ones you will have flowers—the negative kind grows weeds," says **Sonya Wildgrace**. "So too in birth: if you keep hearing tragic stories you begin to believe that is all there is. When you want to prepare for a natural birth you don't hang out at a caesarean support group.

You must at some point reach out to women who can give you positive feedback about their empowered natural birth experience. You must heal from the trauma and look for new evidence from other sources. Get to the place within yourself that is no longer a victim.

You change what you believe about birth by hearing others' positive experiences. Believe it to your core. Then look for evidence that what you are hearing could be true. Then what you desire becomes a knowing within yourself and you can climb mountains. Birth is no longer scary."

She adds: "Your new birth talk is your new beliefs. Your belief eventually becomes your own experience. The more you talk it up the more you believe it into existence. On the other hand, if you feed the fear instead, that is what shows up for you, as evidence.

Positive birth talk becomes infectious. Who you surround yourself with can assist in reinforcing your new beliefs or they can be a hindrance and negatively impact your beliefs according to their own experience of birth."

Shirley-Anne Lawler says the most empowering way to a joyful birth is through asking lots of questions. "Ask questions of your body and what it requires—it has consciousness. Energetically you can receive much awareness of what is the best way forward for you and your baby by checking in energetically."

She explains: "I have found the most useful thing is to be as aware as possible of the negative thoughts and words and clear them and establish questions such as 'what else is possible for an easy joyful birth experience?' and 'what will it take for this to be easy for my body and my baby's body?' These questions also keep you very present in the moment."

Kathryn Williams is also an advocate of positive self-talk. "It's extremely useful to have words like 'open', 'surrender', 'trust'… in preparation, and to be reminded of, in birth. Self-talk is vital.

I personally used the word 'one' to get me through, by focusing on doing just 'one' sensation at a time."

Jo Thomson says if a woman goes into labour believing she won't be able to handle the pain, chances are she'll be right. "One of my favourite quotes is Henry Ford's: '*Whether you think you can or whether you think you can't, you're right'*.

I believe this applies to the birth experience. I've heard more than one woman say 'I can't do this'—what women think and say is the most important aspect when it comes to the birthing experience, as this is ultimately what will guide the choices they make."

Welcome the Contractions - Miren's Story

I gave birth to both of my beautiful children at home: the first one under water and the second one on the grass.

I've always wanted to have children. I was very healthy, had a great first pregnancy and was excited to be growing a baby inside my body. When I was five months pregnant, I travelled to Greece with my partner and spent time on the islands.

I wanted to be in warm weather for my pregnancy and spend some special time with my partner before I gave birth.

It was very clear I felt very strongly about wanting to give birth to my baby at home. I didn't think being pregnant meant I should have to go to hospital. Hospital is where sick people go and being pregnant is not being sick. Giving birth is one of the most amazing things any woman can do and it is a natural part of life.

> **" To grow a human being inside our bodies and then give birth to new life, to love and nurture and take care of this being until we have to let them go, is such a powerful experience and deserves great respect and honouring. "**

I also believed giving birth at home would be much better for me as well as my baby because it was my home and I felt most comfortable there. Feeling comfortable was very important to be able to give birth well. I was in control of my birth and was able to create an atmosphere of serenity and respect with people who were there to support me.

A water birth was at the top of my list because I love water, and I believe it is a much more gentle way to come into this world. Being born is already an intense experience, so to make it a little easier, being born into nice warm water would definitely be less traumatic.

I organised a home birth doctor and two midwives. I think there was only one doctor who did home births at the time in Melbourne, Australia, and he had a group of midwives who worked with him. During the pregnancy, I saw the doctor a few times and got to know and choose which midwife I wanted.

One of the midwives joined me at the birthing classes. I had left my partner in Greece so my father came with me.

> **" We worked mostly on our emotions around the birth and anything else that was happening in our lives. The midwife felt the emotional part of a woman is what either allows the birth to flow smoothly or stops it from doing that. "**

Of course the physical part of the birth process needs to be flowing as well, but the emotions, if not worked through, can stop the physical process of opening up and being able to give birth.

Having just left my partner, I had emotions to deal with, and was concerned this may affect my ability to have a smooth birth, but I was very clear about wanting to have this baby. I actually felt really good, even though the relationship didn't work out, and I did work through everything so I could give it the best chance to go well.

In some ways it was almost better to be able to just concentrate on my baby and myself. I felt completely fulfilled—and the father ended up being around as well. I made a birth plan and really thought about how I wanted it to be and, very importantly, who I wanted to be there.

My mum visited unexpectedly one day. When I opened the door to her, I said, "Welcome to my labour!" I was 10 days early and my mum lived four hours away... so it was quite amazing. She was obviously meant to be there.

Sasha was born under water in a birthing tub in my bedroom with my dear parents beside me, a dear girlfriend who supported me in the tub, a great doctor and two wonderful midwives.

At one stage in the tub, the contractions were quite intense and I was dreading the next one, when my friend who was supporting me in the water, said, "Welcome the contractions"... I learnt this is very important when giving birth, because if you fight against them, things can't flow the way they are supposed to and the birth will be much more difficult.

The mother and baby have to do this together. Breathing, letting go and welcoming the contractions all help the natural process of giving birth.

As I was going through an intense contraction, I had to ask my parents to stop talking ... I think they weren't quite sure what to do and were just chatting with each other. It really disturbed my concentration so I asked them to stop and they did.

Then the midwife said I was welcome to feel the head. This really helped me to embrace the whole process much more because my baby was nearly out. It was amazing to feel the head and know we were nearly there...

My midwife had said to me, "Women birth the way they live." She attended my birth but said I didn't need her to be there because I birthed so well.

“ *It really did flow very naturally and it was one of the most beautiful and amazing experiences of my life.* ”

Tao'ah, my second child, was born very quickly in the backyard of my brother's place in Melbourne.

I moved to Melbourne from East Gippsland, Australia, so I could have a home birth. I again organised a doctor, but this time only one midwife. I planned to have a water birth but didn't have time to get the water happening so I gave birth on the grass instead!

My waters had broken and the contractions came very intensely, very quickly. I ended up on the grass on my hands and knees because I felt I was ready to push the baby out. The midwife and doctor hadn't arrived and I remember someone telling me if you want to slow things down, get on your hands and knees.

Being upright, which I had been since the waters broke, about an hour before, was making things happen too quickly.

The midwife arrived, and after a quick examination, told me I was ready to push the baby out. I gave birth on my knees, with my partner on his knees holding me. I gave birth to the head and then a few minutes went past with no contraction.

My midwife said to push the baby out even without a contraction because his head was going blue and too much time had passed. I asked my partner to help me push out the baby—we did it together and he caught our beautiful baby boy.

It was a beautiful place to give birth. I often drive past the house and remember how special it was. It is quite strange there are people living there now and they don't even know what happened in their backyard.

It actually takes quite a bit of courage and strength to have a home birth because it is going against the norm. To me, the idea of driving to the hospital in the middle of labour is an absurd idea, and to then have to deal with all the people you don't really know, and where there are other people who are sick, is really not something I wanted to do.

" The way giving birth is portrayed in movies is very different to how mine were... no wonder so many women are scared to give birth. "

I think the main reason so many women go to hospital is because of the fear something will go wrong—and also women are just expected to go to hospital to give birth. Many women don't question this at all!

In hospital when interventions start to take place, it disrupts the natural flow and I believe this is why there are so many long, painful births. My first birth was nine hours and the second one was about two.

I believe it is every woman's birthright to give birth as naturally as it was created. I also believe it is the most incredible experience a person can have... because it's creating a life. As women we are amazing beings.

It is an honour to be able to create life. So, with the greatest respect for this incredibly sacred experience, may we flow with life and allow the connection to our intuition to come through us to give birth consciously—with love for our creation and ourselves.

Giving birth is like a sacred dance between mother and child... when they dance well together the dance is a miracle...

> *"We need nothing less than a revolution in our attitudes towards conception, pregnancy, birth and parenting."*
>
> ~ SOPHIE STYLE

Birth is ...

... A miracle, powerful, empowering, orgasmic, spectacular, awe-inspiring, unreal, uplifting, easy, amazing, incredible, surprising, primal, sublime, life-changing, peaceful, challenging, joyful, great, beautiful, grounding, fantastic, bliss, awesome, enjoyable, an achievement, my favourite thing in the universe, best ride of my life, most joyous thing I have ever experienced, loving, magical, freeing, euphoric, a beautiful experience for the soul, tons of great work, calm, connected, emotional, liberated, essential, primal, miraculous, awesome, adventure, beautiful, a journey, loving, magical, gracious, gentle, intimate, intense, terrific, perfect, primal, uplifting, unique, nurturing, natural, fulfilling, expressive, addictive, wonderful, magical, wondrous, welcome ...

9th Insight:
Create a Support Team

"Women's strongest feelings (in terms of their birthings), positive and negative, focus on the way they were treated by their caregivers."

~ ANNIE KENNEDY AND PENNY SIMKIN

*D*o you have the right people on your team? Why is it so important to have the right people supporting you during your pregnancy and birth? It turns out it matters a lot and actually influences the outcomes of labour, as well as how you feel about it afterwards—and that makes the difference between having a natural and empowering experience or not.

Everyone is different and that's why there's no exact formula when it comes to the perfect support team, no "one size fits all". For instance, one woman may want her mother to be present during her labour, while another wouldn't dream of it (case in point: one friend confessed when she drove past her mother's house during labour, her contractions stopped!).

Some women are solitary birthers and want to be left alone, while others want hands-on support of their closest family members or friends, attending to them with heat packs, massages, or to simply be held. Whatever makes you feel most comfortable, safe and supported is right for you.

Some of us are lucky to have supportive partners who are there to hold our hand and give us strength, massage our back to ease the discomfort, or offer encouraging words to build our spirit and confidence when we need it most.

In some cases, we may not have the perfect support team around us, meeting all our needs, but we find the strength we are looking for within ourselves and this can still contribute to a positive experience.

Husbands or partners often don't realise how important their presence is to the woman. They may feel like they are not "doing" very much, or even needed, but often just "being" there is enough, ensuring the woman is comfortable, feeling loved and cared for.

What we do know is women who feel emotionally supported during labour have fewer complications, less pain, shorter labours and less chance of postnatal depression[19].

I was very fortunate when it came to my caregivers. My obstetrician was gentle and calm-by-nature with a less interventionist approach, which suited me perfectly and helped to calm the nerves. He did, however, manage to miss the big event altogether until the ribbon cutting ceremony at the end (cutting the cord), yet I still had to pay him a fortune!

My only gripe was that each routine visit during my pregnancy, I would read virtually every magazine in the waiting room before my obstetrician would see me—and then it was only for five to 10 minutes at a time, even though I was paying top dollar for his services.

Meanwhile, my private midwife would spend a leisurely hour with me during each visit over a relaxing cup of tea, discussing my feelings and any fears or concerns. She also helped me to be educated on all of my options—providing me with the latest research material on areas of interest—so I knew exactly what I wanted.

It was very empowering to say the least! She was very naturally-minded like myself, very passionate about giving the power back to women in birth and very much into conscious living. A real gem!

Of course, I can't even imagine my births without my husband, my amazing soul mate and number one supporter!

When it comes to caregivers, find someone you feel comfortable with and who will calm your fears, especially if you know you are a stress-head like me! One of the best things about my obstetrician was his calm energy. The tone of his voice never gave me cause for alarm.

Unfortunately, the midwives on duty were a bit hit and miss, since it was just luck-of-the-draw with who showed up that day. They were also complete strangers, which didn't help.

I learnt there was an enormous difference between the midwives in the hospital and the one I had brought in with me, BYO-style!

My first labour was a 12-hour marathon and crossed over different hospital staff shifts. The first midwife on duty had been so lovely and kind, more naturally-minded and aligned with my values. She had attended many natural home births and happily supported my birth wishes.

We clicked immediately. Unfortunately, when she finished her shift mid-labour, she was replaced by a new midwife who was trained for hospital emergencies and was a bit cold and stern—a different creature altogether.

Needless to say, I had been much more relaxed and comfortable with the first midwife who was very kind-natured and let me go at my own pace. Now I really didn't appreciate being hurried along. That's where my support team of hubby and private midwife was priceless.

They encouraged me, believed in me, stood up for me to negotiate the extra time to do what I needed to do without any intervention, fuelled me to give me that last energy boost when I couldn't give any more, and gave me permission to rest when I really needed it. As Kate Filmer, co-author of *Hidden Path Book and Journal* says, "If it doesn't flow, let it go." Sometimes struggling is counter-productive and this was one of these times.

How can caregivers or the support team ensure the best conditions for the birthing mother, so she can have a positive, empowering experience?

In *Do Not Disturb: The Importance of Privacy in Labor*, author Judith A. Lothian[31], poses the question: "Can labour-support create a bubble, a cocoon, around the labouring woman?" Within the bubble, privacy is protected: Strangers are kept away (as much as possible), information is filtered, and questions, interruptions, and intrusions are kept to a minimum.

Continuously supported, protected, and cared for, but not disturbed, the labouring woman can let go of fear even in a busy maternity hospital. However, she will be disturbed if she feels she is in a fish bowl being observed and evaluated.

A birthing woman will also be disturbed if she feels pressured to progress quickly because the clock is ticking. Ideally, she is surrounded by family and professionals who listen, watch, and quietly and patiently encourage her, making sure she is not disturbed and has the privacy she needs to do the work of labour.

"All that is needed for the majority of labours to go well is a healthy, pregnant woman who has loving support in labour, self-confidence, and attendants with infinite patience." ~ Sheila Kitzinger

Nurtured by Sisterhood, Protected by Gorilla

It is important to have your own "gorilla" at your labour. For me, that was unquestionably my husband, who gave me emotional and physical support during labour, and ensured my rights were protected and birth wishes were followed in hospital.

He acted as my best supporter and advocate when I was too vulnerable to communicate my wishes. Feeling safe and protected is crucial to having an empowered experience.

My private BYO-style midwife, who shared the journey with me throughout my first pregnancy, was invaluable. I learnt that night not all midwives are created equal, as well as the importance of having a relationship with your support team! She helped me feel supported and empowered, and most likely contributed to my positive outcome the first time around.

It looks like I am not alone. Numerous studies show small maternity units plus midwifery care is the best choice for the physical and emotional health of the majority of women and their babies[15,16,17].

The Magic of Midwifery

Whilst midwives work across the full spectrum of women's birth experiences, they are specialists in normal physiological birth. Midwives also have the deep appreciation of the importance of mother/baby interaction during pregnancy, birth and the immediate postnatal period, since the quality of that interaction sets the tone for the future life of the infant[27-29].

In *The Midwife Challenge*, natural childbirth activist, honorary professor and world-renowned author on childbirth and pregnancy, Sheila Kitzinger, describes a midwife's important role: *"The essence of midwifery is staying sensitively in the moment—in other words, being humble and paying attention. But this focus can be easily destroyed by the desire for control... The wise midwife... understands ebb and flow."*

*"**Without the presence and acceptance of the midwife, obstetrics becomes aggressive, technological and inhumane.**" ~ Professor GJ Kloosterman, formerly of the Department of Obstetrics and Gynacology, University of Amsterdam Hospital, the Netherlands[37].*

Feeling Safe and Supported: Keeping Key People by Your Side - Mothers' Wisdom

"A doula is an amazing source of spiritual and emotional support. My doula opened my eyes to the options available to me. Thank the divine universe for her in my life! Best decision ever!" ~ Leonie

"I had my own private midwife. She is amazing with years of experience and I trusted her completely. This trust was validated when we ended up in hospital and she was able to manage the labour and perform obstetric procedures that the hospital doctors couldn't. I liked having my family around. My sister was amazing at both births and made a world of difference." ~ Heidi

"I had an obstetrician but the midwives are the ones who really helped— we made this choice again based on family history and he was great. (I) was not excited about some stranger delivering our baby if we did need to have a c-section. My husband was my main supporter and yes it did make a huge difference—he wouldn't have missed it for anything!" ~ Cory

"I chose to have a midwife with a support team consisting of my husband, father, mother and stepfather. It was great to have them all around me." ~ Wendy

"I had a midwife. My husband was there with me but I just wanted him to sit and stare with a look of concern on his face and not get involved. He tried at one point to massage me and I said, 'don't touch me'. I told my husband to leave me alone at one point and was on my own for a few hours. When he came back, he was refreshed and happy and was there when the process sped up and the baby was born." ~ Kate

"I wanted my support person or midwife to know me from beginning all the way through and form a relationship. I knew what I wanted. So I looked up the homebirth midwives website and found a support person." ~ Rebecca

*"**Only with trust, faith, and support can the woman allow the birth experience to enlighten and empower her.**" ~ Claudia Lowe*

Supported or Alone: Mums Share their Experiences

"I felt supported during labour but not as much as I would have liked. I wanted my mother with me but wasn't allowed." ~ Leonie

"My mother was present at my first and fourth births, but this was a mistake. Hence, there were difficulties with the birthing. My husband was present at three of my births. I found I felt more empowered with certain friends present and a midwife I had built up a relationship with." ~ Vickie

"I had felt quite alone during my first birth experience and was determined not to feel that way again. I spent a great deal of time discussing with my husband what I would need second time around and he was much more available to me then. I felt much more supported the second time around. Yet I still feel that a female support person wouldn't go astray!" ~ Rachel

"I felt supported during birth—not due to the people around me, (I) just felt confident and comfortable in myself." ~ Kate

"I felt quite supported during pregnancy and birth. If anything, there may have been a lack of emotional support from my partner. There were times when I wondered if I was the only woman who has ever felt this way or that way, ever felt this fear or that fear, ever had doubts...

And there is a sense of aloneness when you realise that ultimately the birth of this child is up to you." ~ Natalie

"During my birth at a birthing centre, only assisted by midwives and no doctors present, I felt total respect from the midwives around me—no one disturbed me—they were honouring that power within me to give birth. I felt supported." ~ Robyn

Safety In Numbers - Experts Say

Davini Malcolm, a Director of the International College of Spiritual Midwifery, says, "I believe that having the right support person(s) before, during and after birth, who will walk the road with you, is an invaluable asset.

Historically this support for the birthing woman came from female family members or community, but these days you have other options too.

This person may be your husband, midwife, doula, mother, best friend, aunty, brother, male friend or a combination of these people. There is no rulebook here! Just get it right for yourself.

I encourage you to really feel into what you need and to ask for that support. This support helps to provide a safe space where you feel, loved, held and protected at this special time."

Shivam Rachana advises new mothers to have the pregnancy and birth well supported. "Have a natural birth in a safe and supported environment, surrounded by people who support her wishes, be fit, well-rested and healthy to give birth to her baby.

If a woman feels safe in a hospital then that is where she should be, due to our inherited situation we are in. We have come to need back-up intervention and that is how it is. If a natural birth is to be supported, we need to open up our body to let the baby out—we need to examine our self and our beliefs by reliving our own birth to let any issues go."

"With the support of friends who are sensitive to your needs, quick to respond to your wishes, who are emotionally nurturing and who above all believe in you and your ability to give birth, childbirth can be an adventure in physical sensation and intense emotion, a journey of discovery of your own inner power that is exhilarating, sensuous and satisfying." ~ *Sheila Kitzinger*

A Speedy Arrival After a Change of Caregivers - Kate's Story

My first pregnancy with Tara had gone well, delivering her in a drug-free labour with a doula in a private hospital. The only intervention was breaking waters, so when I fell pregnant the second time I imagined I would birth the same way and hopefully have no intervention.

I booked in with the same obstetrician but when we turned up, he smelt strongly of cigarette smoke so I phoned to cancel his services and booked into another highly recommended obstetrician.

This one greeted me with negativity and pushiness.

I wasn't pleased to be told, "Big sweet tooth, big baby, big forceps," when my gestational diabetes test came back border line, nor did I appreciate him suggesting being induced at 37 weeks when my pregnancy had no complications—it may have had something to do with my due date of December 28. I wouldn't want to disrupt his Christmas functions!

So I had a meeting with my doula and told her I had always been interested in homebirth but at 33 weeks, thought it wouldn't be possible to organise it now.

She said, "Look into it and if you find a brick wall, you know it's not meant to be but if it goes ahead smoothly then you know it is right." I rang a midwife who was happy to take me on, even though I only had seven weeks to go and was expecting a Christmas baby.

My obstetrician gave me a full refund after I told him I no longer wanted his services. My husband, Garrett, came around to the idea of a homebirth after a few meetings with our midwife.

Christmas day came and I was woken at 2am with a few niggles and a dull ache in my lower back. I had a sense this was "it" but managed to push it to the back of my mind for most of the day so I could enjoy Christmas with Tara.

I was determined for the baby not to be born on Christmas day, as I really wanted him to have his own day. Sensations were getting more intense during the day but I tried to keep rested as I thought I might be in for a long night as my first labour was 36 hours and started exactly like this.

We put Tara to bed after she pointed out my tummy was "very hard". I said her baby brother was ready to come out tomorrow or the next day. I tucked myself into bed around 10pm and tried to get some rest but I couldn't get comfortable.

At midnight, I decided to leave everyone asleep and head to our garage where I had set up a rug, beanbag, candles, music and oils.

" I walked around to ease the discomfort. I continued walking around until I felt a contraction, and then swayed from side-to-side like I was dancing with my baby. "

I was using my iPhone contraction timer. I took a dose of Caulophyllum (herbs) from my Ainsworth homeopathy kit, hoping to reduce the labour length. At 2am, I was coping okay with conscious breathing but I could feel the intensity of the sensations rise, so I messaged my doula, Jan, and asked her to join me for some support.

After a few more sensations, I woke Garrett up so he could start setting up the birth pool. He spoke to my parents and asked them to come over but thought if it was anything like my last labour, we would still have a good 24 hours to go.

My parents came over to watch Tara while she slept. Gran came into the garage and got heat packs ready. She suggested I should get the midwife to come, as it was an hour drive for her. By 2.30am, Jan arrived and gave me a welcoming hug and told me this is where I'm supposed to be and to "relax and let go".

I told her my legs were tired from walking around, but I struggled to find a comfortable seated position. We simply sat down, with mum holding a heat pack on my back and using an endorphin release technique of scratching nails down my back and legs. Jan sat in front of me, talking me through each sensation.

I sat with eyes closed I told myself to relax every other muscle I could while having a contraction, as I had learnt in my birth course, and focused on opening up. I was imagining my cervix opening.

I spoke to Jan about my worries as I wanted to acknowledge them, then let them go so I could be free. I was worried I had called everyone out when it wasn't the real thing. She reminded me I needed to stop thinking and relax and surrender to the labour.

I felt so much pressure below that I grabbed the beanbag and leaned over it. I felt a huge release of fluid and was so shocked; I asked my doula if it was my waters breaking. My mum was behind me and said it wasn't a lot, but yes it was. I was so surprised as I really wanted them to break naturally this time.

After that release, I felt the intensity and said to my doula that he was coming. They said they would help me to the birth pool, as it was quite a distance. I have never been on such a mission. I had visualised having a morning water birth so I was determined to get to the pool before he was born.

I didn't wait for mum or Jan, I just got up and waddled as fast as I could to the birth pool. I saw Garrett filling the pool, which was now only half full, but I got straight in and knelt down and felt between my legs.

I could feel the softest hair I had ever felt, waving gently in the pool water. I said, "His head is right there!" I don't think anyone, even myself, believed all of this was happening so quickly. Garrett rang our midwife to see how far away she was.

As I felt the next wave of sensation, I looked at Jan and a fear broke out in me. I'm not sure why I was fearful but I think it was because my vision of my homebirth included my midwife.

My doula looked at me intensely and said, "You are okay, this is fine." I felt an urge to push but kept my hand flat across his head, as I wasn't ready for him to come.

Mum went to get Garrett and Jan told him to take his place in front of me. Mum stood behind me. I looked strongly into Garrett's eyes while I got another urge to push.

66 I birthed his head slowly, this time feeling the "ring of fire" but not being afraid of it. 99

I slowly pushed through it and said to Garrett that his head was out. With the next quick urge, I pushed out the baby's shoulders slowly without a tear and pulled him up onto my chest and sat down in the pool. Amazing!

Exactly how I saw my water birth going, except not as quickly. Mason Rook was born 10 minutes later, just as I heard my midwife's car pull up.

An important part of my birth plan was to finish by birthing the placenta. With my first birth, the obstetrician used cord traction to release it, as it had already separated, but I was so exhausted I couldn't get up to birth it.

Mason and I sat in the pool for an hour just cuddling, waiting for the placenta to detach. It was the only unknown to me as I had done everything else before, so I felt tension I needed to let go of. I needed to relax but my brain was spinning... thinking about being transferred to hospital if it didn't detach.

My midwife, doula and mum stepped outside to give me space to relax and to have time with my new family, Garrett, Mason and myself.

I felt contractions intensely while I took Mason to the breast for the first time. I wasn't sure what to do with them—if I needed to push or not. My midwife explained, just like I know when to push Mason out, I will know when to push out the placenta.

I just had to listen to my body. My midwife said I could cut the cord and let Mason go to Garrett while I birthed the placenta but I had an image of Mason attached to it so I wanted it to be birthed with him.

Jan, my doula, knew I was contemplating a lotus birth[12] and that this stage meant a lot to me. Soon we could see it had separated. I handed Mason to Garrett who was on the side of the pool. I finally felt the urge to push. It came out in one go and I lifted it up to the surface: full, complete and beautiful!

We decided it was time to cut the cord about one and a half hours after he was born. I bet a hospital wouldn't let me wait that long!

We estimated established labour was only one-and-a-half hours with no interventions, internals or foetal monitoring at all!

My daughter Tara had slept through the whole thing so we went to wake her up at 6.30am to meet her new brother and we all sat around eating breakfast and watching the sunrise as the gentle rain set in.

We planted Mason's placenta under a Bird of Paradise tree, as his middle name Rook is a strong and intelligent bird of prey found in paradise. We often see crows gather around it and like to think they are his deceased loved ones protecting him.

"When the staff believe that labor pain equals suffering, they convey that belief to the woman and her partner, and, instead of offering support and guidance for comfort, they offer pain medication. If that's the only option, women will grasp for it."

~ PENNY SIMKIN

10th Insight:
Your Birth, Your Body

"Every intervention is a lesson in who really owns your body and your baby's body."

~ JOCK DOUBLEDAY, NATURAL WOMAN, NATURAL MAN, INC.

The use of drugs during labour can mean a loss of control and connection to what is going on in the body, and you may feel like your body is no longer yours. With epidurals, where you can't feel when to push the baby out, there is no other option but to rely on "experts", such as a midwife or doctor, to tell you what to do with your own body and when.

Yet feeling in control of your own birth experience, and that your power is not taken away, is one of the key factors that determines whether you feel empowered by the experience or not.

Empowering Tip:

Always remember you have a choice. Don't simply do what you are told without question. This is your body, your birth and your baby. Rather than feeling reassured that you are in "good hands", find a deep place of inner reassurance and confidence. Your body is the ultimate expert on giving birth—trust in that instead. You are much more powerful than you know.

Who Needs Drugs Anyway?

When left to its own devices and undisturbed, the body does a brilliant job of making its own natural pain relief in the form of oxytocin and endorphins. This was part of nature's plan all along—we are never given more than we can handle. When did you last see an animal in labour begging for an epidural?

My first labour was a marathon—and yes, I felt every bit of it!

Even though I was almost fully dilated on arrival at hospital, my waters wouldn't break for a long time, which held up proceedings. I was set on being undisturbed throughout the process and planned to do everything myself.

In fact, looking back, I think I was more fearful of the medical interventions and being out of control (that is, procedures being done to me without my permission) than the birth itself.

I was also well aware of the possible risks to the baby associated with having the drugs. My intense fear of needles and anything remotely invasive, meant my decision to go natural and drug-free was as strong as ever. This phobia worked in my favour, as using drugs never entered my mind. It was never an option.

> *"The more we use technology for uncomplicated labours, the more we undermine women's confidence in their own ability to give birth."* ~ Author Unknown

Location, Location - Mothers' Wisdom

"I decided to have my baby in a hospital birthing suite. I wanted very little, if any, doctor intervention and a midwife to be present. The idea of a home birth appealed, yet I wanted the safety of hospital just in case. I found it reassuring to have my baby at a birthing suite as it has both." ~ Amanda

"I went to a hospital for a water birth the first time as I thought it was the only option. I then planned a home water birth for the second, but had a free birth. I decided it was a better option for bub and me." ~ Leonie

"I decided to have my babies at hospital—I wanted a natural birth, yet wanted to be in a place where, if anything went wrong, everything was there to help to ensure safety. I felt more relaxed, knowing if anything went wrong there was care there." ~ Kate

"I chose a birthing centre with a really small group of midwives who look after you. You meet them during pregnancy so they are not strangers you have never met before. I chose a public hospital as I was low risk." ~ Rebecca

"Our baby girl was born in a private hospital that offered lots of fantastic birthing methods. Our family has a long history of big babies and caesareans and even though this was not going to be our experience, we were keen to cover all bases." ~ Cory

"Both my girls were born in hospital as I felt this was the 'safest' place to bring them into the world, but I would love to have a home birth for my next one!" ~ Rachael

"I chose home births for both my babies. I have never been one for doctors or medical intervention unless absolutely necessary and had opted for alternative therapies instead.

I could not think of anything more beautiful than being able to birth my baby into an environment that was purposefully created to provide the most blissful energy I could. I also loved the fact that it was my home and that after the birth I could have the comfort and privacy of my own room." ~ Natalie

"I chose a birthing centre, due to the fact that medical intervention scares me and I detest hospitals and sickness. However, I also wanted the safety of a hospital nearby in case I needed medical intervention. I needed a melding of the two—the comfort of home with the safety of medical intervention, as I was aware that I had a condition that could require medical attention. As it turned out, I began haemorrhaging and did need intervention." ~ Wendy

"During hospital birth, I was really anxious and fearful, hated the environment and was really scared. I felt there was no compassion or gentleness or even consideration that this is my body and my baby. During my homebirths, I felt in control or at least with the birthing process part ... felt empowered, totally present." ~ Vickie

Reclaim Your Birth Power - Experts Say

Sonya Wildgrace believes the biggest challenge is to give birthing back to the mother and father. "We cannot afford to 'need' medical assistance to birth," she says. "We need to take the panic out of birth. Natural, undisturbed birth needs little to no 'management'.

Birth when undisturbed, is not as dangerous as we are led to believe.

We just have to find out the true meaning of 'undisturbed' and how we can achieve it. The medical model needs to release the choke hold it has on normal birth and refocus on the true high risk pregnancies."

According to **Shivam Rachana**, curbing big pharmaceutical's influence and vested interest in the birth process is vital. "We must ask who owns the process?" she says. "Supporting, encouraging and rewarding women to take responsibility for their bodies and their babies will reduce much of the difficulties associated with high levels of intervention, low breastfeeding rates and postnatal depression."

Diane Gardner also suggests trusting the body's ability to give birth. "Look inside to find the answers—every woman has the instinct to birth a baby. Know how to stand up for your rights... how to find your birth power," she says.

"Everything is choice," says **Shirley-Anne Lawler**. "The important thing is that each pregnant woman choose from an informed point of view. All pregnant women must feel comfortable with the choices they make as this will eliminate guilt later on."

Kathryn Williams adds: "When a woman holds the power in birth, she holds the power in her life. Our role in birth can have permanent ramifications for our role as mothers and women."

Jo Thomson believes the majority of women are in good hands with doctors. "For the most part they have a choice whether to take the care option suggested by the doctor and if they have doubts, they shouldn't be afraid to ask questions until they're happy with the answers."

"Childbirth isn't something that is done to you, or for you; it is something you do yourself. Women give birth. Doctors, hospitals and nurses don't." ~ *Lester Dessez Hazell, author of Commonsense Childbirth*

Everything is Perfect! - Rachael's Story

For the last few days of my pregnancy I started to think our baby was trying to tease us—we knew we were about to become parents, just exactly when was up to our little one. I went about my usual daily activities, booking appointments days in advance, in hope of having to cancel.

Reluctantly, I got ready for bed one night and thought to myself, well another day down and another day closer to being a mother.

At about 2am, I woke up and felt some cramping and decided to give Brett a shove to let him know. Over the next few minutes I became more aware our journey had begun—how exciting! I asked him to ring our amazing midwife, Jenny, to let her know things were happening.

I could sense he would have preferred me to make the call, as I could describe what was going on and so forth—I just wanted to concentrate on what I was feeling.

The cramping was getting a lot more intense and was continual— not the wave of pains I was expecting or had heard so much about. Jenny explained to Brett this was quite normal at the start of labour.

She wasn't concerned, as they would subside and then become more predictable and rhythmic. She suggested we should go back to bed, as it (the birth) would be some time away. I took great relief in her advice and went back to bed.

As we were wide-awake, it seemed almost impossible to go back to sleep, although I knew I would need to sustain some energy. I was squirming around the bed, while the cramping only got more intense. I had to breathe through it.

I convinced myself I had a long way to go, so relax, take some deep breaths and go to sleep in order to wake up feeling refreshed and ready for a long day ahead. Just as I had finished giving myself this pep talk, my waters broke.

❝ I leapt out of bed with excitement and anxiousness, wanting to do a back flip with anticipation over what we had waited so long for. ❞

Brett phoned Jenny again. She said as the trip would take her around two hours, she would come—exciting to know she was now coming for the big event we had so carefully and eagerly planned for.

Brett launched into full activity by blowing up the pool and filling it with water. I was in the shower and quite enjoying the sensation when he came in and reminded me we don't have endless hot water and I should conserve the water for later when I really need it.

After my shower, I put on my pyjama top, lit some candles and turned out the lights. Brett was busily boiling water as he had filled the pool with the hose from the garden tap and the water was absolutely freezing, but with many more hours ahead of us, it was of no great concern.

I was wandering around the house but kept sitting in the bathroom as it was very supporting and I felt most comfortable there, although I did want to be closer to Brett. I dragged the blanket to the lounge where he was still busying himself with the water.

I lay on the mat beside the pool just to be near him. As soon as I lay down, I very quickly decided that position was not the way to go and headed back to the bathroom where I stayed for a few hours.

Brett would slide down the hallway on his socks, stopping just in time to ask how I was doing, and then head straight back to his water boiling duties—he needn't have worried how he would fill in the time!

I called him a couple of times to come and hold my hand as the contractions didn't seem to be subsiding and there was next to no break between them. I didn't know whether I just wasn't coping well or this was actually how it was.

I was having this all-over body trembling that left me shaking as though I was absolutely freezing, although I didn't feel cold.

" Most of the time I had my eyes closed to internalise the feelings going through my body both mentally and physically. This made it easy to stay on top of things and helped me to fully experience my labour. "

At about 5.10am, I opened my eyes and saw headlights approaching our house. I knew Jenny had arrived. She was the most welcome and warming sight—just her presence made everything seem real and made me realise this was no dress rehearsal.

This was time to put all our dreams and plans into action.

Jenny found a footstool and sat in the hallway, watching me as each contraction came back-to-back. We had a brief chat as only Jenny knows how—communicating in so few words but knowing exactly where I was at.

Brett came and I held onto his hands for another few contractions and then he went back to his water boiling again. Jenny watched as one contraction was peaking, and then it seemed to pick up a gear like it was grabbing hold of me before it was about to let go again.

Another contraction like this followed with no break. Next thing I knew, I felt like I could push, although I wasn't sure it was time to, as this hadn't been going on for 10 hours.

Maybe I needed to go on a bit more? I didn't feel too overwhelmed. I guess that's why I doubted it was time for the next stage. Jenny suggested maybe the pool was a good idea and that the water was warmer now.

She held my hand and we walked down the hallway into the lounge. Brett was a picture of calm and peacefulness.

❝ The entire lounge room was steamy; windows fogged up, the candles were burning to provide just enough light and the oil burner had a wonderful aroma just like all the warm baths I had been having in the weeks before the birth. ❞

I stepped into the pool where I just seemed to melt—what a wonderful feeling for someone who isn't so keen on water! It felt so great, I didn't know whether to lie, squat, sit or what to do and I seemed to be moving all around just to find the right position, which was kneeling with my arms resting on the side of the pool.

Jenny again was sitting on the footstool close enough and also giving us all the space we needed. We were grateful just for her presence. Another contraction came and it didn't seem nearly as intense as it was before and I felt soft and warm.

Now I found the next few contractions were creeping up on me and I suddenly felt it was really happening the way I expected it to be. I caught myself thinking it had to become more difficult before it got easier.

I was panting my way through the peak of another contraction, I couldn't imagine how panting would help before I did it! Just as I would start to pant, it would build and build to a point where I thought panting was not doing any good and then I would groan low and deep.

" After panting my way through about three
I could feel the baby's head move down and then b
again—what a crazy sensation that was—not at all painf
exhilarating. "

It never did seem appropriate to scream. The groaning noises helped me to internalise again and move through the contraction.

At the end of these full-on contractions, Jenny asked how I was doing and how the baby was—to both questions, I answered we were doing fine. Brett had climbed into the pool behind me and was holding onto my hips.

He kept saying, "You are doing well sweetie, keep going," and, "You are awesome, doing great." My confidence in how I was coping was growing and I felt more and more capable.

The baby's head moved down again with the next contraction and when it subsided, Jenny asked me to feel where the baby was. I reluctantly put my hand into the water and I could feel my baby's head, and the enormity of what was now just so close, really washed over me.

The next contraction came and the baby's head moved down again but this time it didn't go back up again. When I said this out loud, I knew I was making the final step to becoming a mother.

Jenny moved toward the pool, told me that I was soft, open and relaxed and to just breathe low and deep into the next contraction and see how that felt.

The next contraction arrived and I felt very ready, although had no idea what was about to happen. I thought this was just the start of hours of pushing and straining. Yet, just as the contraction started to peak, I groaned low and deep and felt this stretching sensation and the head was born.

This caught me by complete surprise and before I could register what had happened, the rest of the baby was in the water. Brett helped the baby float to the surface by pushing it between my legs and in front of me.

I then leaned back onto Brett and scooped up this tight pink ball from the water. Just as you expect a flower to open into the warm sunlight, our baby uncurled itself in my arms and took its first breath as its eyes opened to greet us.

Amazing how our child came to be with us, just as the sun was peeking through our windows, warming us and greeting the new day.

ıst completely drifts away into that very
ıto our memory for eternity. The big round
at us, reflecting a little of Brett and me—

vered in a chalky white coat and was absolutely
ot occur to me to cry. We simply lay in each other's
in total wonder at what we had done. The radio
on automatically in the room. After a few photos and
ng, I delivered a very healthy looking, intact placenta.

Oɪ... ɛ cord became pale and very limp, Brett cut it and we held our baby close. About 40 minutes after the baby was born, we got out of the pool, wrapped her in a towel and lay on the lounge with the blanket over me.

Once we were all relaxed and comfortable, Brett picked up the phone and called our parents. I lay on the lounge watching and listening to my dear husband announcing to the world through his tears, "We have just had a baby girl and she is beautiful. We have named our daughter Jade K Leckie and she has large round blue eyes and dark hair. Everything is perfect."

"When enough women realise that birth is a time of great opportunity to get in touch with their true power, and when they are willing to assume responsibility for this, we will reclaim the power of birth and help move technology where it belongs—in the service of birthing women, not their master."

~ DR CHRISTIANE NORTHRUP, MD, AUTHOR

11th Insight:
Doctors and Drugs are Optional

> "*Midwives see birth as a miracle and only mess with it if there's a problem; doctors see birth as a problem and if they don't mess with it, it's a miracle!*"
>
> ~ BARBARA HARPER IN GENTLE BIRTH CHOICES

*D*id you know the word obstetrics comes from the Latin word stare, which means, "to stand by"? However, in her book, *Women's Bodies, Women's Wisdom*, Dr Christiane Northrup confirms what many of our empowered mothers had to say: "*Modern obstetrics has changed from a natural, patient 'standing by' and allowing the woman's body to respond naturally, into a domineering and often invasive practise[22].*" Look how far we have strayed from the original intent!

The truth is, "*A woman's body knows how to give birth instinctively and will respond in settings in which she is encouraged to move in the ways that feel right, and make the sounds she needs to make[22].*"

"*Despite what we may have been led to believe, pregnancy is not a condition, and birth is not an emergency.*" *~ April Asorson*

Due to cultural conditioning, we are taught to give our power over to the medical "experts", when our bodies have been the real experts all along. It seems we have lost touch with our inner wisdom and power as women.

Doctors rely on tests and machines to tell them how to help women during pregnancy and then "help" women during labour with drugs and other invasive procedures that all carry risks they don't really tell us about.

Here is some food for thought...

> *"A study of interactions between women and obstetricians offers an explanation. It described three levels of increasing power imbalance: In the first, you fight and lose; in the second you don't fight because you know you can't win.*
>
> *However, in the highest level of power differential, your preferences are so manipulated that you act against your own interests, but you are content. Elective repeat caesarean exemplifies that highest level."* ~ Henci Goer, The Thinking Woman's Guide to a Better Birth

According to Marsden Wagner, MD, in an article called *Fish Can't See Water, the Need to Humanise Birth in Australia,* the biggest challenge with modern obstetrics is fish can't see the water they are swimming in and the current system tends to de-humanise birth, and in doing so, disempowers the birthing mothers in the process[20].

Humanising birth and empowered birth are really the same things. In medical birth, the doctor is always in control, while the key element in humanised birth is, the woman is in control of her own birthing experience.

Natural Birth, an Endangered Human Right

> *"By separating a woman from her own environment and surrounding her with strange people using strange machines to do strange things to her in an effort to assist her, the woman's state of mind and body is so altered that her way of carrying through this intimate act must also be altered and the state of the baby born must equally be altered.*
>
> *The result is that it is no longer possible to know what births would have been like before these manipulations. Most health care providers no longer know what 'non-medical' birth is. The entire modern obstetric and neonatological literature is essentially based on observations of 'medical' birth."*
> ~ World Health Organisation(20)

Having experienced the natural high of two drug-free labours, I say who needs drugs when your body makes its own! Read more about these wonderful happy hormones in Insight 15 and in our special interview with Dr Sarah Buckley, MD, in the afterword.

What Your Doc Won't Tell You - Mothers' Wisdom

I wish someone had told me...

- ℘ *...we are no different than our mothers and their mothers who have been birthing for thousands of years. I'm the personification of thousands of years of beautiful natural birthing and because of that, I not only have the ability, but also the natural intuition to birth my baby."*

- ℘ *...stepping into a hospital is stepping into unnatural birthing conditions. Your body knows better than anyone how to birth your baby. Say no to hospitals, medication, intervention, to tests and machines."*

- ℘ *...with my first born how much safer and easier it is to birth my baby in my own home! Thank the divine universe I got to experience true natural empowering birth at home!"*

- ℘ *...to research for myself and not take the medical 'professionals' word for it. They unfortunately don't have me and my baby's best interest at heart, but time and money."*

- ℘ *...about doulas and lotus births ... surround your chosen birth place with people who trust and believe in your ability to birth your baby in your way and time." ~ Leonie*

"In hospital they only seemed to interfere, whereas at home everything happened easily." ~ Kiera

"Birth is a natural thing that has nothing to do with the hospital." ~ Tammy

"Women are not realising that obstetricians are surgeons! Not midwives!" ~ Kelly

"I am against intervention if it's unnecessary. It happens for no good reason in a normal hospital ward." ~ *Amanda*

"I discovered how much doctors push you to have gas or drugs—be strong enough to say you don't need it and trust your instincts." ~ *Kayla*

"My hospital birth left me feeling worse than a 'rape' victim, especially as it was expressed as 'normal' and 'natural'. I felt powerless, humiliated, and no-one actually spoke about what happened and why ... I was left mutilated and not informed of what was happening with my baby either." ~ *Vickie*

"Women who opt for a caesar or ask for epidurals, gas etc don't know what they are missing. As for elective caesar—are you kidding? You are not up and about out of bed straight away after delivery and it takes much longer to recover. I say feel it, experience it—you don't do it very often." ~ *Robyn*

"As for epidurals during labour, I don't understand what that's all about. I would hate to do it that way. My birth was the most amazing thing that has ever happened to me." ~ *Rachel*

"Just because it's covered by private health cover doesn't mean you need the lot. Just because all your friends used interventions in their births, doesn't mean you need to as well. Do your due diligence and decide what is right for you." ~ *Leonie*

If you are still uncertain whether you should use medical interventions to birth your baby, consider this:

> ***"Only about 15 percent of medical interventions are supported by solid scientific evidence... This is partly because only one percent of the studies in medical journals are scientifically sound and partly because many treatments have not been assessed at all."*** ~ *Richard Smith, Editor, British Medical Journal*

The Biggest Challenges in Midwifery and Obstetrics - Experts Say

Nicole MacFadyen says intervention is the biggest challenge in obstetrics. "Antenatal classes need better education around other options, rather than just orthodox ones. Doctors, and the first people you come into contact with, need to give natural therapies as real options and discuss them in just as much detail as drugs."

"The biggest challenge is to be patient and leave things alone without jumping in too quickly," **Diane Gardner** says. "The medical profession has too many agendas with too much pressure to get people in and out—midwives are controlled by the hospital system and they are also pressured to get births happening quickly, rather than allowing the process to just unfold and occur naturally."

"Women are choosing to have pain relief, which often leads to a cascade of intervention," **Jo Thomson** says. "Women experiencing this cascade of intervention can be traumatised by it. There is so much focus on the birth itself and not what happens afterwards.

More education needs to be done on being more emotionally prepared as this is just skimmed over in the birth classes. They are more focused on the mechanics of birth and the drugs that are available."

The Intention of Intervention: Why Modern Medicine Needs to Look to Nature

Jo Thomson, who works as a midwife in the private hospital system reveals, "I want to get out of midwifery as I am not keen on all the interventions and don't enjoy it as much as I once did. I now want to help women in a different way." She adds, "Doctors err on the side of caution and caesareans are often due to litigation issues."

Shivam Rachana says, "It is wonderful what we can do safely these days with technology, however, the caesarean rates are a total disgrace. Massive emotional and physical health implications are involved with major abdominal surgery. Mental health is becoming a real issue with postnatal depression."

"There is a deep-rooted and widespread misunderstanding of birth physiology," **Rachana** says. "The maternity care system is sectioned and this has become reflected in the appallingly high rate of c-sections. The facilities where women are expected to give birth are devoid of the basic needs of a birthing mammal.

People with the knowledge need to be appreciated for their expertise, listened to and provided with the support needed to enable women to have access to this level of care."

Nicole agrees: "The liberal use of surgical births and medical interventions is horrifying, sad and disappointing for women".

Unmani believes birth technology is being misused. "You need to make assumptions—if you go to a dentist he or she will look at your teeth, an acupuncturist will put needles in you and if you go to a surgeon (ie obstetrician), he will want to get out the knife and that is what he is good at, and what you will get. However is that what is really needed?"

Empowering Tips

Preparing the Mind and Body to Help Avoid Interventions

"If truth be known, many so-called caesarean emergencies could certainly be avoided by mind and body preparation," says Sonya Wildgrace. She teaches that for a woman to give birth, she needs four basic ingredients:

1. She must feel safe. *A woman will only open up to birth her baby where she feels safest (that may be in a hospital or home environment, depending on her own upbringing and her social norms). She must also feel safe with her chosen support people.*

2. She must understand cognitively that she has all she needs. *Her body is just like all women who birth. If she believes she will need something (such as pain relief, epidural or caesarean) then she hasn't grasped the assistance on offer from her natural opiates and ecstatic hormones. She may need to settle some fears and get some more information, talk to someone who knows what true undisturbed birth is. Nut it out and bring it into feeling.*

3. She needs to let go. *Let go of the need to control it with her mind. She knows how it works (see point 2). Now she just needs to let her body do what it knows. Birth has no place for mundane thinking. She must remove her analytical mind to stay in her body, hormones and heightened senses.*

4. She needs to be supported by her partner and/or own independent midwife and/or doula. *These chosen support people must know the woman intimately and also understand undisturbed natural birth and how to create and hold that space for the woman, and fiercely protect it as if their life depended on it. They also need to know how to serve the birthing woman and be selfless in their support, such as leave their own fears and insecurities at the door.*

"We've put birth in the same category with illness and disease and it's never belonged here. Birth is naturally safe, but we've allowed it to be taken over by the medical community."

~ Carla Hartley, founder Trust in Birth and the Ancient Art of Midwifery Institute

A Fearless Home Birth - Rina's Story

My first birth was at a hospital and it wasn't traumatic, but it wasn't ideal. I was very scared and didn't believe I could give birth naturally. The epidural during my first birth was awful; I had the shakes and it stalled my labour for several hours.

It took three hours to push because I couldn't feel anything to push productively. I also had terrible back pain at the epidural site for six months afterwards.

I wanted to avoid all of that the second time—and I did—no stalled labour due to drugs, pushing went much faster and I have no back pain from that huge needle in my spine.

My second birth was drug-free and at home. It went much smoother and I recovered quickly. Knowing I would give birth at home with my midwife Nancy, assisting midwife Noel and doula Machelle, was a huge comfort.

❝ It was a relief to know I would be labouring in familiar surrounds and recovering without interruptions from nurses and visitors. ❞

During my last trimester, whenever I complained about pregnancy-related discomfort, my husband, Aaron, would ask if he needed to take me home (instead of to the hospital) in case I went into labour. It made me smile every time.

My pregnancy was healthy. Nancy and Machelle came to my house for prenatal visits and it was nice to be able to relax and talk with them in the comfort of home. I was tired much of the time, but baby and I were doing very well. I was anticipating I would be overdue, like I was with my first baby.

So you can imagine my surprise when one Thursday evening, early labour began. I was having a lot of back contractions, felt very restless and the only way I could get comfortable was to sit on my exercise ball and rock back and forth.

I began thinking, "This could be it! I could be in labour ... but I'm just not sure." That night, I was so tired but sleeping was a challenge.

The next morning I woke up and felt like I had a million things to do. I felt this intense need to have everything organised and ready. Around 10.30am, I began working on converting a crib into a safe co-sleeper when the contractions became more intense.

I was incredibly irritable and short-tempered with my son Keaton and I knew I needed help. I called Aaron around 11.30am and asked him to come home and help me care for our son.

Around 12pm, my waters broke in a huge gush, all over the kitchen floor. It was quite a surprise and, at first, I didn't believe this could be happening. But as I had more contractions, it continued. I called Aaron again and told him he had to hurry home! I called Nancy.

Then Nancy called Machelle to have her come to my house to take the baby's heart tones. Thankfully, Machelle arrived soon after and cleaned up the mess. We talked a bit; she listened to the baby's heart tones and started setting up the birthing pool.

Aaron arrived home about 1pm. It was a huge relief to have him at the house to take care of Keaton. Nancy and her assisting midwife, Noel, arrived soon after. Around 1.30pm, I entered active labour. Things became hazy after that and I closed my eyes and concentrated.

❝ I rocked back and forth and rested between contractions as they continued to grow longer and stronger. To my amazement, hours were passing by in the blink of an eye. ❞

Nancy and Machelle reminded me to eat frequently for the baby and to keep my strength up, even though I had no appetite.

Aside, from getting me food and checking the baby's heartbeat, they pretty much let me do my own thing and allowed me to move around as I needed. Machelle would apply a heating pad to my lower abdomen, which was incredibly soothing.

A few times she used a Rebozo wrap [13] to lift my belly, which was very helpful. I was walking around, leaning over my exercise ball, labouring standing up, and walking some more.

Eventually I decided I wanted to be in the birthing pool. One interesting sensation was feeling my hipbones moving and spreading. It wasn't painful, more like an intense pressure as my baby was bearing down on my pelvis with each contraction.

Once out of the pool, it was nice to get my land legs back but I wanted to get back into the birthing pool as each contraction came. The birthing pool was an immense help because the warm water relaxed my muscles and allowed my belly to be buoyant.

Machelle gave me a back massage and reminded me to relax my face. I recall hearing Nancy and Noel talking quietly on the sofa while Machelle was next to me as I was labouring in the birthing pool.

Listening to them talk was a very nice distraction. I had my eyes closed but hearing their voices helped me relax because I was reassured to know where they were. Nancy was able to take the baby's heart tones while I was in the water and it was helpful to know he was doing as well as I was.

In the midst of labour, Keaton became concerned and anxious. He kept coming over to give me hugs and kisses to make me feel better. He even attempted to get in the pool but we had to gently tell him "no". Instead, he would put his hands in the water and move them back and forth. He so badly wanted to be close to me and offer me love.

Unfortunately, having my son upset began to slow down my labour and my contractions would stop while I tried to comfort him. I became emotional so Aaron and I decided it would be best for them to go for a drive and get some fresh air.

Once Aaron and Keaton left, my labour became more productive. I was bellowing and groaning to cope better and it really worked.

" Vocalising and swaying back and forth made it more tolerable. I thought I would be scared of the pain but I really wasn't. "

I took it one contraction at a time, and all the hormones kept me going strong. There were a few times I felt like I couldn't do it anymore but I remembered something Nancy told me: "The pain of labour is a productive pain." That helped me to stay positive. I could actually feel my baby rotating in the birth canal.

Before I knew it, my son was crowning. Deckard was born at 7.02pm but he had a short umbilical cord that was tightly wrapped around his neck. Nancy somersaulted him in the water, leaving the umbilical cord intact, and placed him on my chest.

He was blue and not breathing. Nancy put him on a warm tray next to me and gave him two puffs of air while Noel turned the oxygen tank on. Then, an ambu bag[7] was placed over his face. I was holding my breath and Machelle told me to start talking to my baby.

> **" With tears in my eyes, I told him his name for the first time and told him how much I loved him. I told him he was so beautiful and I asked him to open his eyes. "**

As I rubbed his back, I watched the pink colour return to his skin and his chest began to rise and fall. He looked at me with a confused look on his face, like he was thinking, "How did I get out here?" and he whimpered. Then, he started to cry and I was so happy! All of this took place in less than three minutes.

Shortly after birth, while Deckard and I were still in the birthing tub, I called Aaron to come home. As luck would have it, Aaron and Keaton had already pulled into the garage and were on their way to the door.

They got to meet Deckard at the perfect time; they avoided all the scary, icky stuff but got to meet him when he had stopped crying and was alert. Aaron had a proud look on his face and Keaton was super excited to see his baby brother.

Deckard and I stayed in the birth tub a little while longer to catch our breath. I awkwardly held him against my chest but we could tell he was getting cold. I carefully lowered him into the water, with my hand supporting his head and back so he was floating and staying warm.

As we were resting and enjoying the warm water, I delivered my placenta and when the umbilical cord stopped pulsating, it was cut.

Once I was ready, Nancy, Machelle and Noel, helped me slowly walk over to my living room sofa where I settled in and bonded with my baby. He was very alert as I held him skin-to-skin while I gazed at him. Breastfeeding went off without a hitch about 45 minutes later and we've been going strong ever since.

Aaron and I talked about how beneficial and lifesaving it was to leave Deckard's umbilical cord intact after it had been wrapped around his neck, because he was still receiving 70 percent oxygen.

We talked about water birth and I told them how appreciative I was to have had the birthing tub available because it was instrumental in coping with the pain.

We talked about how home birth is very safe for a mother and baby when they are healthy, and also how perfect and healthy my labour was and how natural homebirth is. We commented on how handsome and healthy Deckard was.

It was such a calming experience to sit and talk in the dim light and warmth of our home, while we discussed the events of my labour.

After a while, I gave Deckard to my husband to hold and I went up to our bedroom, with Nancy, Machelle and Noel, to have a tear stitched up.

Then, my son was brought to me while I lay in bed. Nancy weighed him, did a health check and made sure all his fingers and toes were accounted for. He weighed 4.5 kilos and was 55.9 cm long. What a big, healthy boy!

Around 10pm, Nancy, Machelle and Noel said their goodbyes while Deckard and I snuggled in bed. It was a very restful experience, to sleep in my own bed with my newborn son, undisrupted by nurses and visitors. Just peace and quiet as I got to know my baby.

Giving birth at home, on my own terms, surrounded by three strong women was an amazing experience! I am so glad I had the courage to bring my second son into this world drug-free and in the security of my own home. I can't say enough how peaceful and natural it was.

" Home birth gave me confidence; if I could give birth at home, I could be fearless and I could do anything! "

I had tons of endorphins and oxytocin rushing through my body and I felt alive! Home birth was exactly what I needed. I only wish now I had allowed pictures to be taken of the birth because it was such a beautiful experience.

During the early weeks after birth, I got to see Nancy and Machelle on a regular basis for home visits. Deckard was gaining very well, and we were both very healthy. I realised that emotionally, I was doing much better than I had after my first birth.

Last time, I knew intellectually I had had a baby, but instinctively, I felt unsettled and confused. I remember crying in the shower the next morning, like I had lost someone very dear to me.

I realise now I was grieving because I had been disconnected from the birth due to the painkillers and instinctively I was mourning a loss. I had the baby blues and then postpartum depression the first time, which seemed to drag on and on.

This time, both instinctively and intellectually, I felt at peace because experiencing childbirth in my own home was what my mind and body needed.

I did have the baby blues for a few weeks and I do feel tired most days and overwhelmed sometimes, but there are no signs of postpartum depression.

I feel my home birth has contributed to my state of mind because it was a very healing, enlightening and empowering experience. I felt closer to my newborn son and I felt like I could take on the world. What a blessing homebirth can be. It was hard work and I did it!

> *"Mothers need to know that their care and their choices won't be compromised by birth politics."*
>
> ~ JENNIFER ROSENBERG

12th Insight:
A Whole World of Tips and Tricks

> *"Birth is not only about making babies. Birth is about making mothers—strong, competent, capable mothers—who trust themselves and know their inner strength."*
>
> **~ BARBARA KATZ ROTHMAN, PROFESSOR OF SOCIOLOGY AT THE CITY UNIVERSITY OF NEW YORK**

From my understanding, hospital antenatal classes give you all the medical options on the menu to deal with birth, but do not put enough emphasis on, or give practical guidance about, natural, drug-free options.

They often tend to instil fear in already impressionable pregnant women, who, more often than not, have been presented with only medicalised births shown in graphic movies, leaving an indelible impression that medical pain relief will be needed.

Knowing this, I made a conscious decision not to attend hospital classes, as I was set on a natural, drug-free birth. I didn't want to pollute my mind or feed the fear.

Empowering Tips
Recipe for a Drug-Free Birth

Stay at home as long as possible. *My first, and most helpful, technique was to stay at home for as long as possible. What really stayed with me from the hypnobirthing course was that, "The first intervention is when you leave home."*

That really rang true for me, since home is where it all flowed easily and was very comfortable, with the help of breathing techniques I learned from the birth course. Also, no one was prodding, poking or examining me and I felt the most "normal", whereas the hospital environment felt very different, even with the best of preparations.

Get in the zone. *After the initial examination, I lay down and rested with my wonderful hypnobirthing (guided visualisation) CD for the first 15 minutes to "get into the zone". Then I remained upright and active for the remainder of the birth, as I had envisaged, and avoided lying down on the bed like a patient.*

Make use of water therapy. *I was supported with heat packs and massages thanks to my husband (and also my midwife the first time around) and made good use of the hot shower, which felt incredibly soothing on my lower back. "Birthing women are exempt from water restrictions," joked the midwife, "So enjoy the hot shower for as long as it feels good." That sounded great to me!*

Fuel yourself (and hydrate) like an athlete. *After many hours of active labour, it felt like the last stretch of a marathon. Just like an athlete who needs extra endurance to last the distance when they are exhausted, and there is nothing left to give, I had to push through to get to the finish line—in this case the beginning line! I fuelled myself well beforehand with a good nourishing meal in pre-labour but couldn't stomach a thing during birth. I kept hydrated, conserved energy, kept calm and focused on my breathing as I had been taught in the course.*

Clock off and listen to your body. *I admit, the first time, things got a little shaky when I reached the pushing stage, as I had been in labour for so long already, hadn't eaten for many hours and this part was more difficult than I had anticipated.*

I now realise it was my environment, not my body that was the cause of the "difficulty", since there were unnatural time pressures being placed on me to perform or else they were "calling in the doctor". The time pressure and threats slowed things down as it totally put me out of the zone and fear crept in for the first time. Looking back, I would refuse the initial examination altogether.

That way I would avoid playing the game of being on a controlled hospital time system and all of the pressures and associated stress could have been avoided. If you are not being timed, then they can't hurry you along and you are able to birth at your own pace, which is how it should be!

See the fruits of your labour. *When we were finally making progress, I asked for a mirror so I could see the baby's head coming out. This was the best thing I did. As soon as I saw the head emerging, it gave me just the encouragement I needed and last bit of strength (I was completely exhausted by this stage) to push her out. The forced pushing caused tearing, but it didn't really bother me—I must have been high on those happy birth hormones.*

I now realise every woman and her birth experience is different, so I asked numerous mums who had a natural, empowering birth, what drug-free tools or techniques they used during their births to make it better, easier or simply more comfortable, so I could learn a few tips. I also got a sneak peek into their hospital bags to see what they packed and find out if they brought along a bag of tricks for the birth to get some more ideas and whether it was actually helpful in the birthing process.

The exciting news? It turned out there were as many unique births as women and a whole world of drug-free options just waiting for the willing woman to explore!

"Attending births is like growing roses. You have to marvel at the ones that just open up and bloom at the first kiss of the sun but you wouldn't dream of pulling open the petals of the tightly closed buds and forcing them to blossom to your time line." ~
Gloria Lemay, birth attendant and Wise Woman's Way of Birthing teacher

Natural Birthing Tips - Mothers' Wisdom

"For my first birth there were lots of hospital intervention and drugs. For my next three births, when I was more empowered, I used natural methods instead: Heat packs, massage, homeopathic drops, bath, rescue remedy, candles, essential oils, rose." ~ Vickie

"Being in water was most important for me. It was relaxing and helped me to feel at peace. Also massages, essential oils and nice classical music—all these tools worked wonders." ~ Wendy

"At the hospital I used the shower and the bath. During my second birth, my sister massaged my back. I had essential oils but the smell was too strong so we didn't use them. The birth pool was amazing. Access to water was the most important thing for me during birth." ~ Heidi

"For my first birth, the most helpful tool was the water birth and breathing techniques. For my second birth, I used a combination of music, scented candles and yoga stretches for my back and to open my pelvis. Also massage oil and positive mantras." ~ Leonie

"I used everything I had read about, including special aromatherapy blends, fit balls, massage, warm spa bath, heat packs, meditation and an affirmation, which I had from the start of the pregnancy. Oh and there was a little swearing so I am told!" ~ Cory

"I did pregnancy yoga and used every position we'd learned. I used vocalisation and heat on my back. I used the shower, the birth pool and mobilisation. I think I danced my baby out." ~ Cas

"I used body pillows and relaxed between contractions during labour. Don't stress out about what's to come. Take it all in, listen to all the sounds around you. Do what you need to do. Take it as it comes." ~ Rachel

"Breathing, meditating and going within and not relying on anyone to touch me or massage me. I was prepared for massage, but the only words I spoke during labour were 'don't touch me'." ~ Kate

"No drugs required, just a kit of alternative treatments including homeopathics, herbs, tea, rescue remedy and of course the warm water (birth pool) was the ultimate pain reliever. I had also practised meditation, visualisation and perennial massage[2] before both births and this helped me to cope throughout." ~ Natalie

"I wasn't really happy with anything on my body like heat packs. I used a TENS machine(9) whilst at home but it annoyed me in the hospital. The second time around, I used breathing techniques, brought along music and had the lights dimmed. I was attempting to make the environment less clinical. It helped to an extent." ~ Rachel

"I told myself I just have to do what I need to do. I used prenatal yoga figure of eights: hips straight with a belly-dancing move. Imagine a pencil continually drawing a figure of eight on the ground—and keep everything moving—I did this in the shower for a couple of hours!" ~ Rebecca

The Road to Birthing Bliss - Experts Say

Diane Gardner says, "The most effective tool is understanding how the body works, since bodies know how to birth babies, brains don't. Remember, the blueprint to birth was already there from the moment you were conceived as a female so just allow your body to birth your baby.

You don't need to teach the body how to birth—just keep out of its way and support it with relaxation and good breathing. Work with the body, not against it."

Jo Thomson is an advocate of self-hypnosis and guided visualisation. "It works," she says. "Music can also be a valuable tool as it keeps the mother calm and relaxed."

Sonya Wildgrace believes the most effective techniques for a more positive birth experience are to know how the birthing brain works in labour, how to subdue the thinking brain and stay in your primal birthing space.

"The challenge is to know what disturbs the process, how to educate your support people and then trust you have taught them well enough (so) they can protect your space as you just immerse yourself in what your body does naturally," she says.

Sonya's tips for a positive birth:

    ℘ Darkness, dim lights, warmth, whispers, water, breath and soft rhythmic touch and a birth plan in bold, explaining why, to satisfy the curious staff.

- ❧ No loud voices and bright fluorescent lights, clocks, intrusive strangers, unwanted, excessive staff with silly irrelevant questions and references to anything that requires the birthing woman to "think"—bringing her out of her primal, instinctual brain, into pain and fear and present-time thinking.

- ❧ Natural, undisturbed birth must not be timed by the birthing woman—or anyone else, out loud.

"Keeping active during labour and adopting natural, upright or crouching positions is the safest, most enjoyable, most economical and sensible way for the majority of women to give birth." ~ Janet Balaskas, active birth pioneer

I Have Never Felt So Alive and So Proud of Myself! - Meagan's story

I expected you early and you came oh so late—the day before I was to be induced, in fact. Luckily, your big brother, who was born 30-something hours after my waters broke, had prepared me for a long wait. I had my first rush at around 9pm on a Saturday.

Each one was far apart, but I knew from the first that these were no Braxton Hicks. Your Dada and I called the hospital and told them to expect me at some point during the night and then went back to bed. I knew this time it was important to conserve my energy and rest.

I was amazed at how deeply I could sleep, in between the intensity of my rushes. When one began, I would wake up, breathe through it and go right back to sleep. By 6am the next morning, I had had enough of lying down and was eager to get things going, so I suggested Dada, North (my son) and I go for a brisk march along the beach. It was a cool crisp day, but the sun was shining.

❝ I stopped every so often through a wave and focused on my breathing and, above all else, stayed calm and relaxed. ❞

When we arrived home, the boys headed to the park while I stayed behind in the safety and comfort of our bedroom.

I felt sleepy so I decided to have a nap, even though I knew this might keep things going slowly. This was the best decision I could have made. I listened to my body and what it needed instead of trying to figure out what I should have been doing to help labour progress.

When the boys came home, I nibbled on half a sandwich and drank some raspberry leaf tea and stayed in the bedroom for a little while longer. After North's nap, I decided we'd better go for another walk if I wanted my rushes to get closer together and if I wanted my waters to break soon.

So, we set off to the playground on our last outing as three. Every so often your brother would ask, "What you doing, Mama?" as I leaned over the pram and huffed and puffed. Dada told him you were coming soon and I was just feeling a little funny in my tummy.

I felt inspired to pick a few flowers on the way, as many wise women had suggested using them for visualisation. I trekked around a footy field a few times, gripping onto the little stems for strength and gazing down at the colourful petals.

❝ With every wave, I imagined my uterus blossoming and growing. At times I truly believed this technique was working and I could feel myself opening up. ❞

When we got home, everything felt more intense. The rushes were much closer together.

It was now 5pm on Sunday. I knelt on the floor against the bed, slipping and sliding on my knees for the duration of each rush. Long, deep exhales helped me to get through each wave and I often reminded myself to rest in between rushes. I calmly welcomed each contraction with the knowledge they were bringing you closer to me.

At one point I panicked and began to wonder whether I could give birth without an epidural, or some form of pain relief, and then remembered Ina May's saying about the power of words. In the privacy of my bedroom as I writhed around on the floor, I said out loud to myself, "I can do this, I can do this."

At around six o'clock my waters broke. We called Grandma and Papa and told them to hurry. I slid down against the wall and breathed through another big wave. They were now only minutes away from each other.

We got to the hospital in less than 10 minutes and walked up to the labour ward, it was 6.45pm.

The midwives were waiting for me when we arrived, questions were asked and then, after what seemed like ages, they checked my progress. I was six centimetres dilated and during contractions was stretching as far as eight.

I was emotional, moving from calm lucid moments to a wild animal-like state. I tried to ask the midwife how long she thought I had to go, as I again doubted my ability to go on.

She asked me if I had the urge to push and I replied desperately, "Kind of... but I don't know how." Right then as another wave took over me, I let out a monstrous roar and my whole body took over and I gave a huge push and out popped your entire head!

The midwives were now scrambling around trying to prepare everything in time for your arrival. With the next contraction your shoulders came out, and the next, your legs and feet. I only pushed three times. You were born one hour after we arrived at the hospital.

You found your way to my breast right away and suckled for over an hour. I pushed out the placenta with ease, and two hours later I had a shower and ate an egg salad sandwich. I had no tears, no stitches and no wires or cords attached to my wrists.

“ I have never felt so alive, I have never felt more proud of myself, and I have never felt more feminine. I felt so connected with our Mother Earth and to every other mother who has ever given birth. ”

Thank you my daughter. Thank you so much, for giving me this gift. It will stay with me forever—you have taught me a great lesson—to love and trust my body, to listen and learn from it.

I truly wish every mother could experience childbirth the way I did that evening, because after all is said and done, it really honestly feels so right and so good.

"A woman in birth is at once her most powerful, and most vulnerable. But any woman who has birthed unhindered understands that we are stronger than we know."

~ MARCIE MACARI, AUTHOR OF A MODERN WOMAN'S GUIDEBOOK FOR AN ANCIENT RITE OF PASSAGE

13th Insight:
Deal With Your Monsters

"Anything I've ever done that ultimately was worthwhile… initially scared me to death."

~ BETTY BENDER

The mere thought of going to hospital for the first time was scary in itself. Therefore, I had instinctively helped myself create a safe space by touring and hovering around the maternity ward and making it familiar to me every time I went for antenatal visits to the obstetrician.

This really helped me feel more comfortable with the idea, especially being someone who had never been to hospital before (I pride myself on being exceptionally healthy!). I also associated it with pain, illness and emergency—and drugs, needles and surgery… all the things I detested under one roof!

Therefore, there was a lot of psyching-up to do beforehand. To combat my phobia, I convinced myself I was not a patient going to hospital. I was perfectly healthy and no one was going to do anything to me without my permission.

I was simply hiring the room and the staff in it to do what I needed to do, which was to birth my baby. I was employing them to support me. That turned everything around in my mind, put me back in the driver's seat and made me feel better about the whole thing.

We have all experienced pain in our lives; we all have doubts, insecurities, fears and uncertainties about ourselves. This is normal, however, if these feelings are not released by the time birth arrives, these uncertainties often come up during birth in the form of complications[29].

If you are feeling fearful of the birth process, know it's absolutely normal and a process to work through. In a fascinating article, *Babies Are Overlooked in Labour*, Frederick Leboyer says, *"All pregnant women are frightened.*

What a woman has to do is admit her fear and look at what she is really afraid of. Only then can she begin to work through it and embrace the physical challenge of giving birth."

Although Leboyer has delivered thousands of babies, he hasn't much time for doctors and even less for procedures. He is an old-fashioned advocate of the natural way.

He says, *"Birth is a challenge for a woman. To do her best for her baby, she has to face up to that challenge and not chicken out and have a caesarean instead. Having a caesarean is like reading a book and missing out a crucial chapter of the story—the most important chapter, in fact."*

He likens labour to a storm, through which a woman must sail her boat. *"She has to remain the captain of her ship—it's that straightforward,"* he says. He's also hopelessly romantic about childbirth, maintaining it's *"a woman's secret garden ... it's the moment when a maiden dies and a mature woman is born*[33]*."*

The Best Antidotes for the Biggest Fears - Mothers' Wisdom

> *"You gain strength, courage and confidence by every experience in which you really stop to look fear in the face."* ~ Eleanor Roosevelt

"Getting through the labour was my biggest fear but once it started, I didn't think about it and just got through it." ~ Amanda

"My biggest fear was probably about losing control. That is why I tried throughout my pregnancy to be flexible and just go with the flow." ~ Rachel

"The fear of ending up in an emergency caesarean. I overcame that by imagining I can do it and praying often!" ~ Leonie

"A few times I was scared of giving birth but then thought about it and told myself, billions of people have had babies in this world, some even had babies in the field alone and then continued working." ~ Eva

Rising Above Anxiousness

"Overall, I was calm and in control but certainly there were moments of anxiety, doubt, tension. It is a little bit like riding a roller coaster—you choose to go on the ride and there is no getting off. It's exciting, but boy some of those dips are scary!" ~ Natalie

"I think I felt every emotion. At one point I said to my husband that I didn't want to play this game anymore and could we go home? Ha! There was mixed emotion throughout the day and I would suspect having only done this once, it's the unknown that really fuels those thoughts." ~ Cory

"I felt calm while I was in control of my experience while labouring at home, yet all of that changed in the hospital environment. I was feeling more stressed and out of control at hospital as I was told what to do and when." ~ Leonie

"With the first I felt incredibly anxious, same with the second. With the third I drifted between anxiety and calm. I'm amazed my oxytocin receptors were able to get through that at all." ~ Cas

"Being at home or immersed in water was the key to feeling calm. As soon as I left the water (my first mistake!) I lost control and that's when the interventions began. For my second birth, I was so relaxed that I almost gave birth alone at home! I became a little concerned during transition and then before I knew it, I was holding my bub in my arms!" ~ Rachel

"I felt calm and very much in control—I firmly decided on no drugs as I didn't have any control that way." ~ Kate

"I felt calm and found it was not overwhelmingly painful." ~ Amanda

"Fear can be overcome only by faith." ~ Dr Grantly Dick-Read

Dealing With a Scared Society - Experts Say

Diane Gardner believes women can be influenced by the horror stories they hear, creating fear about their ability to birth their own babies.

"The women who are talking about their negative birth experiences are trying to debrief after what happened to them, and hope that if they tell it often enough they will finally understand what happened," she says.

"Also, synthetic hormone drugs interfere with the body's natural hormones stopping them from working—they give up, and the body becomes dependant on the drugs, so the natural process is inhibited so often can cause a negative experience within the birthing process."

Shivam Rachana says, "It is an inherited situation midwives and pregnant women have taken on. We have inherited a model that doesn't work—an emphasis based towards illness, fear and what goes wrong, so we manifest this as our reality."

We need to enter into it a different way with a holistic approach," she says. "We have a good population of women with good sanitation and good nutrition, yet we still have major abdominal surgery to give birth, which is where the system is failing women. We are not honouring nature.

Men and women are not equal, as the world needs women to perpetuate it. Women need to understand their important role for the species—enjoy being pregnant and take it for the job that it is—listen to our bodies. Birth is part of the continuum."

Most babies are born afraid and imprinted with fear and panic, which they carry throughout their lives, says **Rachana**. "Birth is just another thing to be afraid of (and) the media doesn't help in this regard. There is a lack of good stories and good literature on the subject and positive education needs to start earlier."

Feel the Fear and Give Birth Anyway!

Sonya Wildgrace advises: "Fears are healthy in pregnancy as long as you explore them thoroughly and develop a close connection to your baby throughout your pregnancy. Get to know this little person on an intimate sensory level. You have nine months together in one body so use the time wisely."

The best advice, says **Unmani**, is to surround mothers with positive stories. Attend supportive groups. "Often our own birthing experience can be linked back to unresolved issues in our own birth," she says.

Jo Thomson reminds us the pain is not going to last forever and it is only one day out of your life—and you get an awesome present after it so it is well worth the effort.

"There is too much focus on the birth so it tends to be forgotten about what comes after," she says.

Jo believes it is important to identify what you are fearful of in regards to going into labour and work on the fears before going into the actual situation.

"Women are born to do this," says **Nicole MacFadyen**. "Yet we get too caught up trying to conceive, scared during pregnancy and apprehensive about birth." She tells her clients the only role we have been born to do is to have babies and to trust that.

"We forget that it is our job. The body has an amazing capacity: when we damage the body, it heals itself. The body does an amazing job most of the time, it is clever and we need to trust it. Give it the right tools and it will."

Davini adds: "I worked with my fear of giving birth by getting in my body. I dealt with issues I didn't know were there before I had bodywork. I also did rebirthing, women's circles and yoga. These helped me to work through fears and become deeply acquainted with my body, my emotions and my breath.

Does this guarantee the outcome you wish? Not necessarily, but the surrender that is born out of this type of birth preparation provides a strong foundation for whatever unfolds and allows a more readily accessible communication with yourself in labour and beyond into motherhood."

Confronting Fear

"Birth is the strongest force a woman normally experiences. If there is harmony with this force, your body and mind will enter into a different state, one that surrenders totally to natural forces. The face loses self-consciousness; it is a quiet state ... gentle and profound.

Sometimes I think the ease of a birth has to do with complete surrender to nature; an acceptance of being part of something greater than the individual self, like a beautiful spring, or the first heavy rains, or the sounds and rhythm of the sea.

Labour and birth are a matter of believing, trusting and listening to your instincts—a matter of getting close enough to yourself and to the information you are receiving from your body. You must rely on yourself. Unfold your inherent birth knowledge.

Use your own rhythm, get behind it and don't have your mind in any time dimension except the present.

Accept each contraction, one at a time, just as you accept the sun rising each morning. Without question, one day at a time." ~ Osho [48]

In other words, the real enemy to conquer is not the pain but fear itself.

"A factor in labour is the intense sensation. It is beyond the expectations of anyone who has never given birth. This intense sensation is simply a part of the whole, and when there is no fear, it simply is." ~ Osho

Still Waiting for the Pain! - Tammy's Story

Tammy was no stranger to dealing with challenges or living with pain, having had a major car accident a number of years ago. This, she says, made her strong and gave her an increased pain threshold.

Like many first time mothers, Tammy's greatest fear when she became pregnant was, "How am I going to give birth?"

She chose to have her baby in a birthing centre supported by midwives, as she is a firm believer that "birth is a natural thing that has nothing to do with the hospital". She says she always wanted to give as birth naturally as possible and wanted the same for her baby—not come into the world drugged.

She knew that who was there at the birth was important, so hired her own midwife, Clare, who was recommended by her course instructor. She was able to get to know Clare and bond with her prior to the birth.

Tammy undertook a traditional birth course as well as an "awesome" independent birthing course to prepare her mind. The latter taught her "birth is not pain, it is just muscles stretching".

❝ *Knowing the uterus is a huge muscle, and what optimum conditions the body needs, this changed her perception of what to expect during labour.* ❞

She also learnt we are still mammals and instinctively switch to "fight or flight" when we feel unsafe—only now there is no wild tiger, there are humans involved!

I spoke to Tammy shortly after she had attended the independent course. She was a changed woman; so strong and empowered and ready to take charge of her birthing experience! I was so amazed and proud of her and knew in my heart she would have the natural drug-free birth she had dearly wanted.

In preparation for labour, Tammy ate well, as she understood the baby comes from the building blocks of what the mother is eating. She also stayed active no matter what, despite her back injury. She drank dandelion and raspberry teas daily, Evergreen for a rich source of chlorophyll and did plenty of walking to keep active.

Her pregnancy was a truly magical experience: "I loved the whole thing and felt on top of the world, like this is what I am made for." Her skin and hair were amazing.

" She was also able to share the dream with someone else; every night her hubby massaged her tummy with oil and they sat together in silence listening to the baby. It was a very special bonding experience for the three of them. "

Tammy tried to be as happy as possible and enjoy every moment as she knew the pregnancy wasn't going to last forever.

She felt spiritually connected and in tune with her baby and that they were communicating. In fact, they had a huge talk towards the end of her pregnancy and she sensed her baby was going to be there the next week. She knew the baby was ready to come out. It was an intuitive thing, she says. Sure enough, the following week, Tammy went into labour.

In pre-labour she sniffed clary sage and drove to the beach to relax with her husband. She had contractions throughout the whole journey and thought they would continue for up to four days. She deeply breathed in each contraction and took the time to feel each one, stretching, moving and progressing.

"My body had begun its metamorphosis," Tammy says. "Eventually, I told myself, it will turn into pain, it's to be expected. I repeatedly told myself this is what I am designed to do, the pain will come in four days. Be strong and be calm."

After the beach, Tammy's husband took her to their favourite Thai restaurant. "We were planning to take walks the next two to three days and keep active; we also wanted to bake a welcome home cake, but that night at around 11pm I began to get uncomfortable,"

Tammy recalls. "I kept wriggling on the gym ball; I found it hard to settle, I really wanted to shower but didn't want to stand so I tried to get some sleep.

Four hours later the contractions got stronger; we phoned the birth centre and were told to take (a painkiller) and sleep. I barely got to sleep another 20 minutes.

Leo had a contraction timer and I would say 'start' and 'stop' at every contraction. I tried to stay happy and laughed lots since this would last for another two to three days."

Tammy says they didn't want to go to the birthing centre early and needed the contractions to be greater than two minutes and 30 seconds apart.

"At 7am we had our first two-minute contraction," Tammy says. "We phoned the birth centre again and Sue guided me through the whole contraction, I focused on her kind voice and felt good again. At the end of the call she said 'see you soon', I hung up and laughed, thinking no, I'll be there in another two days, I'm still in pre-labour!"

The next seven hours, Tammy says, were a blur. "I recall Leo telling me 'don't worry, the work you're doing now, you wont have to do again'. I was convinced I was in pre-labour. My waters seemed to break at 2pm. I felt different.

It was then Leo phoned our midwife Clare. As soon as she arrived she hopped on our bed, had a look and said, 'Tammy you're fully dilated and ready to push!'

I couldn't believe it, the time had come, I was going to meet our baby today, and not in two days! I got into Clare's car and 'ha ha hooed' for the whole 10-minute trip!"

Empowering herself with knowledge from the course and taking good care of her health was the best thing she did in preparation for her baby girl's arrival.

66 *Her birth was completely natural and drug-free and she was still waiting for the pain!* 99

She says she learnt human mammals are the most vulnerable. "When oxytocin is up then everything is perfect, however, when you become stressed, the stress produces adrenaline, which shuts the labour down so it is really important to stay relaxed," Tammy explains. "Then you have to work hard to 'chill out' to get back in the zone. "I hated the cold doppler at every push.

I feel I worked harder at getting my brain to relax to come back into the zone than at pushing. I'm looking forward to a home birth next time!" She suggests to, "Stay in the zone during labour—we go there instinctively and this is what gets us through. The best medicine is to be in the zone."

Tammy believes women who choose to have an elective caesarean, or those who are still wondering why they haven't made birth pain-free, are being "robbed of natural enlightenment". "We enjoy natural oxytocin for a reason", she says.

"Unless there is a medical condition with special needs, I hope women can learn to hear the positive stories rather than the scary ones and try to focus on positive energy surrounding them and think of the laws of attraction. If you focus on the negatives, they will find you. Only hold positive thoughts in your head."

❝ While she doesn't recall many of the details of her very quick and easy labour, she found the experience to be "beautiful" and "exhilarating". ❞

It was only one brief hour in the birthing centre! She had no intervention at all, just as she had hoped.

Her advice for new mothers? "Do research to know what is happening and do not have one milligram of fear. As for the 'what ifs', leave them with the birth plan when the time comes to make a decision.

Discuss it with your midwife in hospital. With the right midwife, you can give birth to twins in breech! You need to completely trust in her."

Above all, she says, "Remember that birth is physiological."

"Giving birth should be your greatest achievement, not your greatest fear."

~ JANE WEIDEMAN

14th Insight:
Pain is Good or Nothing at All

> *"Whatever you fight, you strengthen, and what you resist, persists."*
>
> ~ ECKHART TOLLE

There is so much truth in Eckhart Tolle's teachings. The lesson here is if you just release, let go and simply allow the birth to unfold, it will be beautiful! As always, it is our head that gets in the way. So get back into your body and accept and surrender to the miraculous process, rather than resisting it.

Perhaps one of the biggest fears surrounding birth in our modern world is the overwhelming fear of the possible pain involved and whether we are equipped to handle it. This is especially the case for first-time mothers who don't know what to expect.

It is probably one of the biggest considerations when making the decision to go natural and drug-free, or not. Whatever we decide, it's comforting to know we are not alone in our fears.

Aside from being filled with positive anticipation and excitement about the arrival of a new baby, the fear of the unknown and the dreaded pain factor was always top-of-mind or just beneath the surface as a first time mother-to-be. I assumed pain would be part of the experience, as it has always been depicted that way in the movies—and by every woman who has shared her warrior stories.

The expectation of pain was something that clouded the beauty and filled me with intense fear and panic whenever I thought of how I was going to get this baby out.

That was until I empowered myself with extensive research, attended a fabulous natural birth course, which taught me about the possibility of a pain-free birth and showed movies and stories of peaceful and joyous birth experiences. I also employed an independent midwife who took the time to work through my fears and concerns and enlighten me with her knowledge.

Make Peace with Your Monsters

I finally learnt the real truth about birth—the real monster was not the pain but fear itself. It is the fear that promotes the pain. We are taught to fear birth because we are told it is overwhelmingly painful, but what if this was just a myth we have all bought into? What if it could be a pain-free or even joyful experience, if only we would think differently about it?

According to British obstetrician Dr Grantly Dick-Read, "*The fear of pain actually produces true pain through the medium of pathological tension. The most important contributory cause of pain in otherwise normal labour is fear*[40]." When this idea really starts to sink in, it is nothing less than revolutionary!

Another truth I have gained from hearing other women's experiences is that the long-term pain of emotional trauma from *not* having the birth you want is far greater than any short-term physical pain or discomfort you may experience during the course of labour.

So while there are no guarantees in life, or birth for that matter, it is worth the effort to consciously prepare and do everything in your power to have the birth you want and truly deserve.

On that note, I am happy to say my birth experiences were both drug-free and virtually pain-free ones, not due to "good luck" or having a "high pain threshold" as many friends would suggest, but due to my conscious mind-body preparations, mindset and teachings.

Empowering Tip:

See your contractions as waves of energy. Ride the waves, rather than resisting them. Then simply focus on welcoming each one, one wave at a time and know that every wave is bringing your baby closer to you.

The first time I went into labour, it all started one Monday evening at around 8.30pm. The waves continued through the night while I paced around the living room and let my husband sleep, then through the next day, gradually building up in intensity, yet were very comfortable and manageable thanks to my hypnobirthing techniques. I just focused and breathed through them and rested in between.

As the labour progressed, I experienced moments of comfort and ease, discomfort, very intense and strong sensations that I have no real name for, except to say they required my full attention. These culminated in a sense of incredible joy, relief and euphoria at the end when I got to hold my baby for the first time.

It certainly was not a walk in the park by any means—it required real mental and physical stamina (especially the first time as it was a lot longer) and concentrated effort, beyond anything I have ever experienced, which is perhaps why they call it "labour". Yet the fact it required real effort to birth my baby, meant the rewards were far greater and I was able to enjoy a greater sense of satisfaction and achievement afterwards... like I could take on the world.

I have spoken to women who have had ecstatic birth experiences way beyond anything I could imagine. You will hear from some of them in this book. While there are no guarantees and you can't place your order, it does happen and it is not just a wild fantasy, but a real possibility (for some women) if you are committed.

Empowering Tip:

As Ina May Gaskin says, "Don't think of it as pain. Think of it as an interesting sensation that requires all of your attention."

What a great way to turn it around, just by changing our perception of the experience! I took a similar approach to my own births; I spoke of "waves" rather than contractions, and described the feelings as "intense" rather than "painful" and that is exactly what I experienced. It's all about the power of words to create our reality or how we talk to ourselves that makes the world of difference.

"No other natural bodily function is painful and childbirth should not be an exception." ~ *Dr Grantly Dick-Read*

What Birth is Really Like - Mothers' Wisdom

"It's not a bad pain, it's a beautiful pain that only we can have. When you have an epidural, you miss out on that experience and it only lasts for several hours max. Yeah it hurts but it's so worth the end product. It didn't worry me that much. I just slept through contractions." ~ Rachel

"What pain? I learnt in the natural birth preparation course that 'birth is not pain, it is just muscles stretching." ~ Tammy

"I dealt with it just by focusing on what was coming. A gorgeous little person, that was enough." ~ Kellie

"It was a lot more intense than I imagined it to be but not as painful as I imagined it to be. I felt like I'd gained this amazing insight into birth and how our bodies are amazingly made to cope with birth when the environment is right." ~ Cas

"My baby girl was born with little or NO PAIN! The three of us were on a natural high! We kept giggling and saying we can't believe it happened so quick and easy." ~ Leonie

"The contractions hurt, but they were never bigger than me." ~ Kiera

"After being immersed in the water, another contraction came and it didn't seem nearly as intense as it was on land. I caught myself thinking that this had to become more difficult before it got easier...

After panting my way through about three contractions I could feel the baby's head move down and then back up again—what a crazy sensation that was—not at all painful but exhilarating." ~ Rachel

"My second birth was so easy. I had a birth pool ready but decided to stay out of the water until the pain was too much. But it never reached that point. After only two hours I was ready to push and so I figured I had better get in the pool or I would miss the opportunity to use it!" ~ Heidi

"When the pushing urge came, it hurt, yet I greeted it gladly and with joy."
~ Vickie

A Pain-Free Birth: Fantasy or Reality?
- Experts Say

Diane Gardner says although there are no guarantees, "It is absolutely possible to not feel any pain during the birthing process, just intense pressure."

"I have witnessed it with my own eyes and have also experienced it," says **Sonya Wildgrace**. "For me, it seemed to relate to my attachment to my birth at the time. My state of surrender and the care and support I had created for myself. I believed in myself."

"The clients I supported, attributed their pain-free births to their total trust and surrender to the process. They didn't have anyone in the room that they didn't like either. They went 'within' and stayed there. Like there is this mystical place where they go, to skip and play and lie in the sun or swing in a hammock somewhere. They only briefly came out to give short direct instructions, only to quickly disappear again. Truly amazing to witness."

Jo Thomson suggests embracing the pain rather than fighting it. She reminds women it is only one day or so out of their lives and that it will soon pass.

Unmani says, "Pain is what happens, however a woman needs to know she is the one in control and that it is not overwhelming for her. That is, it is not too much and she can do it."

Shivam Rachana believes, "Pain is subjective—it is how you approach the pain and work with the body, not against it, that makes all the difference."

"We are made to do this work and it's not easy ... I would say that pain is part of the glory, or the tremendous mystery of life. And that if anything, it's a kind of privilege to stand so close to such an incredible miracle." ~ Simone in Klasson

Nothing to Fear but a Lot to Love - Bronwyn's Story

The birth of my beautiful daughter began with a sneeze. Hard to believe such a seemingly insignificant but natural bodily function led to that most divine act of creation all living creatures are capable of: introducing a new life into the world.

The sneeze was the catalyst, which led to a chain of events that had me induced in the early hours of a Monday morning in November. I got out of bed and as my feet hit the floor, "Ka-choo!" Initially, when I felt the trickle down my leg I thought I'd had a bit of an accident. But when the trickle didn't stop after a few seconds, I realised I'd sprung a leak of the amniotic fluid kind!

Being my first pregnancy experience and having just hit the 38-week mark, I promptly called the hospital and spoke to a midwife who suggested I come in for a check up. So off we went at around midnight. I was poked and prodded as they "tested" for any sign of amniotic fluid where it shouldn't be—outside of my uterus!

It was determined my cervix was nowhere near "ripe" and although I insisted it was not the case, the rather stern midwife insisted I had simply "wet myself" and should go home and wait for the real deal. I was ushered out of the birthing room with an air of condescension, but my internal voice kept telling me otherwise!

❝ From that moment I realised when it comes to birth, no one knows their own body better than the woman who is nurturing a growing life within. ❞

Intuition is the most powerful biological tool at our disposal and if I could give any expectant mother advice, it would be to quiet all external noise and listen very carefully to that little voice or niggling feeling within—it's always right!

The next day, I was still uneasy and called my obstetrician. She squeezed me into her schedule the following day to conduct a "more reliable" test than the one they had done at the hospital, which would prove with 100 percent certainty whether my gut feeling was on the money.

I wondered why they hadn't done the "more reliable" test in the hospital, but felt relieved to be getting a second opinion from someone I had come to trust.

Of course my gut had not let me down and because of her concern as to the potential for an infection, my obstetrician booked me in for an induction two days later. I was devastated at the prospect of being induced rather than experiencing a natural labour.

We had a huge bath and I had visions of indulging in a large expanse of warm water as I laboured for as long as possible at home. But I wanted what was best for my baby, so I put aside my doubts and went with the chain of events that were unfolding.

Mind you, I didn't sleep a wink the night before, knowing tomorrow was going to bring an unknown experience of enormous magnitude and change our lives forever.

I had been looking forward to going into labour with excited and nervous anticipation, but when my obstetrician inserted a synthetic hormone designed to encourage my uncooperative cervix to start dilating, the gravity of what I was about to do really hit home.

I managed to calm myself by drawing on my background in meditation. As a student and teacher of the art for many years, I knew all too well the benefits of mind over matter and felt it was critical to draw on that knowledge for the journey I was now on.

Waiting for the contractions to start in earnest felt like an eternity, before the small niggles I felt from time-to-time started to pack a bit more punch. The staff kept telling me nothing would happen until much later the next day, as inductions were a long process and insisted on sending my partner home that night.

We argued the point, but they told us it was "hospital policy" and wouldn't budge. They reassured him they'd call if anything happened... although they didn't expect anything until the following evening.

Obviously, they were unaware of my agenda and the fact I am a tad impatient and more than just a bit of a control freak!

" As the contractions grew to an astounding intensity, I started my internal dialogue and filled my body with light energy. "

Then I began to visualize the amazing internal workings that would bring about the birth of our daughter. Knowing the experience of "pain" is merely a perception helped tremendously. I decided this feeling was "good", and as each contraction took hold with what I came to recognise as my own life force helping me toward the birth, I imagined my cervix opening up and my baby moving further and further down.

It must have worked because only a few hours after my partner was ushered out the door, the midwife came in to find me breathing and concentrating with as much gusto as I could muster. She was still sceptical as to how far along I might be, but upon examination, looked rather shocked and took off to call my partner. I had gone from an unripe cervix to four centimetres dilated within two hours.

When Jason arrived, we made our way to the birthing room, and having had no sleep for two nights and feeling exhausted but energised all at once, I assumed the most comfy position I could manage on the bed. It was now about 3am and the midwife—who was wonderfully reassuring and encouraging—told Jason things would progress slowly, with one centimetre of dilation every hour or so.

She was amazed at how I was cracking jokes in between contractions, but as soon as another one took hold, I went straight back into my own internal world. It was just me, my baby and the divine power willing me along. I wanted nothing to distract me from the job at hand!

I told the midwife I felt a strong urge to push only a couple of hours later, so she conducted another internal and announced in amazement that I was eight centimetres dilated and she'd better call my obstetrician. Then, all of a sudden, I felt a build up of pressure, followed by a huge gush: my waters had broken.

When the obstetrician arrived, she found me in a state of calm concentration and fully dilated. I knew I had to make every effort to deliver as soon as possible because I was so tired and running on adrenaline and sheer willpower.

As I pushed my way through each contraction—with the help of a super-strong core due to the Pilates I'd done for a back injury—I made a few little noises and the midwife and obstetrician instructed me to internalise those noises and use them to make my efforts more productive.

I followed their advice without any argument. They had done this quite a bit so I thought it was a good idea to go with their suggestion!

After maybe half an hour of pushing, I heard my obstetrician announce she could see the baby's head. She explained to Jason that with each contraction, the head would go back in, and then come out again. This could occur quite a few times before our little girl finally made a complete appearance.

Upon hearing those words and feeling completely exhausted but still on my adrenaline high, I determined I would prove her wrong!

With the next push, out came the baby's head, much to everyone's surprise! In fact, the obstetrician let out a shocked "oh!" as she assumed a catcher's position!

She told me to pant and wait a moment, but with a strong urge to keep things rolling, I paused for a moment, took a breath and pushed the entire body of our little girl out in one go. The obstetrician just caught her in time and both her and the midwife started laughing at how quickly the whole thing had happened.

They slid our gorgeous little girl onto my chest and almost immediately she started suckling like a pro!

❝ I was overwhelmed with emotion and fell instantly in love, feeling an overwhelming urge to protect and nurture this tiny being. It was worth all of the exhaustion and every last contraction! ❞

Needless to say, I provided a good story for the midwives to share, and every time a different one came in to attend to my little girl and I, they started out with something along the lines of, "Oh, you're the one who proved us all wrong!"

My entire labour lasted three hours. I've always been the type to do things my own way and in my own timeframe—even giving birth!

Our second child, a little boy, came into the world even quicker— one-and-a-half hours and three pushes and he was out, once more with the same focus and meditation. The only thing happening in the world at that moment (in my mind) was his birth.

Unfortunately, my most recent birth experience with our third—a surprise baby—didn't go quite so smoothly. After being head down until 35 weeks, he decided to do a somersault and ended up in breech position.

I'd had a few blood pressure issues and a dreadful virus for the last two months of my pregnancy and didn't want to take any risks with a natural breech delivery.

I discussed my options with the obstetrician and we decided she'd attempt to turn him in hospital at 37 weeks and four days, as my births were so quick, she didn't want to chance a breech birth on the side of the highway (we were more than an hour from the hospital).

Spot on 37 weeks, around midnight, I started having some full on contractions. They immediately fell into a regular pattern of three-minute intervals and I quickly called my sister-in-law to come and look after our two sleeping children.

By the time she arrived, I was up and ready to go, knowing time was of the essence! With each contraction, I stopped talking and focused all of my energy on keeping the baby in!

Jason—a paramedic—called on his driving skills and we made it to the hospital an hour later. I was terrified at the prospect of undergoing surgery, but calmed myself with the thought that I would soon be nursing our third little miracle and that was all that mattered.

I explained to the anaesthetist that I was scared of the spinal and he reassured me wonderfully that all would be fine. All those attending were amazed that in between contractions I was joking and in good humour. Just before they took me in to have the c-section, my waters broke and everyone quickly picked up the pace.

I drew on my meditation breathing to calm my nerves and let the professionals do their job, all the time feeling a little irritated I'd gone through an entire labour without the bliss of pushing out a baby at the end!

At 5.43am, Reilly Elijah entered the world through an incision in my abdomen. They had to resuscitate him and worked for around nine minutes to get a response from his tiny body, but once he got going, he started breathing like a trooper!

**   “ *Having experienced almost every possible birthing situation there is, I have to confess I love the experience of a natural labour and birth.* ”**

Nothing compares to the elation you feel when you achieve such an amazing outcome and your baby is immediately on your chest. Every bit of the process is a true blessing to experience. It is the closest we can ever get, as human beings, to whatever divine power you choose to believe in and the most holy act of creation.

There is nothing to fear, but an awful lot to love. I would never even use the word "pain" in connection with giving birth—it simply cannot exist in the amazing gift of life we've been blessed with as women.

The power and intensity of your contractions cannot be stronger than you, because it is you.

~ UNKNOWN

15th Insight:
Harness Your Hormones

> *"Never underestimate the beautiful orchestra of the birth hormones. Surrendering your body to work with them and not against them assists with the magic of birth."*
>
> ~ LISA, CENTRAL COAST CALMBIRTH

*L*abour and birth is driven by an incredible hormonal system. Oxytocin is the primary hormone of birth. Also known as the hormone of love, it is secreted during orgasm, following ovulation, and is responsible for the release of milk during breastfeeding.

It makes women feel nurturing and loving. The baby also produces oxytocin during un-medicated labour, so in the minutes after birth, mother and baby are bathed in an ecstatic blend of hormones. The perfect recipe for the beginning of a lifelong love story!

If you are still wondering why humans seem to be the only mammals that "need" pain relief during labour, then consider that we are probably the only mammals who are fearful of the process and so we create more pain than necessary. There is also an in-built expectation that we "need help" to give birth, rather than being perfectly capable of doing it on our own.

When we put ourselves in a medical environment that is generally what we get. Know that being in a hospital means you are going against the wave and will need to take extra steps—just as I did—to ensure a natural birth outcome in a place that favours intervention and considers it to be "normal".

Unfortunately, undisturbed birth is a rarity these days.

As stated by Michael Odent, MD, in a new Australian documentary called *The Face of Birth*, is, "*The number of women today who are birthing their babies in these hormones of love is close to zero!*" The reason for this?

Medical births have become the norm and actually mess with this beautiful orchestra of hormones, which has changed the nature of birth. As Dr Sarah Buckley, MD, says in the afterword, "*When you mess with the hormones, you mess up the birth!*"

When you really think about it, we are all made in love. So it makes sense we should be born in love! Call me a hopeless romantic, but I think there is reason and sense to the madness!

The good news is the body makes its own natural pain relief during labour—so long as we are not disturbed or interfered with. How incredible is that?

Another important hormone involved in birth is endorphins. Endorphins are calming and pain-relieving hormones that people produce in response to stress and pain. High endorphin levels during labour and birth can produce an altered state of consciousness that helps women flow with the process, even when it is long and arduous.

Despite the hard work of labour and birth, a woman with high endorphin levels can feel alert, attentive, and even euphoric during her labour and after the birth. Endorphins and oxytocin play an important role in strengthening the mother-baby relationship at this time. It has been shown these hormones drop significantly with use of epidural or opioid pain medication.

Consequently, women who have had a surgical birth or drugs in labour do not experience the same hormonal euphoria at the births of their babies.

Happy Hormones in Action - Mothers' Wisdom

"*The first thing I said after I gave birth was 'I can't wait to do this again!'*"
~ Rachel

"*There is a love cocktail that you drink during natural childbirth. Enjoy it.*" ~ Kelly

"Mine kicked in well when I was in labour (ecstatic birth hormones)—I loved it—not to say I didn't feel pain but there was also a euphoria. I've had it really strong the last three deliveries. I just wish I could bottle it up!"
~ Rebecca

"I felt mine immediately after she was born ... but honestly ... I don't remember anything hurting at all after she was born... I was on such a high. I was just so full of love and butterflies I couldn't fall asleep!

I've never felt anything like that in my life, and haven't felt anything so wonderful since! When they say you feel like you've been to the moon and back... that's exactly how I would describe it... complete with that weightless feeling and fireworks. I still get butterflies thinking about it." ~ Katie

"Some of the best experiences of my life were attributed to the high of the love cocktail. I have also had quite a few of my doula clients say the same."
~ Kelley

"My younger sister made it to my place about half-an-hour after my first birth. One of her first comments was, 'you look high or drunk'. I was just on natural hormones. Incredible. This is what women are being robbed of with our current birth practices, the ecstasy of birth." ~ Nancy

"You just feel like you are in dream land. It's amazing to be able to finally meet your baby, especially after all that hard work." ~ Ellie

"I felt the push as his head came out then I had to push the rest of him out and that felt great! Relieving and exciting... full of energy, hungry and no pain with the push!" ~ Rebel

"My birth crew reckon I looked like I had just spent the afternoon at a cocktail party—pretty relaxed, up for a chat and couldn't wipe the grin off my face... midwife came back three days later and said the birth energy was still high at our house!" ~ Rachael

Labour of Love - Experts Say

Shivam Rachana, who first gave birth 38 years ago, says the pain was "full on" for the first part of labour and then, to her surprise, it changed and ended up being an "orgasmic experience" that blew her mind. This gave her the impetus to do whatever she could to enable other women to have the opportunity for the same experience.

According to **Sonya Wildgrace**, the secret to harnessing your hormones to achieve an ecstatic birth is to understand how to let go and switch off the neocortex (the part of the brain we use for cognitive thought). "We have to know that there is a way to do it, so that we maintain the flow of oxytocin (love hormone)," she says.

"Find a birth educator who is passionate about the subject; don't assume that all are the same and that they 'get it'. All five of my midwives for my births had very different knowledge bases and none of them knew about the ramifications of disturbing natural birth with any interventions and the effect it has on your own ecstatic hormones."

"If a women doesn't feel safe, or feel love and connection to her partner, this too can interfere with her own ability to produce her ecstatic hormones to birth naturally or even go into natural labour for that matter," she adds.

"Some women who are exposed to chronic fear, like victims of domestic violence, may be so used to having adrenalin coursing through their veins that they have pre-term babies or have to have overdue caesareans because their body is so protective, that it does not respond to medical induction either. These women's own protective mechanisms will fight the drugs and may make it impossible for her to have a natural birth."

Kathryn Williams says, "It's achievable to have an undisturbed birth but the modern-day woman needs to research and be aware of her rights and power to achieve this."

> *"At the time when Mother Nature prescribes awe and ecstasy, we have injections, examinations, and clamping and pulling on the cord... Where time should stand still for those eternal moments of first contact, as mother and baby fall deeply in love, we have haste to deliver the placenta and clean up for the next 'case'."*
> ~ Dr Sarah Buckley, MD

On Top of the World After a Natural, Undisturbed Birth - Bec's Story

My birthing story starts at 41 weeks gestation. My actual expected due date was August 26, which happened to be our first wedding anniversary. I woke on September 2, thinking, "I wonder if today is the day?" as I was starting to wonder if this baby was ever going to come and the fears about induction had started to set in!

I had this insane obsession that the house had to be spotless, so I cleaned madly for hours, then rested on the couch for about 20 minutes.

Our midwife was due to visit at 1pm to see how I was and discuss what would happen in preparation for the next week.

At about 12.50pm, as my husband rang to say he was leaving work for our appointment, my waters broke with one almighty gush all over my nice clean floor! I was beside myself with excitement, thinking, "Wow, this is really happening."

We decided to meet our midwife at the hospital to have some swabs and check bub's heart rate. All was okay, and I remember thinking, "Oh hurry up already." I was having irregular contractions, so we ventured home.

At about 4.30pm, I remember saying to my husband, "This is it babe, we are on the rollercoaster now, and there is no turning back."

At 5.30pm, we started timing contractions. My husband encouraged me to stay active, but I found it too difficult to move, so I opted for leaning over the kitchen bench. We rang our midwife at 6.30pm and she confirmed yes, I was definitely in labour and things would really start to kick up a notch soon... then I started to get really worried.

We decided a shower would be nice, although I didn't enjoy it. All I wanted to do was lie down and go to sleep, as I felt super drowsy.

At 9.30pm, things were really kicking in. I called my mum and dad, saying, "Oh my God mum this hurts so much, I want to cry but I can't!" She reminded me to take a few breaths, to trust my body and that it will all be worth it in the end.

We rang our midwife and I think I almost begged her to come into the birthing centre as I was starting to feel a little scared being at home, especially with my hubby who doesn't have a strong stomach when it comes to bodily functions.

The drive to hospital was quite an ordeal. As it was after 10pm, we had to enter the hospital through the Accident and Emergency Department. We waited at the door for what seemed like an hour (most likely five minutes) for someone to let me in so we could go up to the birthing centre rooms.

Finally upstairs, I was so tense, I needed to lie down for five minutes to gather myself. Our midwife was still with another lady who had birthed a few hours prior, so one of her colleagues saw us. My mum and dad visited me on their way home. I was still really drowsy and could hardly open my eyes.

I moved off the bed and onto all fours, leaning over a beanbag. Finally I was comfortable and back in the zone.

I held my husband's hand and the midwife's hand with each contraction. Somehow I just needed reassurance they were there, but I did not want to be touched.

After almost every contraction, my husband offered me water because the midwife said I needed to stay hydrated. I swear, by the end I was ready to jam that water somewhere else!

I literally crawled to the shower around 11pm as I found it so difficult to walk. This time the water was a godsend. I was very close, or in transition, at this stage.

" I felt like I was so high on (natural) drugs—in a completely different world, almost euphoric. "

At the time I was almost scared, but in hindsight, I understand how utterly important the feeling is. I do, however, remember my husband sitting on the bouncing ball holding the showerhead on my back. He asked me, "Are you having fun babe?" My reply was certainly not what I would call polite!

My uterus had started the "forcing down" contractions and the urge to push was starting to get beyond controllable, so I just went with it. I had asked the midwife to run the birth pool, but it was not full enough, so I returned to my trusty beanbag on all fours.

Still completely in my own world, I found humming was really helping me through the contractions and to stay focused (something I had practised very regularly during my pregnancy in my yoga and meditation classes).

It was midnight when I got into the bath, and oh my, what a relief. It was like total bliss. I started to relax even more when our original midwife returned to us. The urge to push was getting stronger and stronger until it was so overwhelming that I just closed my eyes and let my body take over.

I did feel that the pushing part of labour was easier. I was more alert and I got more of a chance to relax between contractions. I was in an upright position, leaning backwards with my husband behind me, holding my head up.

I remember being able to feel a little head inside at one stage that it gave me that spark I needed to keep going. I was pushing so hard, when our midwife said I needed to push harder and more effectively.

Bubba's head kept coming and then sliding back, until finally I gave one almighty push—and I think my first scream—and bubba's head was out. It was such a surreal feeling, kind of like a popping feeling.

When I looked, bubba's head wasn't completely out; it was only out to under the eyes. That's when we realised bub was posterior.

Bub had its eyes open and was looking around under the water. With the final push, bub was completely out and straight up onto my chest at 1.22am. Best of all, she was a little girl! I was so excited as I was convinced I was having a boy.

The tears started to flow as I realised just what I had accomplished and that our daughter was here, safe and sound. I remember my husband whispering in my ear, "I am so proud of you."

After about five minutes I started to feel really cold. My husband and our midwife helped me up and out of the bath and to the bed. My legs were like jelly!

" I brought our daughter straight to the boob, just staring at her in an oxytocin-induced love bubble. "

She suckled for almost an hour until I delivered the placenta. We all had a look at this beautiful "thing" that had nourished our daughter and discovered it was still very healthy despite being eight days "overdue". My husband then cut the cord.

I felt on top of the world. Life felt complete at that very moment. However, as I needed a few stitches, it was time for my husband to have his very first cuddles. He took off his shirt for some skin bonding time.

I remember looking over at them whilst being stitched up, and the tears started flowing and my heart just melted.

We rang both our parents around 4am to share the wonderful news. My parents had to come to the hospital to meet their very first grandchild on their 25th wedding anniversary! It was only as they were arriving that my daughter was weighed and had her first check over. She weighed in at a healthy 3.6 kilograms.

We left the hospital at 5.30am, and wow, what a surreal drive home.

&& I was still on top of the world and just kept thinking about what I had achieved. It honestly was such an empowering experience that I just wanted to tell the whole world! I'm sure I stayed on that high for weeks.))

In hindsight, I remember and see so many things that just make sense about the whole birthing process. Reading about birth and giving birth really are worlds apart. It would be my wish for more women to experience such an empowered undisturbed birth and realise just how natural and instinctive birth is.

Now as I approach the planned home water birth of my second child, the mental preparation has started and I look upon this story with so much emotion as the memories come flooding back.

Without a doubt, I had such a wonderful first time experience, however this time I feel I am even more educated and informed, and am looking forward to the birth, much more than I could ever have expected.

"No one can sufficiently capture in words the euphoria, the gratitude, and the total delight which can follow a natural birth. The high of these moments is spiritual to the utmost, while remaining utterly physical."

~ QAHIRA QALBI

16th Insight:

The Easy Way is Not So Easy

> *"We have a secret in our culture, and it's not that birth is painful. It's that women are strong."*
>
> ~ LAURA STAVOE HARM

I was fortunate to have the trip of a lifetime with my husband when I was five months pregnant with our first baby. We were on a tour bus in Beijing, China.

It was very humid and misty, and as we approached one of the wonders of the world, the Great Wall, in all its glory, the tour guide said something I will never forget: *"There are two ways to climb The Wall— you can either go the hard way or the easy way."*

He added, *"Only the hard way is not so hard and the easy way is not so easy."* At that point we were thoroughly confused!

My husband's eyes lit up and, loving a good challenge, he exclaimed, *"Let's go the hard way!"* I took one look at him and knowing it was very steep and so many steps to climb with my pregnant belly, I said to him, *"Thanks a LOT!"*

In the end, we did go the hard way and my husband had to hold my hand every step of the way for support as we climbed the steep steps. It was an incredible experience and I certainly had no shortage of exercise during that first pregnancy!

This curious riddle back in China managed to get stuck in my head and quite literally "drove me up the wall!" It really got me thinking, many months later, after the birth of my baby, about its deeper meaning.

I started to relate it to the journey into motherhood and life in general. There was so much wisdom there!

For instance, sometimes modern women believe booking themselves into an elective caesarean ("too posh to push" or just plain scared) or taking all the drugs is the easy way out because then they don't have to feel anything, or can bypass the whole process.

Yet when you look at the big picture, it is actually not so easy after all—in fact, I would say the opposite: a medical or surgical birth is taking the hard road.

As we have already seen, the use of drugs or a surgical birth can lead to serious complications and have far-reaching consequences for mother and baby.

Those who bypass a natural birth also miss out on the euphoria, or natural high, the body produces and may have difficulties with breastfeeding and/or bonding with their baby[36].

I have spoken to numerous women who are still in emotional pain many years later because they missed out on that first crucial hour with their newborn baby and didn't get that special bonding time together. That special time can never be replaced.

Having an epidural[1] so you don't have to experience the pain might seem like the easy option, until you realise it will have other negative consequences.

As you will discover in the afterword, there are real risks associated with common interventions, such as epidurals, that we don't really hear about.

Having a caesarean involves major abdominal surgery, which carries much greater risks than going natural. It also makes the entry into motherhood much more difficult than it needs to be and requires a lot longer to recover.

If you are still uncertain as to whether you can give birth naturally, consider this:

"Your body is not a lemon. You are not a machine. The Creator is not a careless mechanic. Human female bodies have the same potential to give birth as well as aardvarks, lions, rhinoceri, elephants, moose, and water buffalo.

Even if it has not been your habit throughout your life so far, I recommend that you learn to think positively about your body."
~ Ina May Gaskin

Take the Road Less Travelled

What kind of births are your friends having? If you are lucky to be surrounded by inspirational women who live consciously, think freely and are the creators of their own destiny, rather than being the victim of it, then you are in good company. Hopefully they have had a wonderful birth experience to match.

If so, soak it up and learn everything you can. However, for most women in our modern society, this is not the case. Life (and birth) is something that just happens to them and they believe having a natural or positive birth experience is a matter of luck or chance, not conscious choice. I would say otherwise!

Like everything else in life, take a look around you. If you don't like the results everyone else is getting, then decide to do things differently. Be prepared to open your mind and look for different possibilities and solutions. Ask more questions!

Find or create a support group or positive birth community of likeminded women to meet or communicate regularly. Meet women who have already done it and who inspire you, not the ones who drag you down. The secret is simply to be conscious. Most people are too busy living unconsciously in all aspects of their life and birth is just one of them.

"Two roads diverged in the wood and I took the road less travelled by, and that has made all the difference." ~ Robert Frost

Dare to Be Different

I am no stranger to being different from the crowd, I have had good practise, having spent my whole life being an individual, a freethinker and analysing and questioning almost everything, rather than taking things at face value. I have always had a strong mind and never succumbed to peer pressure.

While it is not easy to be different from the crowd in childhood or the teenage years, this attitude has served me well and turned out to be the best blessing when it came to my births.

It meant I was able to discover a different world and learn the secrets and tools to have a more conscious life and birth, and have a very different experience compared to so many around me.

From everything I have seen and experienced, I encourage you to dare to be different from the crowd and choose your own path. It takes faith and courage to go against the wave and do what you believe is right, even when others around you don't agree or understand—and even criticise you—for your decisions.

Yet I assure you, it will be worth it as there is nothing more important.

With this approach, you will give yourself the best possible chance to have the positive experience you have always wanted. I have done it, countless other women who have gone before me have done it, and so can you. While birth is not always 100 percent predictable, you can certainly do a lot to put "good luck" in your favour.

Take the Nine-Month Challenge

I encourage you to take the nine-month challenge to honour yourself as a mother. Dedicate yourself to the ultimate level of self-care, nurturing, inner calm and connection that you and your baby deserve. Focus only on the beauty, magic and miracle of creating new life and you will never look back.

Take a walk in the park and listen to the healing sounds of the birds or take a leisurely walk along the beach and inhale the fresh air to give good oxygen to your baby. Be in the magic and serenity as you take in the beauty. Create positive daily rituals that support your path towards a natural and empowering birth.

During this time, remember nothing else matters except for your wellbeing, which is your baby's whole world. Everything outside of you should pale in significance, in comparison to this marvel that is happening within you. This is a time to tune in and listen to the needs of your body and your baby for guidance.

Then ensure your external environment is supportive. Surround yourself with positive women with inspiring stories, read empowering books, do your research and have a birth plan. If everyone else is having the drugs, then consider going drug-free.

Choose Your Own Adventure

So what to do when you are going against the wave and taking the road less travelled? This is where birth preparation tools such as our inspirational cards (*available via www.inspiringbirthstories.com.au*) and the positive stories and quotes within this book are so valuable. Reading and repeating positive statements are the key to natural birth preparation.

Pay attention to how you speak to yourself. Ina May Gaskin says positive self-talk can, "*Help us deal with deep fears since the very act of making positive statements is empowering.*" Ultimately, the one thing you have complete control over in your labour is your own mind. So use it wisely!

It is no coincidence, mothers we interviewed who had an empowering experience were fully awake and conscious for the entire birth. The biggest factor that affected the quality of their experience and feeling of satisfaction afterwards, was whether they chose to have medical pain relief, whether their birth wishes were respected and honoured and whether they were involved in the decision-making process.

A Conscious Birth Experience
- Mothers' Wisdom

"After my first birth, I felt like I had failed and that my body had failed. After my second I felt strong and empowered but after my third I felt amazing, like I could do anything." ~ Cas

"I was happy to experience everything and just relaxed between contractions. Don't stress about what's to come—just take it all in, listen to all the sounds around you, do what you need to do and just take it as it comes." ~ Rachel

"I was fully conscious for both births, however I was given pethidine for my first and whilst it allowed me to sleep, I felt a little 'trapped' in my own body as I couldn't communicate for a while. I was much more at ease with a clear head during my second birth." ~ Rachel

"I had a fully conscious birth with no drugs. I remember it all but sometimes it felt like a dream." ~ Eva

Saying No to Drugs

"I did it all with a bit of gas. I got through the pain, nine hours of it with the first. With my last birth, my waters didn't break until I pushed his head out (with my first push) and one more push and he was out—that was amazing!" ~ Kellie

"Having a water birth meant that there was no need to use any medical pain relief." ~ Amanda

"It was a quick birth so it was not needed, however I was strong-minded that I didn't want any medical intervention. I took naturopathics during the whole procedure." ~ Kayla

"I had no drugs the first time but ended up having lots of interventions and procedures. At the time I was unaware that it was not contributing to a positive birth. For my second birth, I was very firm about no drugs, no interventions and no procedures!" ~ Leonie

Mums on Medical Interventions

"Offer hugs, not drugs." ~ Adina Lebowitz

"I am against having medical interventions and procedures during birth if unnecessary. In a normal hospital ward, you can have intervention for no good reason. Doctors are there to treat illnesses and you are not sick when you are pregnant!" ~ Amanda

"Medical interventions should only be performed when absolutely necessary. You need to have someone who you can trust to make the call about what is necessary." ~ Heidi

"There are options, which is a good thing, but it's good to know that I can say 'yes' or 'no'. They made suggestions but I said I was okay. I really had my heart set on a natural birth." ~ Eva

"People rely on it too much—I hear people comment that they are having all the drugs they can get, before they even walk in—people numb themselves to life." ~ Kate

"Women need to take responsibility for the birthing process, not just leave it up to the 'professionals'. They are not the ones who are bringing this child into the world. Opting for procedures out of convenience or vanity belies the gift and blessing of being able to give birth… of being a woman." ~ Natalie

"There is too much medical intervention and animals in nature just do it. The body does it all for you and to push the baby out is a very natural thing. It is a shame the power has been taken away from women." ~ Wendy

Finding the Wild Woman Within - Experts Say

Nicole MacFadyen teaches: "Women are born to do this, yet we get too caught up trying to conceive, scared during pregnancy and apprehensive about birth.

She tells her clients the only role we have been born to do is have babies and to trust that. We forget that it is our job.

The body has an amazing capacity—when we damage the body it heals itself. The body does an amazing job most of the time, it is clever and we need to trust it. Give it the right tools and it will."

Sonya Wildgrace says, "The more empowered women are the ones who are not afraid to ask the big questions, and scream like hell until they are heard. Nice girls get overlooked and have no place in birth. I get women to find that wild woman inside and bring her out into the light.

A wild woman will protect her baby and her space with everything she has. Just the way nature would have it. By accessing her wild woman, she embraces her birth and becomes a fierce guardian of her own sacred space. She is less likely to be bowled over by unnecessary interventions."

"There is one simple, yet profound birth truth: Birth is safe; Interference is risky!" ~ Carla Hartley, founder of Trust Birth and the Ancient Art Midwifery Institute

From Unsupported and Afraid to Queen of the World - Kiera's Story

My Hospital Birth

When I was pregnant with my first child, my experiences of pregnancy and birth were what I'd seen on TV, and what my mum had shared with me through the births of her five daughters. Quite frankly, I thought I knew a lot.

So when those two blue lines appeared on my pregnancy test, I wasn't panicked, I was assured I'd be in the best care in the private health system. My doctor simply assumed I'd be birthing in a private hospital, when I told her I had private health insurance.

So a referral was written, an appointment was made, and soon I was sitting in the offices of a lovely obstetrician. She made me feel very special, showing me our nine-week-old baby on the ultrasound machine, and explained that at 20 weeks, if I hadn't miscarried, she'd require half of her fee.

I walked away from that appointment in awe of the tiny creature inside of me, with no feelings other than utter excitement, and a hint of nausea (morning sickness). My subsequent appointments involved a similar routine.

Arrive, pee, weigh in, blush, wait, see the obstetrician, and see the baby, pay at the door.

> ❝ *Perhaps it was the elation of seeing the baby on the screen; perhaps it was my confidence in my knowledge that I was in good hands, but I felt safe, and well looked after at each visit.* ❞

The 20-week appointment arrived, and my husband and I decided now was a good time to broach the subject of birth plans, and vaccinations with our obstetrician.

I'd spent the past 10 weeks reading Janet Balakas' New Active Birth, and while I wasn't certain I felt safe homebirthing, I knew I wanted a natural childbirth, with minimal intervention, and the ability to move around during my labour.

My obstetrician was very receptive, and explained her job was to ensure a healthy mum and a healthy baby, in that order.

And if I was happy to cooperate with those terms, we'd get along like a house on fire. I came away from that appointment appeased, and confident my ideal birth was a real possibility. Of course, I knew my doctor would look after me, should things go wrong.

Weeks passed and I began to feel what I assumed was normal for being so pregnant. I was eating take away foods as the cravings hit me—drinking cola, lots of coffee, and generally ignoring the bathroom scales, as the weight piled on at an alarming rate.

My hands were swollen, I felt constantly out of breath, and my groin, hips and back ached constantly.

At 38 weeks pregnant, my blood pressure was too high, according to my obstetrician. A quick ultrasound was done, my husband was called in, and hospital bags were packed. So began the journey to my first birth.

I sat shivering in my obstetrician's room, on her paper-covered table, with no one to hold my hand, as she told me it was time to meet our baby. She briefly explained the induction process, saying she'd start with a stretch and sweep. Gel would be administered later that night, and I'd birth in the morning on a Pitocin (synthetic oxytocin) drip.

I lay there as she performed the stretch and sweep, clenching my teeth as my unready cervix was wrenched and twisted. My obstetrician apologised for the discomfort, and gave me directions to a hospital room. I sat and waited, my husband arrived, and we waited alone together, with no real idea what was going on.

At about midnight, a midwife popped in and explained she would administer the gel—and do another stretch and sweep. This time, I lay on the bed, writhing away from her hands, sobbing in agony, as the gel was administered. It wasn't a pleasant time, and I found myself apologising for being so weak. Then, we waited.

We waited for two days for the birthing room to be available. We were told in no uncertain terms that we were "the least of their priorities" so we ate, played cards and waited.

Then came the day of my son's delivery. I trudged down the halls, very large, and very orange in my pyjamas. I was told to undress and change into a hospital gown. Then the midwife said, "Let's find out how brave you are."

All of a sudden, I was simply a number, and another process on the clock. A cannula was inserted into my arm, and the contractions began. With each contraction, my plans for a natural childbirth seemed more and more distant.

I was unable to move, unsupported and afraid. Machines made noises that irritated me, the floor was cold, and the bed was hard. My husband tried to support me, but was as new to the process as I was, and felt helpless with me in so much pain.

After enduring three hours of seemingly constant contractions, I begged for an epidural. It was administered nearly immediately, as though they were simply waiting for me to cave in. Then, again, I waited.

Three hours later, my son was imminent. The obstetrician arrived, and some nameless midwives stood peering up my vagina. I was told to push. So I pushed. I was told to hold, so I held. I was told to wait, so I waited.

I was told to look away, so I did, and in that moment, I was given an episiotomy, and my son was born. The best part about his birth was my baby. Everything else, I'd gladly forget.

My Home Birth

My second son was born at home with a midwife present. My pregnancy was so much more positive. I was a healthier, happier, fitter, and more focused me. I met our wonderful doula, and our plans for a homebirth began.

> **This pregnancy was a journey of healing for me, where I revisited the hospital birth of my first son, and picked every second of it to pieces, eventually coming to terms and peace with it. 99**

Our midwife was brilliant, lovely, warm, and accepting of our birthing choices. She seemed as excited as I was that a baby was arriving, and made me feel like the only woman in the world to birth, as well as connected to every other birthing woman.

Each month, my antenatal visits were in my home. I saw the same midwife and student midwife, and chatted about my concerns or plans over a cup of tea. I never felt rushed, and I always felt listened to.

I felt surrounded by support throughout the entire pregnancy. My doula listened to my concerns, and helped me chat through them; she provided me with books and resources to ensure I felt empowered and knowledgeable, and recommended books to help me make healthy choices.

Despite the support, and encouragement, while I felt safe birthing at home, I was never able to visualise the birth of my child. I could never picture him arriving into my arms.

The evening of his birth, I felt edgy and "nesty". I couldn't get comfortable, and all of a sudden, the birth I hadn't been able to visualise was forefront in my mind.

I knew our baby was arriving, and I relished the idea that I was about to birth, and I was going to do it in my dining room, with my husband and son present.

The contractions began, I put on my special birthing necklace, which was made by lovely friends, and climbed into bed to see if I could sleep. As the contractions got stronger, I danced around my bedroom, moaning a little, and chatting to the baby in between.

Pretty soon, I was convinced I was in labour, so I woke my husband, who began fetching heat packs and re-inflating our birthing pool. We began to get a bit excited, and a bit nervous.

❝ The contractions hurt, but they were never bigger than me. ❞

My doula arrived and sent us on a walk around the block. As we walked I clung to my husband through the contractions, and breathed. It was surprisingly cold for February, and I couldn't stop shivering, so we came home.

In the dark of my lounge room, I leaned over the couch, as my doula encouraged me, rubbed my back, and ate chicken sandwiches. I managed to laugh, and even sleep a little.

Then my labour really began. I bounced on a fitball, and squatted through each contraction, trying to mentally welcome them. Then, bliss of all bliss, my doula suggested I get into the birth pool.

The warm water was delicious on my back, and all of a sudden, my mind relaxed, and I remembered I was having a baby, and I was feeling my own labour.

My wonderful midwives arrived, and snuck silently into the house, asking permission before they checked the baby's heart rate, or checked me. Other than that, they sat and held my hands when I needed it and helped me work through each contraction.

My doula, my midwife, and my amazing husband kept me grounded... kept me moaning nice and low to the baby, and held my hands through each contraction.

Labour progressed pretty quickly, and there were moments when I felt I couldn't continue, but as the contraction passed I was relishing the fact I could feel my body working.

Then, it happened: I got to experience it, every bit of it, as my body began to push my baby out. I could hear myself making new sounds, but I wasn't in control, something bigger than me was bringing my baby into this world. I wasn't afraid, I was birthing.

And then, there he was, arms, legs, open eyes—and a cord thicker than I'd ever seen— looking up at me in the water of the pool. I scooped him up. I had done it. I had birthed my baby. It was just he and I. The whole world didn't matter for a moment. We'd done it!

As my little baby and I sat in the pool, we breastfed, snuggled, and got to know each other. His cord remained attached until it stopped pulsing, then his daddy cut it. I birthed the placenta in the pool, and ate a sandwich, and a delicious hot, sweet cup of tea.

Looking back, I don't regret my first birth. I did the very best I could with the knowledge I had.

❝ My homebirth was so healing, and so empowering, that for months afterwards I felt like queen of the world. ❞

It was wonderful for my husband too, and he has become the world's greatest homebirth advocate.

"You're braver than you believe, stronger than you seem and smarter than you think."

~ CHRISTOPHER ROBIN, DISNEY'S POOH'S GRAND ADVENTURE

17th Insight:
Birth Is Beautiful

"There is such a special sweetness in being able to participate in creation."

~ PAMELA NADAV

Birth should be honoured as an amazing transformational experience where women are gifted with participating in the miracle of creation. Instead, it is often reduced to something that mostly happens in a harsh, unnatural clinical environment, with heart monitors beeping, prodding and poking, unwelcome examinations and interference by "experts".

In our modern society, it seems, everything has to be tightly controlled and by entering the system we agree to be part of that model.

Rather than positive expectation in the process and an inner trust that the woman's body is perfectly designed, that she is the ultimate expert who intuitively knows what to do for her body and baby, the power has been handed over to the "experts" whom we are told, know best. No wonder the women are often left disempowered in the process!

A Life-Changing Experience

"There is power that comes to women when they give birth. They don't ask for it, it simply invades them. Accumulates like clouds on the horizon and passes through, carrying the child with it." ~ *Sheryl Feldman*

While pregnancy and birth is one of life's most spectacular mysteries, one thing is for certain: it's a life-changing experience and your world will never be the same again!

Both of my births, although incredibly different, were powerful, empowering and transformational like nothing else I have experienced. They were an opportunity to grow, to listen to my inner guidance, to face my fears, to move beyond what I thought I was capable of and find new inner strength, courage and confidence.

I also felt a sense of satisfaction that I did it the way I wanted to, as much as possible, within the bounds of the hospital system.

Thus, I came out pleasantly exhausted, yet with a sense of immense pride and accomplishment. It gave me a sense of, "If I can do this, I can do anything!" I was so proud of myself after giving birth; you would have thought I was the first woman on the moon or that I had just climbed Mount Everest.

It certainly felt that way. All I wanted to do was shout from the rooftops. It wasn't about bragging either, it was more about feeling compelled to share with others one of my most glorious moments … what I had learned along the way and to tell the world it could be a positive experience after all.

Having had no drugs during labour with both of my girls, I felt so good afterwards. We were both alert and the recovery was easy. The second time was even better as the labour was so quick, I wasn't exhausted by the end of it.

Knowing I had my eldest daughter at home and how great I felt, I was raring to go home the next day but my husband convinced me to stay. He urged me to enjoy the benefits of aftercare and have some alone time with our new baby girl as it wouldn't last long. I am glad I listened to his advice, as it was a very special time of bonding for both of us.

Buzzing with all the natural birth hormones, we got a chance to have our little magical kingdom. We came home from hospital a few days later to begin our new life. I jokingly complained that the birth was so quick I didn't even get a chance to listen to my compilation of birth music we had prepared!

Stronger, Wiser and Fabulously Feminine - Mothers' Wisdom

"I had a bit of postnatal depression about 18 months after my son was born. I thought if I could get through this, I can get through anything. I am so much more resilient, powerful, strong, capable, flexible, deserving and divine than I could ever imagine. I have that within me to deal with all I need to.

When I stepped into motherhood I also stepped into my warrior woman energy. Would I fight to the death for my children? You bet!" ~ Natalie

"I feel so empowered by my natural birth experience. I found a love for a body I had always disliked. I was amazed by how powerful my body truly was. There's a magic that happens with natural childbirth that gets lost with drugs." ~ Jen

"It strengthens you and galvanizes you in ways you can't imagine. You become stronger, more selfless and more compassionate. You have a new respect for every other mother alive, especially your own." ~ Heidi

"It was just amazing. It changes you, your focus and outlook on life. People always say you can't really understand until you are a parent—there is something truly magical that happens when you have your own child." ~ Cory

"Each birth experience was unique and so different, but empowering. I imagine it would feel similar to climbing a mountain and standing on top and looking back at from where we had travelled." ~ Vickie

"I loved my births. I had two very different home water births and I felt strength and power like I have never known. My mum had to deliver my son because he came so fast and she had to step fully into empowerment to do this. It was the most divine time." ~ Natalie

"The births were both empowering in different ways. The first one because I was able to have a natural birth in conditions where it could have easily gone another way and the second one because it felt so natural and easy." ~ Heidi

"I have learnt the magic of motherhood and about being in the magic." ~ Shirley

"I came to the realisation that I am the result of thousands of years of natural birthing. When I listen to and respect my body and baby, I am capable of the most blessed birthing experience.

I learned I am more intuitive than I thought … that I am a strong woman in mind and body. That there is nothing more precious than a mother's love for her baby and the importance of those first undisturbed moments of bonding right after birth." ~ *Leonie*

Become the Birthing Goddess - Experts Say

Sonya Wildgrace says, "I believe that the journey of birth should start from within—that quintessential point where the woman first feels she is pregnant. She is stirred to enter a new phase, to access that knowledge and to seek it from intuitive sources.

A birthing woman who knows herself knows her body and how best to facilitate her birth process. If she doesn't, then she is not yet in her own heart with it all. She may need to stop and allow herself to 'feel' pregnant, by leaving her place of work or by slowing down her busy lifestyle, taking deliberate time to prepare and seek counselling to connect to her unborn baby, so she can hear what her baby is trying to tell her."

She continues: "The power of deep relaxation should never be underestimated. This is the key to unlocking a birthing woman's natural birth chemistry. If she can get to a state of deep relaxation so much as to forget herself, where she is birthing and get out of her head thinking space. Her body can work its magic. All she has to do is breathe and let go in that place."

A New Richness to Life - Rachael's Story

As my second pregnancy was nearing an end, it was easy to let my mind wander to thoughts of the birth of our first daughter Jade, wondering if I had used up all of my great birth energy that time around. How different would this birth be, given I had some level of understanding and expectation that I didn't have with Jade.

❝ Although I had blind faith on my side then—I still had complete trust in my own ability and those around me who came to support and nurture. ❞

The week or so leading up to my due date was encouraging as there were some signs and warm ups for the delivery, which I was thankful for—a good reminder to stay focused and to listen to my body.

After squirming around and feeling slightly uncomfortable during dinner, we proceeded with the usual bedtime rituals for Jade, while I headed to bed at a reasonable hour. I took a cup of raspberry leaf tea to bed and read for a bit, waking at about 1am thanks to drinking tea so late in the evening.

I hopped back into bed and lay there not able to get back to sleep. I felt something had shifted, but not entirely sure my labour had started.

I lay there trying to tune in to see if anything was developing, only to have Brett demanding to know what was going on so he could be involved and ready. I told him I wasn't really sure. Then, not long after, I was certain things were moving.

After our first labour being reasonably quick and expecting a shorter labour this time around, I was keen for our midwife Jenny to head our way. Brett called her at around 2am and said my labour had started, that it was manageable and consistent. We had no desire to be timing contractions. Jenny said she would leave straight away. I took great comfort in knowing she was a few short hours from being here.

Contractions were rhythmic and I was able to move around quite freely to whatever felt most comfortable—propped on the floor on all fours, sitting on the toilet and lying down on the mattress next to the birthing pool.

Brett started filling up the pool. Having learnt from Jade's birth, he hooked the hose directly to the hot water tap from the washing machine. The pool was filling quickly and easily, much better than having to boil pots of water on the stove! He would check in with me every now and then, surprised at how quickly everything was done. It was now just a matter of concentrating on the job at hand.

I continued to lie on my side on the mattress and felt quite relaxed and calm. Contractions were building, although we had not much clue as to how far along we actually were. Brett was pacing around almost making me feel uncomfortable, so I asked him to lie down next to me.

Jenny arrived at around 3.45am and brought all her things from the car, up the stairs to our candlelit "birthing suite". She was her usual picture of calm and instantly made me feel excited, calm and ready. I could sense she felt she had come too early or that perhaps things had eased since we phoned.

This wasn't really the case as I guess I had more time to get into the swing of things after we phoned.

❝ Although it looked like it was low key, I was just feeling more on top of the contractions, even as they were building more and more. ❞

I decided I wanted to get up and move around and go to the toilet. Just as I got to sitting, a full-on contraction caught me by surprise. This was when my waters broke—it was a big relief, although painful. I headed to the bathroom and sat there for a bit. Jenny came to be with me and after two or so contractions, I knew it was time to get into the pool.

I asked Brett to call his folks to come as we both wanted someone to be here for Jade so she was okay and, although we hadn't really discussed it in any detail, at some level I really wanted them to be here and involved at such a special time. Brett told them we were about half way along and all was progressing well.

The walk from the bathroom to the pool was quite short although it felt surreal, as I knew what was about to happen. As I eased my way into the pool, a wave of something swept over me. I was almost caught off-guard.

A sense of knowing what was about to happen hit me; a real déjà-vu experience engulfed me—almost to the point where I felt quite nauseous in a physical sense, but spiritual on another level.

I had flashbacks to Jade's birth, projecting another similar experience for now. This feeling lasted only moments but seemed to go on forever. I was trying really hard to stay present and not get beyond myself. Slowly, the warm water turned from making me feel quite sick to being really supported.

I was thankful to be in a familiar environment that felt so right. The next short while felt like a replay (of my first labour) almost to the point where I could anticipate what was happening next and almost greet it.

Another contraction came and I knew it was time to get moving. I felt between my legs and became even more ready for the moments ahead. That deep, full feeling engulfed my body. It was time to move this little person who had been so much a part of me to another world—one we could all share in.

One contraction later I pushed and the head emerged. Jenny reminded me I could breathe any time I liked as the shoulders were out. Brett was in the pool supporting me from behind and I was leaning on the edge of the pool.

> " *The next contraction came and it was only as I felt a leg brush past mine that I knew our baby had been born.* "

Jenny told Brett to untangle the cord from around the baby's body by pushing the baby around whilst still under the water. The baby kicked to life in Brett's hands, and he brought our baby to the surface.

Again, as with Jade, no emotion seemed adequate for such a moment in your life and we were just still and silent until, of course, the baby let out a full cry against my chest. At that moment, Brett's parents, Don and Jess, reached the top of the stairs all glassy-eyed, demanding to know, "What is it!"

We hadn't had a moment to even contemplate what sex our new child was as the first breaths had just been taken by all of us. Before everyone checked, I had a suspicion as I was holding my newest joy in life, the baby was either a boy or it was a girl with too many bottom cheeks!

What an absolute delight to discover we had a son for us to love and to share a moment of discovery like this with Don, who had so clearly wanted a grandson. We felt like we had won the lottery a hundred times over.

We lay in the pool gathering ourselves, just looking at one another. Jenny took some photographs that we will always adore—images that capture the essence of the journey.

After some encouragement, the placenta came through and was perfectly healthy which I already knew to be the case, as we had such a perfect pregnancy and baby. I hopped out of the pool and curled up in bed, whilst the beaming proud dad and his parents fussed around the baby.

After what seemed like an eternity, Jade woke—her biggest sleep in of the year! She ran towards us to see what was curled up in Brett's arms inside the towel.

It was at this point emotions flooded—no thoughts, just pure, raw emotion that you can't imagine ever capturing again.

Jade had spent so many mornings going through the routine of running up the stairs to see if the baby was here, only to find mummy with her lovely round tummy still intact. This morning she found her new brother. It left our usually chattering toddler speechless.

After a shower and a rest, Brett, Jenny and Jade got on with the statistics of our new babe: he was born 3.7 kilograms and was 52 centimetres long. He looked perfectly delicious to us! After a while, we got around to thinking of a name for our little guy: Lewis J Leckie.

Jenny stayed for a few hours after we all tried to sleep. After she had done a load of "birthing washing" which consisted of a couple of wet towels, she cooked us a lovely meal, and then left us to enjoy our new baby. Her contribution to our experiences cannot be under estimated or over appreciated.

There is absolutely no doubt in my mind the home birth experience gave us the soft landing we so instinctively knew was possible. It has allowed us the confidence, flexibility and trust in our intuitive parenting, now and in the future.

Sitting here, nine weeks on, with Lewis by my feet kicking in the rocker, he is the complete and final piece in the puzzle of my life to date, an absolute delight, a knowing, bright whole person who engages all those whom he meets.

His sister clearly adores him. Daddy thinks he is the "cleverest person ever" and he finds it difficult to understand those who have chosen different paths in life to his.

" *As for me, what a ride! I couldn't love anything more or have anticipated how rich my life could ever be.* **"**

None of this would be possible without the pure love and trust I feel from so many who believe in me, not the least of whom are the children I have borne from my own flesh. How fortunate I am that such unique beings are chosen to be mine to share in this journey.

"The best and most beautiful things in the world cannot be seen or even touched. They must be felt within the heart."

~ HELEN KELLER

18th Insight:
Trust Your Instincts

"The knowledge of how to give birth without outside intervention lies deep within each woman. Successful childbirth depends on an acceptance of the process."

~ SUZANNE ARMS

*L*abour is a magnificent physiological process orchestrated by a very complex array of hormones that we are only just beginning to understand and respect on a great level. We do not need to alter the process, as we return to our mammalian nature during labour. Allowing a labouring woman to go within and rely on natural instinct will assist the body to orchestrate a natural, healthy birth.

My second labour was in full swing. So my husband and I went for a leisurely walk down the street for a change of scenery and to keep things moving. It was a beautiful sunny day and very peaceful. Every 10 metres or so, I would stop to lean against a fence or my husband as if he were a tree, so I could breathe through the wave.

After a little while, we decided to ignore the advice we had been given by the hospital nurse to "wait and see", since the waves were becoming very regular and close together. I had to really concentrate on the sensations and could no longer carry on a normal conversation—and my instincts confirmed this was "it".

So without saying goodbye to our visitors, my husband grabbed the packed bags in a hurry and we drove to the hospital. We arrived at hospital at 5.30pm.

Luckily we arrived when we did, as we would never have guessed in our wildest dreams that our new arrival was to greet us so quickly—at exactly 7pm my little miracle and surprise package was born. It was a baby girl!

Thank goodness I listened to my body and instincts, and not to the nurses, as I probably would not have made it to hospital in time and may have had an unplanned home or car birth!

Don't Push the River, it Flows by Itself

There is a great saying that relates the process of giving birth to other forms of nature: "Don't push the river, it flows by itself." In her book, *Unassisted Childbirth*[41], Laura Shanley challenges the current system and gives a new perspective on birth and life as we know it.

She says, "Giving birth is a creative act, and like all creative acts it cannot be forced to conform to society's unnatural time constraints. The insistence on pushing in labour is simply a reflection of our cultural attitude that force and haste are superior to trust and patience."

I agree wholeheartedly we shouldn't impose unnatural time constraints on birth and to trust our instincts. I also really like the underlying assumption here, that the woman giving birth is the true expert of her own body.

I learnt birth doesn't need to be a struggle or even a forced pushing effort (in fact, forced pushing can be dangerous for the baby[14]). Having had a long struggle during the first birth, I then experienced this "allowing" or "going with the flow" during my second birth. My body birthed her all by itself and I just went along for the ride—it was truly amazing.

Listen to Your Body - Mothers' Wisdom

"Trust yourself. You know your baby better than anyone! I wish more birth courses and manuals would encourage women to talk to other women about birth … about the really beautiful moments that occur during this most intimate of experiences. I was blessed to experience a truly natural birth and I cannot wait to go back for more!" ~ Rachel

"I felt totally present and aware, connected to and tuned into my body and the baby. Each pregnancy and birth were totally different experiences." ~ Vickie

"I spent the most part of both of my pregnancies just trying to stay calm and listen to my body, so I avoided most parenting and birth manuals." ~ Rachel

"I simply obeyed my instincts. When I was pregnant, I would get up and eat in the middle of the night. If I felt like something, I would just go with it. I didn't exercise much throughout my pregnancy.

Fortunately I was fit beforehand which really paid off, as I was not tired or sore. The birthing class was a waste of time—we walked out early." ~ Amanda

"I followed my instincts as the hospital was trying to get me to have a caesar, then they tried to stop me pushing when I felt ready. However, I trusted my instincts and pushed and the baby came out easily." ~ Kayla

"I felt a lot of guilt for needing some interventions during my first birth, even though they were relatively minor. I had a reasonably easy birth; it was just long and intense. I spent the first year of my daughter's life constantly reliving what happened. It was only when I gave birth for a second time that I was able to heal as I allowed my body to do its job in its own time. I was more aware of the process and spent a lot more time at home—almost not making it to the hospital in time!" ~ Rachel

"Listen to the advice of others but in the end follow your own instincts. No one can experience what you are feeling and every woman's birth and parenting experience is unique. Be kind to yourself and honour your own maternal wisdom. Take responsibility for consciously creating the support and procedures that will empower you to 'live' in your pregnancy and birth process to the best of your ability... and then surrender!" ~ Natalie

"I think women have, for too long, kept quiet and accepted the way our births have been taken out of our hands and managed. I think it's time we stand up and proudly take back what belongs to us! The power of intuition!" ~ Leonie

"After being empowered by my midwife, I felt confident and strong about my upcoming birth, yet planned for both eventualities." ~ Rebecca

Be In Your Power - Experts Say

Ellie Burscough believes every woman should have the right to birth "her way". "It is important to listen to your body, nobody knows your body like you do," she says. "By being a strong, powerful woman and firm in your decisions and values you will have the best birth possible. Believe in yourself and anything is possible."

"It is your rite to have your baby in the way you choose. You are actually in charge," says **Davini Malcolm**. "Hear what the doctor says, then go get educated! Take responsibility, after all, post-birth you are then officially a mother and you will be called many times over to take responsibility for choices made on behalf of your child. Notice your fears then start to deal with them in a positive manner.

Some doctors would prefer to treat you as a patient, rather than as a birthing woman. There is a big difference in perspective here... One involves control and fixing and the other is surrender. Even if you do need medical intervention, making those decisions in an educated and informed manner with your partner will be far more empowering than simply being a good girl and doing what you are told. Women give birth, not girls!"

Nicole MacFadyen adds, "Women are over intellectualising it … they should have more faith in Mother Nature."

Learning to Surrender to My Body and Baby: Leonie's Story

For my first birth, I was at home labouring until my contractions were "by the book" and it was time to go to hospital. My contractions stopped in the car on the way.

When I arrived at the hospital and strapped to a machine to be inspected and to "check" my baby's heartbeat, I was made to feel irresponsible because I showed up at the hospital already six centimetres dilated.

I was told to lie in a bed and answer questions about my health history, including allergies.

My labour advanced quickly and, 30 minutes later, it was noted I was eight centimetres dilated and moved to the birthing room where the bathtub was being filled with water.

I was told to lie in the water on my back so my gynaecologist could inspect me. Thirty minutes later I was fully dilated but my water didn't break.

They decided to break my water. About 15 minutes later, after much uncomfortable pushing in a lying position, my baby Marion Gabryelle was born and placed onto my tummy. In that instant, time stopped and I knew my life had changed irreversibly.

" *I was in love with a love only a mother could understand!* "

We asked for the cord to be cut only after it stopped pulsing and hubby did that. After about 10 minutes, Marion was taken away from me to be measured and cleaned. I was told to get out of the water and lie on a bed to birth my placenta after I was given an injection to bring it on.

At the time of birth this all seemed "normal and natural" to me. Only now I'm more informed, do I realise how much more beautiful and easy my birth could have been with less interference and more honouring and respecting of my body and baby. Labour, from first contraction until birth: 15 hours. Baby born on her due date.

For my second birth, we were moving house when I noticed the first signs of labour. I laboured at home while feeding, bathing and putting my little one to bed.

Then we got the birthing room in my house ready with candles, music and the birthing pool.

I was still labouring easily when my doula showed up, saying she felt very restless and had a deep desire to be with me. Thank the Divine she trusted her intuition! We were still getting everything ready when I needed to go to the bathroom.

By this time my contractions were about two minutes apart and mild. My hubby came with me to support me. I felt a contraction coming on, so I stood up and leaned on him. I had a great urge to push and thought it was my tummy going, but soon realised it was my baby's head being born!

When I could eventually breathe, I shouted for my doula to come, as my midwife was on her way, but not there yet. With my baby's head born, my doula and hubby rushed to get towels and blankets to put on the floor where I went on all fours. The next push, my baby was born.

" Caelia Domineke was born with my mucus plug and water still intact! And with little or no pain! The three of us were on a natural high! "

My midwife arrived about 10 minutes later and checked bub, while Caelia was still in my arms.

She waited until the cord stopped pulsing before helping hubby cut the cord. Then she helped me to birth my placenta by blowing on my thumb. My baby wasn't removed from me or taken away to be cleaned.

She was only out of my arms while I took a shower in my own home and then I jumped in bed next to bub to sleep. Labour from first contraction to birth: Just over four hours. Baby was born two days before her due date.

I learnt a vital birth lesson: "Trust that just as God has created your body to care for, nurture and grow a baby in your womb, so he has created your body to know exactly how to birth your baby intuitively.

The moment you surrender to your body and baby, the moment you trust your intuition, you will have the most precious birthing experience. I also feel the way a child is brought into the world determines much about how they manage for the rest of their lives.

"Most of us are in touch with our intuition whether we know it or not, but we're usually in the habit of doubting or contradicting it so automatically, that we don't even know it has spoken."

~ SHAKTI GAWAIN

19th Insight:
Get Your Baby on Board

> *"Pregnancy is a miraculous process and should
> be a time when a woman makes every effort to
> tune into her body and baby with the support of
> her surroundings."*
>
> ~ DR CHRISTIANE NORTHRUP, MD, AUTHOR

ften we think it is just the mother giving birth and that it's a solo sport. We almost forget the other important participant in the process: your baby!

If we remember there is a conscious being growing inside of us who is very much aware and listening to our every emotion and word—if we would only consider birth from the baby's perspective for a moment—we would look at things very differently.

Dr Christiane Northrup, MD in her insightful book, *Women's Bodies, Women's Wisdom,* describes the importance of connecting and communicating positively with your baby while it is still inside the womb, in order to help the baby feel wanted, safe and welcome into the world and to ensure positive birth outcomes[(22)].

My Little Circus Acrobat!

I experienced the importance of this communication firsthand. My second baby decided to perform acrobatics in my belly and managed to turn herself around into the wrong position towards the end of my pregnancy. I have always believed everything happens for a reason, so I was convinced it was not just a matter of "bad luck".

I now believe the baby was picking up on my high stress levels and uncertainty at the time—and the turning was in direct response to it.

If you are experiencing the same situation, consider a deeper emotional meaning or some unresolved feelings that may be behind it, and do what you can to work through them. Some experts believe there is a psychological reason behind babies becoming breech. It is not surprising that women who are anxious and fearful during pregnancy tend to have a higher chance of having breech babies[22].

Another theory is the baby changes position to get closer to the mother's heartbeat and feel more connected to her. Knowing this, the key is to focus on connecting with your baby and releasing tension in the lower part of the body to allow the baby to turn around by itself. This can be achieved through acupressure, breathing techniques or hypnosis. Tuning into my baby and listening to hypnobirthing CDs daily worked for me.

Switching Gears to a More Resourceful State

While I describe this event lightly now (with talk of acrobatics and the like), it was no laughing matter at the time. In fact, my initial reaction was to flip out and panic. At just the mere mention of the word "breech", everything inside me dropped and I instantly feared the worst.

However, I quickly pulled myself together as I knew this was not a resourceful state, and my baby may pick up on my fear and only make the situation worse. Beyond that, I decided to keep this news to myself and not share it with a soul, not even my own mother. I was determined to go natural and didn't want to consider any other option or even entertain the possibility.

Ready for Launch

I knew it was even more important to connect with my baby every day and let her know everything would be okay, how much I was looking forward to meeting her and asking her to turn around. I would close my eyes and visualise the baby turning around into the right position, and then coming out smoothly through the birth canal.

I did this visualisation exercise several times daily. It may sound strange but I really believe I talked my baby into turning around. By the time my baby's birth-day arrived I was ready and had dealt with any fears. My little acrobat had turned around all by herself and was ready for launch. As for me, I was only left with positive anticipation. Phew, what a relief!

Empowering Tips:

Stay calm and positive no matter what happens, *get out of panic mode (avoid telling everyone your woes as it will only make them grow), switch gears into a more resourceful mode and look for ways to address it. There is still time and there is lots you can do, so just take a deep breath and above all, have faith that everything will be okay.*

Be baby-centred. *See this as an opportunity to step into the role of the mother and be strong for your baby. Remember, this little being is listening to your every word and picking up on your emotions. So make sure you let your baby know everything is okay and you are really looking forward to welcoming him or her into the world.*

"If in doubt, breathe out." ~ *Cathy Doberska*

Acrobatics and Inside Tricks You Need to Know

If you have chosen to go through the hospital system, be aware most doctors will not perform breech births and will often go straight to caesarean if the baby has not turned itself around. Only a select few will 'allow' you to deliver naturally.

It's the same scenario, yet a vastly different outcome, simply based on your choice of care provider. Another reason to choose your provider carefully!

Know there are also ways to turn babies around by skilled professionals. So just take a deep breath and above all, have faith everything will be okay.

Embrace Your Pregnancy

It is nature's design for pregnancy to be a beautiful experience of connecting with and nurturing new life inside, honoured by taking extra care of mind, body and spirit. This is the time for slowing down and listening to your body, not racing with the clock and society-imposed deadlines or expectations.

Yet for too many modern women, it has become a time of excitement mixed with overwhelming fear and uncertainty. With the advent of technology, pregnant women are being closely monitored with a series of clinical tests and scans, in the search for problems and possible defects, much the same way as any patient is treated with an existing medical condition!

Positive Birth Experiences Leave Clues

Numerous studies confirm unborn babies can hear and respond to what is going on outside. Just notice how babies kick when they hear sudden loud noises! Even more importantly, they are able to feel their mother's emotions via shared hormonal links from just six months post-conception onwards.

It doesn't take a far stretch to consider our inner life impacts our baby. Now research confirms there is a real connection between what the pregnant mother thinks and feels and how her baby feels, and that anxious mothers do indeed tend to produce anxious babies! So paying attention to our emotional wellbeing is paramount.

We need to embrace our pregnancy and not resent it—and begin the attachment process early with our babies while in utero, or risk having children with emotional problems later on[21].

> *"If you can take even five minutes a day, to think good thoughts, listen to your favourite music, or nourish yourself in any way you want, your kindness will be multiplied a thousand-fold and become an organic part of a person's being for years to come. Five minutes of care is worth years of well-being. What's more, you can talk to the embryo, sending it warm, reassuring messages, even verbal ones."* ~ Laura Huxley in her book, The Child of Your Dreams

In Bloom and Loving It - Mothers' Wisdom

"(I loved) holding them closer than anyone can, being the cradle and the giver of life. Full with infinite possibilities, radiating love inside and out." ~ Sonya

"I felt more like a woman and more feminine than I have ever felt in my whole life! I also loved the attention it drew and how lovely people were to me. I enjoyed meeting complete strangers who would strike up a conversation with me, initiated by my pregnancy!" ~ Kerryn

"Just knowing I am forming a mini human being inside of me energises my soul! Being pregnant is magical." ~ Chasery

"I loved being pregnant. I felt beautiful, radiant, in awe of what I was creating. Feeling the baby moving and growing, the amazing love and connection you have with this child you have not met, even the doubt and fears of how you are going to be as a mum, are all part of the most astounding journey." ~ Natalie

"I feel like a real woman, whole. I just want to curl up in a sunbeam and bask in my glory of motherhood or wander around in 'never-never' land and drool over our creation. Sometimes I want the world to know and worship me, because I'm carrying a baby." ~ Vickie

"The pregnancy was so easy, I didn't even know I was pregnant in the beginning! There were no obvious signs such as morning sickness. I ate healthy and what my baby wanted within reason." ~ Eva

"From the moment we found out I was pregnant, it was amazing, loved it all. I was really well the whole way through. I got to about 40 weeks and my staff kicked me out of the business—I was so huge and had total pregnant brain by then!" ~ Cory

"I was very happy, even though it didn't come easily to me. We had tried for two-and-half years and ended up having intrauterine insemination because of my pinpoint cervix[3]. So it was a dream come true. The second pregnancy happened without any effort. The first birth cured the pinpoint cervix. So for women with this condition, it is really important to try to have a vaginal birth so they can fix it." ~ Heidi

"Super-excited about pregnancy and loved every moment. Had morning sickness any time of day until the day my baby was born but I would do it all again!" ~ Leonie

The Magic of Touch

We all need touch to thrive as human beings, even before we are born. For pregnant and birthing women, touch can be therapeutic, relaxing and naturally pain-relieving in the form of massage.

Women in bloom instinctively rub their belly throughout pregnancy. Touch is one of the first ways we get to connect with our baby and is so important for beginning the bonding process.

It can console an active baby who is kicking in utero. This touch of love teaches your baby that he or she has some control over your ability to console them.

More than just comforting, this is the beginning of his or her emerging self-esteem[39]. And it shouldn't stop there.

Expressing our love to our child via touch should continue in babyhood and throughout their entire lives for our children's wellbeing and to nurture healthy loving relationships.

In *Revolution From Within*, the author Gloria Steinem discusses the importance of touch to thrive as human beings: "In most parts of the world, people massage babies. The Western countries are about the only place this is not routine. We touch each other too little[38]."

So why not start early and give that belly a loving rub and a positive pep talk—and do it often!

Womb Talk - Mothers' Wisdom

"I wish that someone had given me permission to allow the birth to be how it was going to be. I didn't figure the baby in the process, so when the baby presented in a different way than I expected; it shattered the plan I had prepared for...

I also didn't communicate to my baby to know how it was going to happen. I recommend you constantly communicate with the baby about the type of birth that you want to have. Take care of you and your body. Put you first. Connect with the baby, talk to it all the time." ~ Shirley

"I would listen to the classical music before birth as I wanted my baby to hear it when in my tummy, then I played the classical music when my baby was sleeping. I had heard somewhere that classical music was very calming and relaxing." ~ Wendy

"I practised meditation, visualisation and affirmations. I used natural products to nurture my body and mind. I spoke to, read to, played music to my baby and massaged my baby in the womb." ~ Natalie

"Read to your baby in the womb, give the baby a name and talk to it (nickname or real), love the changes in your body, know what you want and go about getting that. Enjoy the journey of pregnancy because its only nine months and it goes so quick and then hang onto your hat after that because it's a fantastic ride." ~ Cory

Experts Say

Shivam Rachana says, "We are not taught to consider birth from our baby's perspective. Primarily most babies are born afraid and then they are imprinted with fear and panic, which they carry throughout their lives. Birth is just another thing to be afraid of—the media doesn't help—there is also a lack of good stories and good literature on birth."

I Delivered My Own Grandchild - Diane's Story

I was awoken at 4.30am by my mobile ringing on January 14, 2011. As I looked and saw Carrie's name, I immediately knew what it was. She said, "Mum, I think I am in labour. I have been up since 2.30am and I'm breathing through my surges, walking and swaying with them. I'm fine, take your time."

I stood there for a few moments trying to clear the sleep cobwebs. As I walked around in circles, I laughed to myself, "Come on Di, get that brain into thinking gear."

This was her second baby. Her first, Jasper, almost four, had arrived two-and-a-half weeks early so I really wasn't surprised by this one being early too. Carrie and Brad had done a refresher hypnobirthing class with me only the night before. I started to get really excited as today we were going to meet our fourth grand baby, little did I know how soon that was going to be.

I told her I would leave in about half-an-hour. I had been washing all the beautiful, tiny baby clothes for her, oooing and ahhhhing at the gorgeousness of them. I had them spread all over the house, trying to get them dry in the humid weather.

All little things gathered, I drove out of our driveway at 5am. In the middle of a thought of "have I got everything?" and only a minute up the road, my mobile rang. It was Brad, Carrie's partner, who asked, "How far away are you Di because she's pushing".

I took a deep breath and said, "I'll be four minutes." My immediate thought was, "I have attended births for a long time but this was my child having her baby and there was a great chance I was going to be catching it."

How did I feel about that? A little amazed, nervous. We had joked only a couple of months earlier about having her baby at home. So many things were going through my mind but I needed to focus on getting there.

I drove just a bit faster than I usually would because I had attended births as a doula for 10 years and knew the pushing stage could be short or it could be long—there was no guarantee of either.

Oh my God, would I make it! I had to make it! I came to a red light and a car went past. I thought, "I haven't got time to wait because Mother Nature isn't." So, with no more cars coming, around the corner I went and arrived in almost four minutes on the dot. Sure enough, there she was, lying on the couch. She said, "Thank goodness you are here mum because I really want to push."

❝ I thought well this is it; there is only me and no time to get her to hospital. I thanked the universe many times over for the knowledge I had gained from the births I had attended. ❞

All my nervousness and doubt went out the window and I just kept saying, "Listen to your body Carrie, it knows what to do and when it asks you to push, do what you need to do and take lots of deep breaths to give your body and baby lots of good oxygen."

I asked Brad to get a couple of towels and I put them under her, as her waters had not broken, then said, "Ring an ambulance." I spoke to the operator for a couple of minutes, and then handed the phone back to Brad, as I needed two hands.

Her waters had just released and the baby was coming fast and I needed to focus. I let Brad speak on the phone. They stayed on the phone with him the entire time until the ambulance arrived.

She was now seriously pushing her baby out and I could see the top of the baby's head. I knew to keep my hands off. Body and baby working together. With each push the baby was easing out more and more until her little head popped out.

As I was about to feel if there was a cord around her neck she slid out a little more and I saw her little hand right there under her chin. What a smart little baby! Her hand had wedged her, slowing her down as she was pushed down the birth canal.

If her hand hadn't been there I would never have made it in time.

> **" At that moment I felt very reassured that this little baby was very smart and knew exactly what she was doing. I got such a strong sense of that. "**

The next push and our beautiful little granddaughter, Iyla, was born into my hands, and as I lifted her up onto Carrie's chest, I felt so ecstatic. It was 5.25am. We had done it together! It was such an intimate moment.

I gave little Iyla some rubs up her back to encourage her to breathe. She was still attached to the umbilical cord so I knew she was still getting blood and oxygen from the placenta, just as she had in utero. In a short time, which always seems like a long time, she took her first breath. Shortly after she was born, my hubby Rob arrived and then not long after, the ambulance turned up to find little Iyla skin-to-skin on Carrie's chest.

They took them both to the hospital where she had been booked into the birth centre. Iyla was still skin-to-skin with Carrie. When they arrived, the birth centre was full so they took her to the labour ward. It was full too.

They had a record number of babies born overnight. I'm absolutely sure this little baby knew all of that and maybe the next best thing was Nanna. Had she been listening to my suggestion to be born at home?

She had done it again, a natural birth, a super mum with no drugs, no gas, no epidural, no tears, and no episiotomy, just the knowledge to trust her body that it knew what to do. And it did. Carrie was just amazing. Truly a woman in her power.

I feel such a sense of honour being trusted to bring our granddaughter into the world. My heart is full and I will never forget the feeling the moment she slipped out into my hands. Thank you little Iyla with all my heart for trusting me.

"There is no way out of the experience except through it, because it is not really your experience at all but the baby's. Your body is the child's instrument of birth."

~ PENELOPE LEACH

20th Insight:

Trust in Nature's Perfect Design

> *"Just as a woman's heart knows how and when to pump, her lungs to inhale, and her hand to pull back from fire, so she knows when and how to give birth."*
>
> ~ **VIRGINIA DI ORI**

One of the most important factors in preparing the mind for a positive birth experience is simply to have faith in the natural and normal outcome of labour. Once we truly understand and trust that nature is perfect in its design—and to meddle with it is to mess with the natural flow and rhythm—then we may think twice before interfering in this intricate process.

Just look at the human body and how miraculous it is in its design. The way the belly grows to accommodate the developing baby; that the mother is perfectly equipped to nourish this baby with everything it needs to grow and develop for nine months, the fact babies are fully aware in utero and are already starting to make sense of the world.

How the baby is given the gift of natural protective flora as it travels through the birth canal as its first line of defence that sets the foundation for immunity for the rest of its life; how breastfeeding gives the mother's uterus the signal to shrink to its original size and naturally helps her to regain her pre-baby body... and I could go on!

Your Body Knows What to Do

As a first time mother, we often don't know what to expect, even with the best intentions, research and preparation. We can be forgiven then, for thinking we don't know what to do—at least our mind doesn't. The good news? As women, our body was expertly programmed and designed to give birth and knows exactly what to do, even when we don't!

I have needed a reminder of this myself on occasion, even as a second-time mother. I had relied on my hypnobirthing teachings throughout my first pregnancy to deeply relax, get into the zone and even experience a virtually pain-free birth with great success.

Having moved house, I had misplaced the course booklet during my second pregnancy and felt lost without it. It was perhaps silly to feel so attached to a piece of paper. Yet sometimes a pregnant mind knows no logic and I felt like everything depended on it, forgetting it was *me* who gave birth the first time, not the booklet. Of course, the knowledge was still within me.

To throw another spanner in the works, personal circumstances meant my midwives were unable to be there for my second birth. At the time, it felt like the rug was pulled from under me, as I had never birthed without female support from someone I knew and trusted.

Two midwives and too many nerves later, it was just my husband and I in the birthing suite and yet it turned out to be the best blessing we could have imagined. Even though we were in a private hospital, I told myself we had just hired a hotel room—and my wish came true—we were given privacy for the most part, since everything was progressing so smoothly.

The atmosphere was as quiet and intimate as it could be. I wasn't making any fuss or much noise or requesting any pain relief; just a whole lot of breathing, kneeling over the bed and burying my head into my husband's chest or a big pillow for support and resting in between, so the midwives went to more complicated births next door where there was more for them to do.

If you have any doubt that your body knows how to birth your baby, consider this: *Women in comas birth babies*. Their bodies, which are too unstable to receive medication, simply give birth without any help from doctors. Doctors just observe the woman's body as it births the baby. Amazing, huh?

A Powerful Force of Nature

This time it was more like a powerful force of nature, and more a sprint than a marathon. I was being swept up in what felt like an enormous tidal wave of something much bigger than myself. It all happened so fast; it was so strong and intense that I just had to go along for the ride and breathe through it! I managed to make good, long use of the hot shower again which was a great help.

I didn't even need to struggle or push this time; my body did it all by itself. No time for any bag of tricks either, as it happened so fast. I suddenly needed to go to the bathroom, or so I thought until I realised it was the baby ready to come out in a big hurry—and there was no stopping her! I shouted out from the bathroom, "The baby is coming!"

For a moment, I thought I was going to give birth right there and then (not the best way to greet the world!) so I managed to hop off just in time to dive into a beanbag on the floor where I gave birth to her upright in the kneeling position.

Only one-and-a-half hours after our arrival, she slid out quickly and effortlessly, like a dream, and was placed on me straight away for feeding. This was the most powerful, amazing and surprising birth experience by far! I felt an instant connection with her and very protective like a mother hen. She was—and still is—an absolute dream.

"Giving birth is not a matter of pushing, expelling the baby, but of yielding, surrendering to birth energy." ~ *Marie Reid*

Nature's Healing Power

So strong was my resolve to be left untouched and my underlying trust in the power of nature, I refused stitches, despite significant tearing. The obstetrician who was ready to start "sewing", must have thought I was completely mad, yet I was firm in my decision, so he respectfully honoured it and put his instruments away. He said he would leave it until the follow up visit and then "see how we go".

The day after the birth while still in hospital, one nurse quietly asked me, "Just between you and me, can you tell me why you refused stitches?" She was visibly concerned, more than a little perplexed and incredibly curious. I confidently replied, "Because the body heals itself." She just looked at me, stunned.

Between birth and my follow-up visit to the doctor, I gave nature a helping hand and proceeded to load up on my nutritional superfoods (*available via www.inspiredwellness.com.au*) to speed up healing and aid recovery, as I was determined to prove the body does indeed heal itself!

I must have been a grand experimental "rat" to the obstetrician. I think he was quietly curious, waiting to see what would happen. Upon inspection at my follow-up visit six weeks later, the obstetrician announced with great surprise, I was an "amazing healer" and was "healing beautifully".

He was simply amazed at my recovery. He then confessed I was the first "patient" he had not sutured in 25 years! I left that doctor's office walking on air. I was so incredibly proud of myself. Furthermore, my trust in nature went through the roof that day. I had just proven it to myself.

The Birth Experience - Mothers' Wisdom

"Women have been giving birth for so long without medical intervention— if a woman in Africa can do it, then so can I." ~ Kate

"The actual birth blew me away! Once I decided to trust my body and baby, I was rewarded by a virtually pain-free, quick birth! The power of being in my own home, surrounded by the things I knew, by only the people I knew and wanted present, meant I had a birth experience that changed the course of my life." ~ Leonie

"For my three homebirths, I had no expectation but openness to what may happen. I allowed my body to birth my babies." ~ Vickie

"Birth is a natural process that all beings and animals go through—we are no different and don't need to be so heavily controlled or afraid that something is going to happen." ~ Wendy

"It is amazing what our bodies are capable of. Don't be scared of it—it is the most magical thing ever. Pain yes, but then you are rewarded (with) the most beautiful thing ever. I wish I could have another baby, and naturally, as I would love to go through the experience again." ~ Amanda

"I swam through my pregnancies; it was a natural progression going to birth in the water. It was a gentle birth option and my baby seemed pretty happy." ~ Wendy

Dispelling Myths - Experts Say

"The pelvic disproportion myth is the biggest one for me. Nine times out of 10, if a woman is having difficulty birthing, it is because something is not right in her birthing environment; the baby's position is not optimal, or her position is not optimal.

Women are lead to believe their bodies are dysfunctional and that is just not true. More often than not, someone has let them down along the way," says **Cas McCullough**.

Sonya Wildgrace adds: "There is nothing else on the planet that equals the benefits to natural birth. I always come back to the butterfly and the chrysalis analogy. Everything in nature is made perfect for the survival of its species.

Caesarean birth promotion weakens the species perception and we have a new generation who believe there is something wrong with their bodies ability to birth."

"Birth is a natural process not a medical one," says **Deanne Schmid**. "Our body has the innate wisdom required to birth our babies without intervention in the vast majority of cases. All we need to do is trust and surrender during the birth process and our baby will work with our body to enter the world as nature intended."

Nicole MacFadyen says pregnancy is not a medical complaint, rather a natural human function. "Don't treat it like an illness, remember you are just giving birth," she says.

A Smooth and Easy Hospital Birth - Katia's Story

I wanted a natural drug-free birth for my child's sake, and mine, and that is what I got. I feel interventions should be kept to a minimum and only be used when it is an absolute medical necessity rather than convenience, such as the obstetrician needing to get to a dinner or start their holidays.

Having said that, I do feel it should be a woman's choice – we are in no position to say, "You have to have a natural birth."

> **" Deciding to have a natural birth was a natural choice for me—this is how it had worked for women across the ages and my body is built for this one job, so I knew I was capable of it. "**

Secondly, I did not want my child to be born drugged and groggy.

This is consistent with some of my choices during pregnancy as well: I ate well, kept physically active, and to deal with my "all day sickness" during pregnancy, I chose to have fortnightly acupuncture to keep it at bay.

I was initially scared of the process and had the "movie birthing scenes" as references stacked in my head. So I made a conscious decision not to attend hospital birth classes, as I had no interest in seeing a tray of implements and hearing their horror stories.

My intention was to go natural all the way.

So we went to hypnobirthing classes instead, where we not only talked about it but also watched videos of empowering births. Afterwards, for the duration of my pregnancy, I went to sleep listening to various hypnobirthing tracks about releasing fear, relaxation and welcoming the baby.

Meanwhile, I did extensive research, so I felt very informed and was making educated decisions, which was important to me. I did a lot of reading about motherhood but most of the books annoyed me, so I stopped. I felt they were very slanted towards mainstream ideas, and not the type of birth I wanted.

I wanted to have a choice of doctor and not have the constant shift changes of the public system, so I decided on a private hospital.

My primary caregiver was an obstetrician, however, I think "checker upper" is a better description.

I also had my own doula who was trained as a midwife and it was the best decision. It allowed me to relax and focus on what I was there to do, rather than worry about "when is it time to go to hospital?" or "is my husband coping?"

She understood what I wanted, made decisions on my behalf and orchestrated what needed to happen for me to get what I wanted. As a result of my preparations, I had overcome my fears and felt totally calm and safe throughout the process, which helped things run smoothly.

My husband and doula were present for the birth—I was very happy with this combination. I would definitely not have wanted my mother there, much to her disappointment! I had a bag of tricks packed but never used them. My key "weapons" were arching back on all fours in a yoga cat stretch and my mantra "relax, breathe, open".

In terms of support, I knew people were there, but they did not concern me—it was just about my "birthing body" and me. Apparently my husband was sent across the road to have dinner.

He was gone for a good half-an-hour, which I knew nothing about. But I guess that means I felt supported because my doula was there with me so I did not feel alone.

"Remember, nature designed us for this purpose. If it was "hard", humans would have gone the way of the dinosaurs and become extinct a long time ago!"

Our experience was very smooth and easy. I was about 10 days past the due date and had been booked for induction by the obstetrician for later that week, but had no intention of getting induced. So I was busy doing five kilometre walks, eating chilli and doing all those old wives tale methods.

I started getting contractions in the evening. I knew lying down would slow me down, so I spoke to my doula and we decided I would try to get sleep that night and really get stuck into it the next morning.

My doula came over in the morning, as did my acupuncturist, and we did acupuncture and hypnobirthing relaxation. By lunchtime, I was having sporadic contractions but I definitely had to stop and breathe and stretch my back through them.

By 4pm, I had called my husband to come home; my doula was on the way and around 6pm, my waters broke.

I was soon in the shower on all fours with water running down my back until the doula, who by then had got my husband to line the car with bags and blankets, said we were ready to start moving to the hospital, which was about 10 minutes (and three unwelcome sets of tram tracks) away.

At hospital, a check-up showed I was eight centimetres dilated; I got back in the shower.

"I spent most of the time during labour in the shower, chatting with my doula. I stayed there until I was well and truly bearing down, at which point I got back out to push."

We were in hospital for only three hours by the time the bub arrived. We had a birth plan and knew what we wanted, and the doula was well worded-up on our desired process.

However, there were a couple of deviations from the plan, which are lessons for the future, but I was happy to accept them.

I wanted to birth not lying on my back, but that is what happened.

Apparently I was asked after they got me up on the bed if I wanted to get up but I said "no", which I do not remember. A girlfriend reported having a similar issue and had instructed her husband in a subsequent birth to not ask but physically move her.

The second deviation was, I believe, as a consequence of lying down. I had an episiotomy, which may have been avoided, had I had the gravity to work with. Overall, the labour was pretty close to how I ideally imagined it to be and I was very pleased. If I could do it all over again, I would not lie down on the bed to push.

The most valuable thing I did to prepare for birth was definitely hypnobirthing and finding a doula. If I could destroy one myth about childbirth, it would be that "it is a painful experience". It is an "intense" experience from my perspective, but not painful.

As for giving advice to a new mummy, I wouldn't—everyone is so busy giving her advice. She just needs headspace to work out what is right for her. What I will say is when they annoyingly say, "Your life is going to change"—which seems so obvious—they are not kidding!

❝   There is so much magic about it. It is a sacred time. I would describe my birth as positive, empowering and magical! I remember holding my son for the first time, looking into his eyes thinking, "Aha... so this is who you are! ❞

"I think one of the best things we could do would be to help women discover their own birth power, from within themselves. And to let them know it's always been there, they just needed to tap into it."

~ JOHN H. KENNELL, MD

21st Insight:
The First Magical Moments

"In the sheltered simplicity of the first few days after a baby is born, one sees again the magical closed circle of two people existing only for each other."

~ SUSIE CAMERON AND KATRINA CROOK, AUTHORS

The most magical memories a woman will ever have are those first precious moments with her newborn baby. The full beauty of these moments can only be experienced during a normal physiological birth—those who have a caesarean unfortunately miss these moments, which is a real shame, as this is biologically a time of bonding bliss and pure love between mother and baby.

A natural drug-free birth ensures mother and baby are immersed in a cocktail of love hormones. This is nature's way of ensuring the mother falls completely in love and is going to respond to her baby's needs, which is crucial for survival.

For many mothers, the magic starts way before that—from the very first movements or flutters of their baby inside of their belly—in that instant, the fact they are growing and nurturing a baby becomes "real" for the first time. For some, it is a case of love at first sight and touch and for others it is a blossoming relationship.

Either way, we are programmed to bond with our child and it is surely life's greatest miracle! No matter what journey lies ahead, with all its joys and challenges, we must embrace it and be grateful every day for this beautiful blessing in our lives.

The Miracle of Birth - Mothers' Wisdom

"The most magical memory about pregnancy was the baby kicking! Nothing can replace that feeling. Then in birth, that euphoria of having just pushed a baby into the world! Such a rush!" ~ Cas

"That first sleepy look that my daughter gave me when the midwife put her in my arms, that's when I felt the most incredible, amazing indescribable feeling in the world, I just became a mummy!" ~ Magdalena

"Picking the babies up for the first time—I picked them all up and put them on my chest myself—was fantastic, all the exhaustion of labour disappears instantly into contentment." ~ Amy

"The absolute wonder of knowing that I had created something so divine and precious. I was in complete awe and gratitude. When my first child started to feed for the first time, I had never felt anything like it. My emotions were so heightened, it was heavenly." ~ Natalie

"Birth is the sudden opening of a window, through which you look out upon a stupendous prospect. For what has happened? A miracle. You have exchanged nothing for the possibility of everything." ~ William MacNeile Dixon

Love at First Sight or a Blossoming Relationship?

"I had already fallen in love with them when they were in the womb. For me, it was more the excitement and expectation of discovering their personality and the delight of getting to know them as a person." ~ Natalie

"After my first birth, I was amazed I had done it. I think I felt a kind of protectiveness first before a loving feeling. I felt I had to protect her from the hospital staff and their procedures. I think that 'oh my God I love you' feeling took until I got home and the three of us all hopped in bed together. After my second birth I felt very soft and calm and there was lots of love very soon after the birth." ~ Heidi

"I felt very proud of myself for being able to do it and drug-free. I don't know that I felt specifically 'love' instantly. He was an extension of me and I felt very attached to him, but I think it took time to bond and fall in love." ~ Katia

"I thought she was amazing from the moment I saw her and a day hasn't passed where I haven't looked at her and thought the same thing." ~ *Cory*

Birth and Bonding - Experts Say

"The moment of skin-on-skin contact that will be imbedded indelibly on both mother and babe... This is a time of the most amazing magic... To welcome the baby to the world, to calm and sooth it...

To tell the baby that it did such an amazing job being born and show it that it is loved and show gratitude for the gift that it is to the world!" says **Shirley-Anne Lawler**.

Kathryn Williams says the moments after birth provide a bonding blueprint between mother and baby. "It is part of nature's plan for the baby to be on the mother's chest and this is the magical beginning of secure and attached human beings."

Davini Malcolm continues: "It has been proven that a baby will seek the eyes of its mother for around 45 minutes after birth," she says. "It may close its eyes and be dreamy but then a moment comes where it will look deeply into her eyes again. Much is communicated between mother and babe at this wonderous time. This is called *The First Gaze*."

She explains, "It is vitally important for us to be present with our child at birth no matter what the circumstances...

If the mother is not able to be that person (ie she is ill, in shock, traumatised or has had an operation and is unconscious or is drugged) then I believe there should be someone who is present completely for the newborn baby taking the time to talk to the little one and explain the situation.

If those first moments are traumatic and the baby is not able feel his connectedness to his mother, all the more reason to be very aware and reassuring with the newborn.

I believe that deep abandonment issues can be seeded at this time if the newborn isn't cared for with great awareness at birth thus impacting the mother and baby relationship on some level."

Birth As a Spiritual Experience
- Mothers' Wisdom

"Many women have described their experiences of childbirth as being associated with a spiritual uplifting, the power of which they have never previously been aware. To such a woman, childbirth is a monument of joy within her memory. She turns to it in thought to seek again an ecstasy which passed too soon." ~ Dr Grantly Dick-Read, Childbirth Without Fear

"Birth is just as much spiritual and emotional as it is physical. And that's why the use of drugs and interference and restriction is so damaging because it breaks that bond. Then birth becomes more difficult than it's meant to be. Birth was an experience where my spirit, mind and body became one and I became the birthing goddess I was meant to be." ~ Leonie

"In a spiritual experience, the body tends to dissolve and you merge blissfully into other states. In birth it is the opposite, everything else dissolves and all that exists is the body and the movements and sounds needed to work with the contractions. It is similar in that the chatter of the mind or the ego ceases for a time and you can lose yourself in the experience. But I would say birth was the most profoundly 'physical' experience I have had." ~ Heidi

"My husband and were just blown away and continue to be every day, by this delightfully spirited little human who has come into my life. My husband is a fairly religious man so I think for him it is a bit different, but for me I am always looking at her in wonder and thinking about the universe and how she has come to be with us." ~ Cory

"Yes it was spiritual. I am pretty sure my angels were there to keep me calm and make sure my baby was safe and came out safely and quickly. Sometimes it felt like a dream, I felt I left my body and I was floating over my bed and watching me give birth naturally." ~ Eva

"I felt such a strong connection to my child, spirit, women all over the world who have given birth and my mum. I also recognised the primitive aspect of myself that had been repeated over thousands of years—there was an eternal quality to it." ~ Natalie

"Birth is a big stretch of mind, body and spirit… not just a physical stretch but also a stretch as a woman." ~ Rebecca

The Trees Looked Greener, I Felt Reborn: Rebecca's Story

The day had arrived to come home from the hospital. It was a windy day with light rain, so Pete drove the new car with the baby capsule up to the end of the shelter outside the hospital. I took you out through two sets of automatic sliding doors and it was surreal. This is the big wide world.

Life seemed so stable for you in the hospital. Yet as those double doors opened, a gust of wind blew across your face for the first time, your eyes closed and your nose crinkled up, as if to say, "What on earth was that?"

I pushed you along in the hospital bassinette to the end of the shelter where dad had parked. As he clutched you up into his arms, and awkwardly put your limp little body into the car seat, there was a brief moment when you moved out from under the shelter and the light drizzle fell on your nose and cheeks.

You shook your little head as if to shake it off. "What is going on here?" you must have thought. We hadn't thought to bring you a blanket—it wasn't on the list of things to take to the hospital—so I had wrapped you in my cardigan, only to have to take it off you to put you into the car seat. With all those presents, no one thought of a blanket. And we were cold. Your face was wet. The wind blew into the car as dad lifted your little arms through the harness.

I sat next to you in the back seat and I looked at the world as you did for the first time. I looked at the rain as though I had never seen or felt it before. I felt the wind on my face, and I felt the cold as I had given you my only warm cardigan.

Normally, if I was cold in the past, Dad would have given me his jacket, yet now for the first time I could remember, there was someone more important than I, and I felt that I wanted to take off my jacket for you.

❝ I felt reborn, watching the hospital fade away as we drove towards our home. I have driven that road so many times before but now the journey seemed so very different. ❞

It was as though the trees were greener. I noticed the construction work that had inconvenienced me every week when I drove to my antenatal checkups, yet now I looked at it as a new beginning.

It even seemed like there was less traffic. As soon as we got home, I took you to the new feeding chair we had set up beside the window to the deck, and I sat down to feed you as Dad unloaded the car.

With your eyes still closed, you went straight to the breast and you were content. "This is home Daniel," I told you.

It was as though hospital boot camp (that was how it felt to me, an intense workout of learning to breastfeed, express, sterilise bottles, change nappies, put a singlet over your head, give you a bath, and try to sleep with a nurse's station bell ringing incessantly for four nights straight) just faded into the distant past.

The hospital stay was like being with you on a space ship—it really seemed out of this world... almost a fabricated life—where my food was brought in on a tray and we weren't really living. Now we were home it felt like my life had started anew again.

I looked around the house. Everything was just where we left it five days before. Except, strangely now, it looked cleaner. Honestly, nothing had changed, but it seemed so relaxed.

" ***The garden looked greener... I swear a whole florist worth of flowers bloomed in the last five days.* "**

As I was still amazed at how the garden seemed to have bloomed, just as my son did, three birds flew up at once and landed on the balustrade of the deck. They hopped down and walked up to the window next to where I was feeding. It was like something out of a Disney cartoon. It was as though the birds had flown in to meet the new baby and bring their good wishes.

They went on, in typical Disney chorus, to sing to you. It was surreal. I thought I would see little music notes float out of their beaks and into the air. I can honestly say this has never happened before or since that day...

Dad put on the kettle, and pondered the empty fridge. "What do you want for lunch?" he said. "We have no food. Should I ask Nana to bring some?" It was the first time he had called my mum "Nana", and she was going to bring food. Now I really knew we were home, and somehow, I couldn't remember my life before.

"Birthing is the most profound initiation to spirituality a woman can have."

~ ROBIN LIM

Afterword

A Special Interview with Dr Sarah J Buckley, Author of Gentle Birth, Gentle Mothering

> *"Women's bodies have their own wisdom, and a system of birth refined over 100,000 generations is not so easily overpowered."*
>
> ~ DR SARAH BUCKLEY, MD.

I'm a big fan of Dr Sarah Buckley. I first read *Gentle Birth, Gentle Mothering,* when I was pregnant for the first time. It was one of many guides I read about birth, as I was so hungry for knowledge, and yet, it was one of the few that really impacted me.

Her natural, holistic approach really resonated with me. I also liked that she spoke as a natural mother and from a doctor's perspective—a rare combination.

I was particularly fascinated that as a medical doctor with an obstetric background, she made the conscious decision to birth her four children naturally at home. So, when I had the pleasure of speaking to her on a recent trip to Queensland, Australia, I knew she would have lots of valuable gems to share…

What is your birth philosophy?

As a society, we have lost the deep-seated belief in our body's ability to give birth. My belief is that our bodies are superbly designed for giving birth and that birth is one of the most powerful experiences you can have.

Why is there such a pervasive fear in society around giving birth and so many horror stories or distorted ideas? Why don't we hear lots of beautiful inspiring stories instead?

We have a negative culture in our Western world and what my friend Carla Hartley calls "birth fright". When women have a bad experience, they are left traumatised and resolve it by talking about it with other women. This permeates our culture, creating fear and negativity and this affects women during pregnancy.

What is the best advice you could give to a new mother to help her to overcome her fears and have a more positive experience?

The antidote is to find a positive birth community, whether it means reading books, online chat groups, meeting and talking to women.

What is an "ecstatic birth"?

It is our birthright and our body's intent to give birth in ecstasy. When we follow Mother Nature's blueprint, natural birthing hormones take us outside our usual state so that we can be transformed on every level as we enter motherhood.

This exquisite hormonal orchestration unfolds optimally when birth is undisturbed, enhancing safety for both mother and baby. An ecstatic birth takes us beyond our self and is the gift of a lifetime! (Read Ecstatic Birth by Dr Sarah Buckley)

What about the possibility of an "ecstatic birth"—is it a fantasy or a reality?

For many women, medicalised birth is the only way they know it can be. In Victorian times, women were taught not to enjoy sex and to lie back and think of England.

These same women would not believe that it is possible for sex to be enjoyable. In regards to positive or ecstatic birth, the same hormonal flow is involved with both birth and sexual activity.

In the same way, those who have not personally experienced or witnessed such a birth, the concept of pain-free or even ecstatic birth would be inconceivable.

Unfortunately, some women only know the panic of medicalised birth. There are many cases where the baby nearly died or were told by medical staff this same message. Often the hospital messed the birth up and had to cover up the mess they had made. This is also known as the cascade of intervention.

As a result, the mother comes out traumatised or believes that the doctor saved her life. In either case, she is imprinted with fear and develops the false belief that birth is dangerous.

(Author's note: this same woman would most likely spread that negative message to other women, especially unsuspecting pregnant women who would then pick up on the same fear, end up having a medicalised and possibly a traumatic experience themselves and perpetuate the cycle of fear and panic. This is why it's so crucial to protect our mental space and choose our inputs and community wisely during pregnancy).

In your book, Ecstatic Birth, you talk a lot about the vital role of hormones. Tell me more about the role of 'ecstatic birth hormones' in birth?

Natural birth is about species survival, since the hormones involved are related to attachment and bonding. When you mess with the hormones, you mess up the birth. These hormones include oxytocin and endorphins—the hormone of pleasure and reward—adrenaline and noradrenaline.

What are some of the risks associated with common modern procedures such as epidurals and caesareans? What are the impacts on mothers and babies?

Choosing to have medical interventions can have serious consequences for both mother and baby. For instance, having an epidural decreases oxytocin production during labour and this is a critical hormone of attachment as shown in animal studies.

Epidurals interfere with all hormones of labour and birth and we don't fully understand all the long-term effects. For instance, when French researchers gave epidurals to labouring sheep, the ewes failed to display their normal mothering behaviour, especially the ewes in their first lambing, which were given epidurals early in labour.

Seven out of eight of these mothers showed no interest in their offspring for at least 30 minutes (Krehbiel, Poindron et al. 1987).

These researchers subsequently showed epidural sheep had lower brain oxytocin levels and also demonstrated a partial reversal of the effects on maternal behaviour when oxytocin was administered directly into the new mother's brain (Levy, Kendrick et al. 1992). Some studies indicate this disturbance may apply to humans also[36].

In one study, mothers given epidurals spent less time with their babies in hospital, in inverse proportion to the dose of drugs they received and the length of the second stage of labour (Sepkoski, Lester et al. 1992). In another study, mothers who had epidurals described their babies as more difficult to care for one month later (Murray, Dolby et al. 1981).

These changes may reflect hormonal dysfunctions and/or drug toxicity and/or the less-than-optimal circumstances that often accompany epidural births such as long labours, forceps, and caesareans.

Epidural studies confirm babies with higher drug levels have worse neurobehavioral scores (Radzyminski 2005) and babies with worse scores have more compromised breastfeeding abilities (Chang and Heaman 2005) including diminished suckling reflexes and capacity (Riordan, Gross et al. 2000).

Two recent studies have particularly implicated epidural opiates in breastfeeding difficulties (Beilin, Bodian et al. 2005)[36]. Drugs administered by epidural enter the mother's bloodstream within minutes and go straight to the baby at equal, and sometimes greater, levels (Brinsmead 1987; Fernando, Bonello et al. 1997).

Some drugs will be preferentially taken up into the baby's brain (Hale 1998), and almost all will take longer to be eliminated from the baby's immature system after the cord is cut, making elevated drug levels likely during the critical newborn hours (Hale 1997)[36].

We are designed to be more sociable after birth thanks to oxytocin, which helps us fall in love with our baby and primes us to be social and accept help, which is especially important in the early days and weeks.

When synthetic oxytocin is administered during labour it decreases oxytocin production during breastfeeding.

What do you say to women who think it's easier to take all the drugs or bypass the whole process by just booking themselves in for an elective caesar, rather than go through the process of a natural labour?

Choosing a medical birth may appear to be the easier road but is actually a much harder road to travel since it doesn't unfold as easily as a normal natural birth.

For those who think having a caesar is the easy way out, consider that it is major surgery and not something to be trifled with. Caesarean section involves major abdominal surgery and has all the same risks associated with any other operation, including blood clots, infections and increased chance of death.

The initiation into motherhood is a huge step in itself and I wouldn't want to deal with recovery from major surgery at the same time—I would not wish that on anybody.

For those that choose to have elective caesar, it has increased risks associated with it. When the mother has a caesarean, she misses out on the ecstatic birth hormones and decreases her chance of successful breastfeeding.

Babies don't get the hormonal preparation that they would during a normal physiological birth and it bypasses the baby's timetable. Babies come out when they are ripe and ready under normal circumstances. For the baby, there are risks with difficulty breathing outside the womb which can be life threatening for a newborn.

It also affects our maternal instincts. When they scanned the brains of women, only four-to-six weeks after giving birth, and made them listen to the sound of their baby crying, those that had a caesarean birth didn't have the same "switching on" of brain centres compared to those mothers who had a normal birth. This is certainly a cause for concern and a lot more research is needed on the subject.

What do you see as the biggest challenge in midwifery or obstetrics today and how do you think it should change?

Medical interventions can be lifesaving and incredibly valuable. All have their place. However in our current society they are overused. Right now there is a one-in-three caesarean rate. In my mind, five percent, or not more than 10 percent, genuinely need it.

In my experience, female doctors tend to have higher intervention rates than the general population, partly because we are trained to believe that the body (especially the female body) is inherently faulty. We rarely see a woman labouring in hospital without drugs and intervention, which reinforces this view.

As patients, doctors also tend to be over-treated in general, and this applies in the birth room. I think we are also susceptible to the contagion of fear in birth, which is reinforced by the distorted births we see.

We can come to believe that childbirth can't happen safely without medical assistance, which becomes self-fulfilling. In my work around the world, I have met maybe 10 or 15 female doctors who have given birth at home, including two transformed obstetricians.

Also, birth is the only place that it happens where you get specialist care in the first instance such as getting a high-risk obstetrician for a low risk pregnant woman. It's a bit like having a headache and going to see a brain surgeon and they end up having a CT scan, and then find something wrong and then it keeps going...

There is a great saying by Dr Marsden Wagner: "Having a highly trained obstetrical surgeon attend a normal birth is analogous to having a paediatric surgeon baby-sit a healthy two year old."

It's costly, not an appropriative use of technology, and leads to a lot of unnecessary intervention.

How much influence do we really have over our birth outcomes and how can we give ourselves the best possible chance of a natural birth?

To optimise our chances of having a positive birth we need to choose our birth environment very carefully, such as where we choose to give birth. Location has a big impact on our outcomes. My personal belief is that staying out of hospital gives women a much greater chance of having a normal birth.

For example, during my obstetric practise, I observed that those women who birthed at night when there were not many people around had better birth outcomes due to having fewer interventions.

Choosing to have a home birth results in 90 percent chance of normal birth and less than 10 percent chance of having a caesarean. If you put the same women in hospital, it will be flipped on its head.

In the hospital environment, 10 percent will have a normal birth and 90 percent will have a medicalised birth. The key is to birth somewhere where we feel private, safe and unobserved to allow the hormonal flow to happen effectively.

What are the most effective tools or techniques for a more positive birth experience?

Social environment matters, so the mother should choose to be with people with whom she feels private, safe and unobserved. We are not designed to be with strangers during birth. It is antagonistic to parts of the brain that shut down in this scenario, yet in hospitals there are many strangers around with change of staff during shifts.

Create a positive birth culture by reading positive books, joining online groups or physically getting together with mothers who have had a good experience is really important to prepare for a positive birth.

Find a supportive community and don't just rely on the medical world for advice or knowledge on birth. Look around at what is available. Seek out good quality information.

Saturate yourself in positive birth experiences. What you read about is really important. When you read about positive experiences of others, it makes you imagine what is going to happen and is the best thing you can do to prepare yourself for birth.

Nutrition is also really important in preparation for a natural birth. Today many people are undernourished and yet over-fed at the same time. Put simply, we are eating a lot of unhelpful foods and not eating enough helpful ones.

Why is this important when it comes to birth? Because our baby is made out of what the mother eats and what the mother has already eaten. Our pre-conception diet is even more important than after conception.

Deal with your fears before birth. During pregnancy we have heightened emotional development. It is a time when things come up for us that have never come up before and are designed to help us to heal. This is an important task to look at those.

We can do this by journaling, doing yoga class, birth preparation class, by talking to our partner or other women. The more you have dealt with during pregnancy the less there is that comes up to deal with during birth.

It's really important to trust your instincts and get back into your body. We can do this by doing physical things such as walking or swimming. We live in an intellectually heavy culture where we are not encouraged to follow our instincts and women have learnt to function in a man's world. Therefore we need to become more grounded in our bodies and gain our trust back in our body.

Historically, all we had was our own instincts and evolution has meant that it has become finely evolved. We are more tuned in or psychic during pregnancy so it enhances our instincts, which gives us the ability to know exactly what to do. We are given special access to the mystery of birth—your body's mystery.

Not following that inner knowing can have unwanted outcomes. For example, I know of one story where the pregnant mother had a strong feeling about getting an induction. She said it felt really wrong at the time but she didn't listen and the baby died. Really listen to that inner voice—this is your intuition.

How important is it to connect with our babies even before they are born?

It's so important to connect with your baby while it is still in the womb. This is something many may take for granted but may be overlooked by some modern women. Pregnancy is an extraordinary time. It's important to get on the baby's wavelength before they are born; it's such a beautiful place to be.

We can do this by listening to recordings with visualisations, meditation or by practising yoga. Others may tune into their baby while they are walking, much like tuning into a radio station. This can really enhance the experience for both mother and baby. Find what it takes for you to tune in.

Birth is a huge experience for the baby as well. As a culture we haven't begun to take into account the baby's perspective. I have witnessed how babies are often not happy when they are born by medicalised births.

Take a look at the difference when you watch positive birth videos—often you will notice the baby is "blissed out". Birth is such a pivotal point for the baby as it is the first experience of life and sets the template of how we experience the world.

What kind of changes would you like to see in the world in regards to birth?

I would like to see the current statistics reversed. That is, 90 percent normal births and only 10 percent with the use of interventions. This would mean women receive appropriate care and the proper use of technology.

Why is it so important to follow Mother Nature's design?

For the mother, the ultimate outcome is that she comes out incredibly empowered with a feeling of achievement that if she can do this, then she can do anything and also the switching on of instinctive mothering behaviours, as it happens with all other animals in nature.

(There is also) incredible ease and pleasure of mothering and when she hears the baby cry, it turns on reward centres which makes the mother respond promptly and fulfil the baby's needs.

This is Mother Nature's design. It's not just about feeling good either, this is about offspring survival. It is the nuts and bolts of evolution to care for your baby since the baby depends on the mother for its survival.

What is the best advice you could give to a new mother?

Don't rely on advice from any medical perspective as your only frame of reference. The hospital is not the expert on natural birth. Midwives or doulas are the real experts. I have heard someone say that it's a bit like going to McDonalds and asking for a sirloin steak—your chances of getting one are pretty low! Remember you are the ultimate expert on your baby and your body.

Those who choose a natural birth go against the whole culture and are the most courageous. Especially those who choose to go natural after caesarean (VBAC).

Our own experience can determine our ideas and beliefs around birth. For instance, an obstetrician, who has dealt with many obstetric emergencies, will truly believe that all women need a medicalised birth.

As women, we are taught to ignore our body and it's a long road to get from there to get into our pelvis.

How important is it for new mothers to properly rest and recover in the first weeks after giving birth? How can new mothers honour themselves for the very best start to motherhood?

I'm a big fan of 40 days rest after birth—every woman should have that experience and get support during that time. I did it myself with my fourth baby and highly recommend it.

No matter how it happens—natural or otherwise—birth is an enormous experience for our body and psyche and we should honour and respect that and approach it with ease and grace.

The role of motherhood is not recognised in our society. We are expected to be superwomen and get back to our normal life immediately. For instance, cook dinner for the whole family, the minute after we give birth!

Yet in Chinese medicine, they recognise the importance of the first few weeks of motherhood and the importance of proper rest and that ignoring this depletes our life force energy, leading to problems at menopause, so allowing ourselves to rest after birth is a long-term investment in our health.

Personally, I didn't get past the letterbox for the first six weeks after giving birth to my fourth baby and that gave me the energy I needed for the first whole year of motherhood! A worthy investment indeed!

People want to support babies; we just have to learn to ask for help. There are wonderful groups like the Australian Breastfeeding Association (ABA) where they offer support by bringing home cooked meals to new mothers and this is far more important than giving gifts to the new baby.

Why do you think many women today experience postnatal depression?

Postnatal depression is often caused by stress and having a difficult birth experience, where women don't get the hormonal flow happening correctly. I believe it's due to lack of proper nutrition, especially essential fatty acids for mother and baby.

Also, lack of support plays a role and the whole societal attitude of "just get on with it", which is a huge detriment to the woman in the early days and weeks of motherhood. That's why it's so important to have a supportive community in the early weeks. Those that are "loved up" and have that community around them, have less postnatal depression.

In terms of support during birth, women are very different. Some are solitary birthers and others need physical support of others during birth, either physically or metaphysically. This could be in the form of hearing someone's voice in your head saying a positive message, like a mantra.

In summary, Dr Buckley urges pregnant and birthing women to trust their body, baby and birth!

Meet Our Experts

Dr Sarah J Buckley

Dr Sarah J Buckley is trained as a general practitioner (GP) with qualifications in GP obstetrics and family planning. Currently Sarah is fully occupied as an internationally acclaimed author and speaker on pregnancy, birth and parenting.

She is best known for her bestselling book, *Gentle Birth, Gentle Mothering: A Doctor's Guide to Natural Childbirth and Gentle Early Parenting Choices*. She is also the mother of four home-born children.

Dr Buckley's work critiques current practices in pregnancy, birth, and parenting from scientific, anthropological, cross-cultural, psychological, and personal perspectives. Her writing has been published internationally, incorporated into numerous parenting books and translated into eight languages.

She has also contributed to many professional texts. Dr Buckley has presented at conferences internationally and has been interviewed on issues related to birth and mothering for TV, radio, newspapers and magazines, and for educational and birth-related DVDs.

You can connect with Sarah and download a free copy of her latest e-book, *Ecstatic Birth*, at *www.sarahbuckley.com*

www.sarahbuckley.com

Diane Gardner

Diane Gardner is a professional doula and hypnobirthing practitioner and has trained more than 500 mothers. She studied the work of Marie Mongan, the founder of Hypnobirthing Institute, and has been a hypnobirthing practitioner since 2001 and an NLP master since 1997.

In 2005, she was instrumental in the early development of the Calmbirth program. She has a Diploma in Professional Counselling and an Advanced Diploma in Solution Oriented Hypnosis.

She is the creator of an advanced birthing program for women to overcome their fears and experience a more gentle, natural and empowering experience. She is passionately involved in helping mothers have a more rewarding birthing experience and believes more than ever, that birth is not meant to be a medical incident, but rather a gentle, natural and empowering experience just like nature intended.

www.dianegardner.com.au

Shivam Rachana

Shivam Rachana is the founding principal of the International College of Spiritual Midwifery and former co-director of the Centre for Human Transformation for 28 years. Rachana's teaching career spans 40 years.

A pioneer of conscious birthing practises since the 1970's, she specialises in water birth and Lotus Birth. She connects women to the source of their feminine power and wisdom and trains doulas and rebirthers. Her book, Lotus Birth, now in its second edition and translated into Italian, Polish and Czech, is a world first publication. She is executive director of the acclaimed DVD The Lotus Birth of the Malcolm Twins and co-author of The Tantric Path.

www.lotusbirth.net

www.womenofspirit.asn.au

Sonya Wildgrace

Sonya Wildgrace is a professional birth trauma counsellor, independent sustainable natural birth educator and experienced doula.

Her birth knowledge comes from more than 14 years of holding the space, listening, supporting and watching women birthing, hearing their stories, sharing their intimate space and seeing the erosion of natural instinctual birth unfold in a non-supportive clinical environment.

Also as a birthing mother, she witnessed the stereotypical management of birth in an industrialised small town hospital. The mother of five began offering private antenatal classes for couples and intimate groups.

Offering mentorship, she encouraged a core group of women to train as doulas in her area to offer more services for birthing women and their families. She ran pregnancy survival workshops and co-facilitated a postnatal support group through the Woman's Health Centre.

Having had four successful vaginal births after caesarean (VBAC), she decided to specialise in VBAC counselling and education and offers classes with small groups of women and their partners wishing to explore their VBAC options.

She works extensively with women and their partners to navigate through the modern minefield of today's obstetric practise, assisting in the reemergence of a new empowered natural birth model.

www.wildgracebabies.com

www.yinhealth.com.au

Cas McCullough

Cas brings a wealth of experience and knowledge to her role as a birth doula and postnatal doula, writer and speaker about pregnancy, birth, and parenting.

Cas is the former editor of Birth Matters Journal, past president of the Maternity Coalition and co-founder of Caesarean Awareness Network Australia.

Since 2008 she has also been listed in Who's Who of Australian Women. Cas provides support services for birthing women and new parents, offering practical assistance and a range of quality resources that promote natural and sustainable family living.

www.mumatopia.com

Nicole MacFadyen

Nicole MacFadyen is a naturopath and natural fertility specialist with more than 15 years of clinical experience. Nicole specialises in pre-conception health, infertility, IVF support, pregnancy and postnatal care, women's health and menopause and children's ailments.

Nicole also works closely with other health professionals to enhance the success of IVF where necessary.

She holds a Diploma of Applied Science, Naturopathy (SSNT) Advanced Certificate in Natural Fertility Management and Better Babies Preconception Health Care and is a Member of the Australian Traditional Medicine Society.

www.botanicanaturopathy.com.au

Shirley-Anne Lawler

Shirley-Anne Lawler, a trained midwife, gives pregnant women tools to make conscious choices for an easy birth. She uses these tools to change the energy of fear, worry and concerns relating to conception, pregnancy and birth.

Shirley-Anne discovered Access Consciousness in 2007 and fast tracked her training to become a facilitator, saying she "finally found a set of tools and processes that allowed me to use my ability to identify and change limiting thought patterns and belief systems."

She says her goal is to increase the happiness quotient on the planet and one of the ways to this is to facilitate an easy, relaxed, joyful pregnancy and birth experience!

www.consciouspregnancyeasybirth.com

Jo Thomson

Jo Thomson has been a private hospital midwife for more than 12 years. In the past two years she has also gained qualifications as a life coach.

This work has highlighted the need for women (and their partners) to be better prepared both emotionally and mentally for birth in order to be empowered throughout and have the birth experience they desire.

With this aim in mind, she will soon be adding Hypnobirth Trainer to her skills. As a life coach, Jo also offers women support through emotional healing if things have not gone to plan and they are feeling at all disempowered by their experience.

www.destinybychoice.com.au

Davini Malcolm

Davini Malcolm has 29 years of experience in film and television as an actress. She was also one of the producers for the internationally released and acclaimed DVD Lotus Birth, featuring the homebirth of her twins in water.

Davini is a director of the International College of Spiritual Midwifery (ICSM) and has been involved in Women's Mystery circles for 20 years. She believes this sacred time in the company of women has created the foundations.

She says she "feels the blessings of this every day." Davini is a mother of four Lotus-born children. She speaks with the informed clarity of a woman who is deeply aware of, and has fully embraced her feminine process, as woman and mother. She shows an authority that is palpable in its ancient knowledge, its wisdom and beauty.

www.lotusbirth.net

Kathryn Williams

Kat is a homebirth midwife and natural birth educator. She has worked in hospital and home environments and has extensive knowledge and experience of natural physiological birth.

Her passion is for women to "realise their inner strength" through birth and for the mother and baby to come through the process emotionally, physically and spiritually intact.

www.birthworker.com

Unmani

Unmani is a teacher of conscious birthing and has been involved with a women's circle for approximately 15 years. She also studied tantra and hypnosis with the Centre for Human Transformation.

www.unmani.com.au/groups.html

Robyn Stitt

Robyn Stitt is a complementary therapist (kinesiology and Reiki) who helps people turn their overwhelmed bodies and lives into calm, confident order, with a special interest in pre-and-postnatal care.

overcomingoverwhelm.blogspot.com

Deanne Schmid

Deanne Schmid is a homebirth mum, former Homebirth Network South Australia Committee Member, natural birth advocate and relaxation therapist.

www.lotusfloating.com.au

Continue The Journey:
Your Empowering Birth Tools

Now that you have finished the book, there is even more to discover!

As a special gift for you, we would like to offer you a few extra practical tools with our compliments, to help you on your journey into motherhood.

Please note this special site is not open to the public and has been created just for you as a valued reader: *www.inspiringbirthstories.com.au/gifts*

So jump online now to receive the following gifts:

1.   **Empowering Daily Affirmations** – handpicked gems for you to program your mind daily with positive thoughts and overcome your fears for good!

2.   **Eat Right Birth Right Nutritional Chart** - for nutritional tips to nourish you and your precious baby

3.   **Empowering Sample Birth Plan** that you can use to create your own + Full Explanation Guide - for your eyes only!!

4.   **Empowering Resources List** including:

     ℰ   Must - read books on pregnancy and birth

     ℰ   Must - see DVDs on the subject of birth

     ℰ   Useful web links to explore

Share the Love

Did you enjoy this book? Once you have finished reading it, please pay it forward by passing this book on to another first time mother-to-be who really needs to hear this message.

If this book impacts positively on your journey into motherhood, I encourage you to let me know what difference it has made in your life, or share your inspiring birth story to help empower other women around the world. I can be contacted at:

katrina@inspiringbirthstories.com.au.

Join Our Empowered Community

We invite you to join our empowered community of women on Facebook for daily inspirations, discussions and latest updates.

Visit www.facebook.com/InspiringBirthStories.

Be part of a positive virtual community, get ongoing support, share ideas and pick up news, tips and handy hints for your journey into motherhood and beyond.

More Inspiring Resources

Explore more inspiring birth stories, get useful tips from our expert articles and live interviews on empowering birth and natural parenting, register for *Empower Yourself* e-news, meet our empowered mums, find more useful tools, resources and inspiring products—or simply share your inspiring birth story at:

www.inspiringbirthstories.com.au

Thank you for joining us on this empowering journey!

Much love and birth blessings,

Katrina Zaslavsky ♥

Footnotes:

1. Epidural: a step in a cascade of intervention that is often given too casually without fully explaining the possible risks to mother and baby. It interrupts the physiological process and can cause intensely painful contractions and carries a risk of paralysis in 1 in 500 cases and three times higher risk of maternal death. It can also lead to lack of oxygen to the foetus. Epidurals also can prolong the second stage of labour inducing the use of forceps and vacuum suction to remove the baby from the womb, often causing problems to the baby such as swelling and bruising to the head. Using a surgical instrument also means the need for an episiotomy. Such invasive surgical procedures can cause damage that last for a long time after giving birth such as perineal pain, bowel problems, hemorrhoids and sexual problems.

2. Perineal massage: Perineal massage is the practise of massaging a pregnant woman's perineum around the vagina in preparation for childbirth. This is to help prevent tearing of the perineum during birth, the need for an episiotomy or an instrument delivery.

3. Pinpoint cervix: narrowing of the cervix.

4. Doula: a person who supports other women during childbirth by helping with breathing patterns, massage, positive visualisation, positioning, and reassurance. Having a doula can lead to: 50 percent fewer cesareans, 25 percent shorter labours with fewer complications, 40 percent less use of pitocin (a labour-inducing drug), 60 percent fewer requests for epidural anesthesia, better success with breastfeeding and less postpartum depression.

5. Fear-Tension-Pain Syndrome: a theory that states fear leads to tension and tension leads to pain in labour by setting off the "fight or flight" response, which takes blood away from the uterine muscle causing unnecessary pain through lack of blood and oxygen to this hard-working muscle.

6. Episiotomy: a surgically planned incision on the perineum and the posterior vaginal wall during second stage of labour. The incision is performed under local anaesthetic and is sutured closed after delivery.

7. Ambu bag: a bag valve mask used for resuscitation.

8. Epi-No: An instrument that helps with perineal massage.

9. TENS machine: A device that sends electrical impulses to parts of the body to help block pain signals.

10. Toxaemia: A condition in pregnancy, also known as pre-eclampsia, characterised by a sharp rise in blood pressure, leakage of large amounts of the protein albumin into the urine and swelling of the hands, feet, and face.

Pre-eclampsia is the most common complication of pregnancy. It affects about five percent of pregnancies and occurs in the third trimester of pregnancy. Source: Medicinenet.com

11. Bloody show: A small amount of blood or blood-tinged mucus through the vagina towards the end of pregnancy. It can occur just before labour or in early labour as the cervix changes shape, freeing mucus and blood. Bloody show is relatively common in pregnancy, and it does not signify increased risk to the mother or baby.

12. Lotus birth: The practise of leaving the umbilical cord uncut, so the baby remains attached to the placenta until the cord naturally separates at the navel—exactly as the cut cord does—at three to 10 days after birth. "This prolonged contact can be seen as a time of transition, allowing the baby to slowly and gently let go of the attachment to the mother's body." ~ Dr Sarah Buckley, MD, Pregnancy magazine, Spring 1998. Receiving the full amount of the valuable cord blood present at birth is of major benefit to the child's ongoing health and wellbeing.

13. Rebozo wrap: A baby sling is a piece of cloth that supports an infant or other small child from a carer's body.

14. Hard pushing: Or "purple pushing", where women hold their breath and push. It can break blood vessels in the eyes, cause headaches, blows air into the carotid glands so women look like bullfrogs and cuts down the blood supply to the baby by holding the breath.

References:

15. Maternity Coalition, AIMS. (Australia) Australian Society of Independent Midwives and Community Midwifery WA Inc. National Maternity Action Plan 2002. www. maternitycoalition.org.au

16. Tracey S Sullivan E Dahlen H Black D Wang YA Tracey M. Does Size Matter? A Population Based Study of Birth in Lower Volume Maternity Hospitals for Low Risk Women. BJOG: 2006; 113:86-96

17. Johnson KC, Daviss A. Outcomes of Homebirths With Certified Professional Midwives; A Large Prospective Study In North America. BMJ:2005; 330;1416-1423

18. Article, In Pursuit of Happiness, DNA Can Be Influenced And Reprogrammed by Words and Frequencies, Aurick, October 30, 2010 via Quantum Pranx www.inpursuitofhappiness. wordpress.com/2011/06/11/our-bodies-are-programmable-by-language-words-sound-and-thought

19. Alternative Medicine, The Definitive Guide, 2002, p858-880 www.alternativemedicine. com, published by Celestial Arts, CA, USA. Distributed In Australia by Simon & Schuster Australia.

20. The Need To Humanize Birth In Australia, Fish Can't See Water, Birth International, Marsden Wagner (MD, MSPH) www.birthinternational.com/articles/birth/18-fish-cant-see-water

21. Article, Why More Moms Are Getting C-Sections, The Bump, The Inside Scoop On Pregnancy, http://pregnant.thebump.com/fertility-pregnancy-parenting-news/pregnancy-news-information/blogs/why-moms-are-getting-c-sections

22. Women's Bodies, Women's Wisdom: The Complete Guide to Women's Health and Wellbeing, Dr Christiane Northrup, MD, 1998, First Published in Great Britain in 1995 by Judy Piatkus (Publishers) Ltd.

23. Article, Stress During Pregnancy can Affect a Child's Health by Vijai P. Sharma, PhD, mind publications www.askdrsears.com/topics/pregnancy-childbirth/fourth-month/7-ways-bond-your-preborn-baby

24. Journal of Obstetric, Gynecologic, & Neonatal Nursing Volume 38, Issue 1. Article first published online: 21 JAN 2009.

25. Axness, Marcy. Parenting for Peace: Raising the Next Generation of Peacemakers. Boulder, CO: Sentient Publications, 2012.

26. Mother Wisdom, For Mothers By Mothers by Susie Cameron and Katrina Crook. First published 2007, Pan McMillan Australia Pty Ltd.

27. Verny T, Kelly J. The Secret Life of the Unborn Child, London. Warner Books 1995.

28. Schore R, Rethinking The Brain, New York, Families and Work Institute, 1997.

29. Schore A, Effects of Early Relational Trauma on Right Brain Development, Affect Regulation and Infant Mental Health. Infant Mental Health Journal 2001:22(1):201-269.

30. Siegal D, The Developing Mind: How Relationships and The Brain Interact To Shape Who We Are. London, The Guildford Press, 2004.

31. The Journal of Perinatal Education, Advancing Normal Birth, Do Not Disturb: The Importance of Privacy in Labor by Judith A. Lothian, RN, PhD, LCCE, FACCE. A Lamaze International publication www.ncbi.nlm.nih.gov/pmc/articles/PMC1595201/

32. Natural Labour Tips, July 2004 issue of Parents magazine www.parents.com/pregnancy/giving-birth/vaginal/natural-labor-tips/

33. The Guardian Life & Style. Frederick Leboyer: Babies are overlooked in labour www.guardian.co.uk/lifeandstyle/2011/jun/25/obstetrician-frederick-leboyer-childbirth

34. Melbourne's Child, Births of a Nation by Dr Sue White, June 2011 p12-13.

35. New Research Proves Mothers Who do this Bond Better With Their Children Posted by Dr Joseph Mercola, July 03 2011. Source: Time Magazine May 20, 2011

36. Ecstatic Birth - Nature's Hormonal Blueprint for Labor, by Dr Sarah J Buckley, MD, 2010

37. The Natural Way to Better Babies by Francesca Naish and Janette Roberts, 2000, Published by Random House Australia Pty Ltd, First published in 1996.

38. Revolution From Within, A Book of Self Esteem by Gloria Steinem, Little, Brown and Co. (Canada), 1993, p201-202.

39. Wirth, F. 2001, Prenatal Parenting: The Complete Psychological and Spiritual Guide to Loving Your Unborn Baby by Frederick Wirth, Regan Books, Harper Collins Publishers, New York.

40. Read, G. D. 1956, Childbirth Without Fear by William Heinemann, Medical Books Ltd, London.

41. Unassisted Childbirth by Laura Shanley www.freebirth.com

42. Natural Childcare, The Complete Natural Guide from Preconception to Preschool for all Thinking Parents by Elyane T. Brightlight PhD, Griffin Press, Brolga Publishing Pty Ltd, Australia, 1999.

43. Birthtalk.org - Makes Birth Better, www.birthtalk.org

44. The Power of Now: A Guide to Spiritual Enlightenment by Eckhart Tolle, New World Library; 1ST edition (September 29, 2004)

45. (Gaskin 2003, pp 4-5)

46. The Relaxation Response and Timeless Healing by Dr Herbert Benson 1996, pp16-17 & 138.

47. Birth Issues 2006:15 (1): 11-17.

48. International College of Spiritual Midwifery - www.womenofspirit.asn.au